THANKS FOR NOTHING

www.rbooks.co.uk

THANKS FOR NOTHING

Jack Dee

BLACK SWAN

TRANSWORLD PUBLISHERS
61–63 Uxbridge Road, London W5 5SA
A Random House Group Company
www.rbooks.co.uk

THANKS FOR NOTHING
A BLACK SWAN BOOK: 9780552775250

First published in Great Britain
in 2009 by Doubleday
an imprint of Transworld Publishers
Black Swan edition published 2010

Addresses for Random House Group Ltd companies outside the UK
can be found at: www.randomhouse.co.uk
The Random House Group Ltd Reg. No. 954009

The Random House Group Limited supports The Forest Stewardship
Council (FSC), the leading international forest certification organisation.
All our titles that are printed on Greenpeace approved FSC certified paper
carry the FSC logo. Our paper procurement policy can be found at
www.rbooks.co.uk/environment

Typeset in 11/16pt Giovanni Book by Falcon Oast Graphic Art Ltd.
Printed in the UK by CPI Cox & Wyman, Reading, RG1 8EX.

2 4 6 8 10 9 7 5 3 1

Acknowledgements

No thanks to the following:

My editor Susanna Wadeson – God, what a pain she was.

The photographer – forgotten his name already. Anyway, he was rubbish. Made me look like I'd put on weight.

Claire Ward for the artwork – like getting blood out of a stone.

Patsy whatshername for her PR. I might as well have ticked the box marked 'No publicity'.

The Sales team. Well, we'll see.

Larry Finlay, CEO Transworld – never even saw him once I'd signed.

Everyone else at Transworld Publishers – talk about overstaffed.

Gary Farrow – for messing up everything he tried to do.

Pete Sinclair – worse than useless. Next time don't bother.

Everyone at Open Mike where I write – maybe in future, at least try to keep quiet. I know you're pretending to be busy but that's taking the piss.

Addison Cresswell – my hopeless agent, who is to literature what napalm is to wild fauna.

But most of all, I must fail to thank my wife and children for their total lack of patience and understanding while I was writing this. Without them I would have got it done miles quicker.

To me,
without whom none of this would have been possible

Preface

I don't read prefaces. They make me suspicious. I always think it looks like the book was handed in with a sick-note.

It's as if the author has got to the end, then suddenly realized that he forgot all sorts of things, so he's stuck in an extra chapter at the beginning just to cover his mistakes.

Well, that's not the case here. Everything I wanted to say, and was legally allowed to, is in the book itself. So why don't you read that instead? Everyone else is on page five by now and here you are, dutifully wasting your time on the preface.

Anyway, because this bit has to have something in it, I might as well give you the basic facts of my early life.

By the way, all this stuff is as I remember it. If I was at school with you or something, and I got the year wrong, then I'm sorry.

Actually, having said that, I'm not sorry. Also, don't try to get in touch.

So, here it is.

1961: Born in Petts Wood, Kent. My mum and dad are Rosemary and Geoff and I have a brother, David, and sister, Joanna, who are five and eight years older than me respectively. We live in Orpington until I am four.

1965: Move to Easton, a village near Winchester. Attend Itchen Abbas Primary School until age seven.

1966: England win World Cup. Like I cared. Or care now.

1968: Start at Pilgrims' School in Winchester.

1969: Moon Landing. Overrated.

1973: Go to Montgomery of Alamein, a local comprehensive.

1977: Attend Peter Symonds sixth-form college.

1981: Start a career in the restaurant trade but, disillusioned, experiment with many other jobs.

1984: Decide to become a priest.

1984: Decide not to.

1986: First step on stage at the Comedy Store as a try-out. Meet Jane.

1989: Give up the day job and turn professional comedian. Marry Jane.

1999: Arndale Centre in Wandsworth demolished.
And that's about it. If that's all you wanted to know, then feel free to put this back on the shelf and walk out of the bookshop without having to part with your money.

But if you're still curious and want to find out more about what shaped me in the past and what makes me tick now, then take it up to the till and pay for it like a man.

Unless you're a woman, in which case pay for it like a woman. Then take it home, decide you don't really like it and put it in your wardrobe, where it will stay for the next seven years.

Contains strong opinions from the outset.

1

I CAN HARDLY BELIEVE how cheap some things are when everything else is so expensive. Not long ago, I bought an alarm clock, a known brand, £2.95, battery included, and it works perfectly. Or rather it did until my daughter borrowed it from my bedside table to take on a school trip. She had a great time. She sailed, trekked, climbed and lost my alarm clock.

But who cares? Certainly not me. It was a pleasure to return to the shop where I got it and just buy another one. I almost felt like buying two and throwing one of them away. Two pounds ninety-five; and I'm pretty sure I've seen ones just like it for £14.95 at an airport shop.

Then, I needed to replace a short piece of piping that had burst between my boiler and the hot-water cylinder. It was that kind of rubberized piping that's coated in a wire mesh to make it stronger while still enabling it to bend into awkward positions. About ten inches of it, I needed. How much do you think that would be?

Sixty-five pounds, not including labour.

The plumber reasoned that it was very good quality, hence the price. 'Hence the previous identical one bursting,' I suggested.

Then the plumber took offence in the way that only somebody who is desperately, vitally needed can afford to do. In other words, he wasn't really offended at all, but he recognized his opportunity to act offended and was going to take full advantage of it.

'Yeah, alright, don't have a go at me, I'm only saying that's how much it cost.'

He knows I need him too much to say, 'Actually I *am* going to have a go at you. I think you are a bastard. Take your grubby bag of spanners and sod off out of my house, I'll fix the boiler myself,' because if I did, he would, and I couldn't.

I don't know what happened in our development as a species, what unfortunate glitch it was in our anthropological journey that led us all to this dependency on stroppy tradesmen for a continued supply of hot water.

I wonder how soon after the discovery of fire, a particularly devious caveman, who by extraordinary coincidence was called The Plumber, started telling everyone that if they didn't boil their water a certain way, on a fire started with a certain twig that only he was qualified to supply, it would blow up and kill them. I imagine it was quite soon, knowing human nature.

I expect that's why there are cave-paintings. It was something to do while they waited in all day Wednesday for The Plumber to turn up with his special CORGI-registered twigs that cost 65 pebbles a go.

In the interests of balance, I can see it must be difficult, if you are a plumber, to gauge your own popularity.

Most reasonable people have a natural sense of how well liked they are.

For example, our postman is nice enough. We're not friends as such, but we are on weather-observing terms. We exchange a few words and that is that. He doesn't go on his way thinking that he is a genius or even especially well liked by me merely because he delivered the post to my house and I remarked on the rain we had at the weekend. He and I both know that talking about the weather is the smallest talk there is. It is a safe bet for anyone who wishes to have a quick, uninvolved chat with no risk of it turning into a proper conversation.

The window-cleaner is Polish. On his twice-yearly visits he likes to get on with his work without chatting, which is fine by me. He seems affable and if my Polish were up to it, I expect we could have a pleasant enough conversation about, I don't know, sponges or ladders or something.

My point here is this: neither the postman nor the window-cleaner leaves my house under the illusion that he is a really great bloke. Why? Two reasons:

1) The circumstances under which they execute their duties are never an emergency. Ever seen a postman or a window-cleaner in a hurry? Exactly. (Obviously the postman in a van, driving round side-streets like a glued-up teenage joy-rider is a different matter. I guarantee he's on his way home, so it doesn't count.)

2) Their jobs are not surrounded by mystery – it is quite easy to see exactly how they do them and they don't cloak them in obscure terminology to make what they do sound more clever. For example, it would be highly unlikely that the postman would need to explain anything beyond the basic jargon of 'letter', 'postcard' and 'parcel'. Likewise nobody really quizzes their window-cleaner about buckets and J-cloths.

The plumber, however, is almost always called to your house when something isn't working properly, like a pipe that's spraying a jet of water all over the bathroom carpet or just leaking sewage into your sitting room. When he walks in and solves the problem, your gratitude is actually disproportionate to the task that he has completed. Which is why he then leaves your house thinking, 'I must be fantastic, because they said I was, just like the people in the last house did, even though I pitched up late there as well.'

'So what?' you may think. 'Don't be so harsh, he did a good job, he deserves praise.' Wrong. He did his job, not a good job. He shouldn't be praised. He should be thanked, of course, but no more than you would thank anybody else for doing the thing that you paid them to do.

But if it's truly deluded self-regard you're after, look no further than the so-called 'professional' whose trade-mark tools are carried in a briefcase.

When my wife Jane and I moved into our first, tiny house in Tooting, south-west London, we congratulated ourselves endlessly on living in such a rough pocket of town. We thought it was quite clever to live in a 'real' urban area, surrounded by people who spent much of their time leaning against things and shouting across the street to each other. All the females from the age of three up until they were grannies (at about thirty-two) had their hair scraped back tightly over their skulls so that their bubble gum wouldn't get tangled in it. The menfolk always walked as if they had nowhere to go, a sort of listless meander that allowed for peering into parked cars and lazily gobbing on the pavement. It was great. We were really pleased that we'd bought there and as soon as we'd had Banham's round to fit collapsible gates on all the windows and a triple-locking deadbolt on the front door, we felt quite cosy.

We bought the house from a vicar and when we went to look around it we were struck by how chillingly breezy it was. I said to Jane that it was just because he was an ascetic who felt closer to God the colder he and his family became. Jane didn't agree and said that we should have a survey done. Once we'd completed and moved in, I realized that his penchant for draftiness was more to do with creating a constant flow of fresh air through the house that would mask the musty smell of damp.

And before you put your penny-worth in, yes we did employ a surveyor, that's my point. All he said in his ever-so-neatly typed report was that it was not possible to inspect under the carpets or wallpaper to check for dry rot and damp, so therefore he couldn't guarantee anything. Which is legalese for 'Sorry, guys, you're on your own.' There was no mention of the tell-tale mustiness. The vicar's little open-window trick had clearly worked on him as well.

Today I am an older and wiser man and know that surveyors are people who take a photograph of the roof of your prospective house, cut and paste a load of generic piffle that would apply to any house in the country and then charge you for their services. At the time, however, I was still working on the premise that they were an essential link in the house-buying chain, or at least had enough basic curiosity to do a half-decent job. It just goes to show how wrong you can be.

Seven hundred pounds spent on a nicely bound document full of statements such as 'It was not possible to gain access to the loft space.' No, fair enough. How could anyone be expected to realize that the hatch in the ceiling was in fact a portal with a folding ladder tucked away inside it? You'd have to be some sort of house expert to spot that.

Wouldn't it be refreshing to get a survey that read 'It was not possible to inspect the condition of the floorboards because it was half past four by then and I was too lazy to get down on my hands and knees and lift the rug'?

I toyed with the idea of tracking the vicar down to his new parish and leafleting the area so that everybody there would know that, despite all his fête-opening and tea-drinking, the man charged with the care of their spiritual needs was a lousy con artist. Perhaps I would sit at the back of his church, wait until he was in the middle of his sermon (hopefully something about honesty or kindness) and then jump up and denounce him and his scone-baking wife as charlatans.

For a while I fancied that this quest would put me into the league of Nazi-hunter Simon Wiesenthal. I liked the idea of monitoring the vicar's movements, letting him go about his daily business not knowing that he was being watched. As he left his new, no doubt damp-free house each morning, he would be unaware of the bronchitic man sitting in the parked car outside, waiting, taking notes, comparing the confident, strolling vicar with a crumply black-and-white photo of a uniformed Waffen SS vicar, younger but unmistakably the same man. Very soon my contacts in Mossad would arrive in Tooting. I'd meet up with them at a safe house, brief them, hand them a dossier of recent photos and leave them to their work.

Some weeks later, I would buy a newspaper from the corner shop and read that the vicar had disappeared from his new parish near Reading. There had been sightings of him being bundled into a black car, flown to Israel, tried and hanged. That's quite a sighting, I would wryly remark to myself. Tough justice but, sadly, no less than he deserved. Who knows how many problematic houses he had sold to unsuspecting first-time buyers?

Anyway, the house needed some work to undampen it. Conveniently the source of the problem lay under the hall floorboards, so once they had been pulled up nobody could enter or leave without walking along the edge of a joist. If you opened the front door in the dark you could quite easily step in and fall two feet on to the earth that the house had originally been built on at the end of the nineteenth century.

Evidently some remedial work had been attempted since that construction. I know this from the presence of builders' rubbish. An empty and very dusty box of Mr Kipling's individual apple pies. The late Victorians enjoyed no such packaged fancies and yet nor was the artwork contemporary, dating the artefact, in my humble opinion, circa 1970. Likewise the discarded box of Swan Vesta matches had a quaintly anachronistic air about them.

How do I know that the culprit was a builder? Do pay attention, Lewis. The chap was a smoker who preferred matches to the elegance of a Ronson or Dunhill lighter and he ate pies by the half-dozen. The bugger may as well have left behind his cloth-cap and trowel. Case closed. Pass me my crossword.

So, to recap, when I was nine years old, some builder was leaving a time capsule of litter under the floorboards of a house that I didn't know existed but which I would one day regret buying. Funny old thing, life.

I had a couple of quotes to deal with the damp, but it appeared to be more difficult to solve than I had hoped, so the boards were hammered back down and the windows opened until eventually we sold. It seemed the only sensible thing to do.

2

THERE ARE SOME PEOPLE who, from an early age, know exactly what they want to be when they grow up. Usually the career path that they assign themselves is a vocational one such as doctor, astronaut or ballerina.

One of my daughters was set on being a traffic warden from about the age of five. She liked the gadgets they have on their belts and the fact that you spend most of the day wandering around, window-shopping and, of course, penalizing drivers for the slightest infringement of our parking laws. She saw that bit as the best part of the job and at the time demonstrated an alarmingly fascistic attitude towards anyone who over-stayed their time on a meter or dared to pull up on a double yellow line. It was a day of enormous excitement for her when a Red Route was introduced on the main road near our house. She wrote a poem about it.

As proud, caring – oh, alright then, snobbish – parents, Jane and I were relieved when this desire to

ticket people for a living gave way to the far more
suitable ambition of opening a five-star hotel just for
dogs. You may be thinking, 'Well, she was only five.
Why get stressed about it?' Frankly, if you think that,
then you deserve to have a child who grows up to be a
traffic warden.

I had good reason to be stressed about it. I imagined
at the time spending my latter years in the absurd
position of defending traffic wardens at dinner parties.
'They really are petty-minded retards, aren't they?'
someone might say as he poured me some more wine,
regaling me with the details of his latest minor violation
that had resulted in a penalty. Whilst agreeing wholeheart-
edly, I would at the same time have to say, out of parental
loyalty, 'Actually, I've found that some of them are very
bright and charming.' And everyone at the table would
laugh, thinking that I was being humorously sarcastic.
Then I'd probably shut up and go home resenting everyone there, and myself even more for not standing up and
tipping the table on its side and storming out shouting
that some traffic wardens are wonderful people.

Being a train-driver always used to be a perfectly
respectable playground ambition. But I suspect that it is
a job that has lost its appeal over the years. Long gone
are the days when you could make toast on the burning
coals and wave to people as you chugged through the
rolling countryside, leaving plumes of billowing
nostalgia in your wake.

The modern counterpart is far less alluring. Train-drivers don't wave to the kiddies any more, presumably for Health and Safety reasons. Either that or they just hate kids. In fairness, if you'd had a workmate beheaded by a paving flag mischievously thrown from a bridge, it might colour your view of the little rascals.

Train-driving is no longer a rough, tough manual job with elements of skill that could make a man proud of his profession. Nowadays a train-driver's day is a timetable of sandwiches and Sudoku. It's like being unemployed except you have to go to work. And even that's confusing because you never get there.

But if you still feel that train-driving is for you, I would at least urge you to think long and hard before working for London Underground. Driving a tube-train is one of the few jobs that you can apparently do without moving any of your limbs. I imagine that at the interview stage you could show promise by turning up late, slumping in the seat and not saying anything for eight hours.

I spent the first twenty-five years of my life not knowing what I wanted to do. As a small child, that is your right. Not knowing what you want to do is a strength and a blessing when you are a child; just as knowing becomes a strength and a blessing in your adult years. It's the transition between those two states that is problematic. If you are lucky, you will be struck with a Eureka moment in which your life is suddenly switched from murky home-video to professional High Definition. Unlucky, and life will play along, unfocused and pointless until the end of the reel. But most commonly, fate reveals itself lethargically, as if nothing can alter its decision anyway. Occasionally, the result is exciting and wonderful. But often it isn't anything more than a slowly emerging, manageable disappointment.

From my teens onwards, I wondered where and how I would fit into the scheme of things. I was obsessed with the notion that life was too extraordinary a fluke for it not to have purpose. Given this, it may seem odd to learn, as you will if you continue reading, that I did remarkably little to ensure any aspect of my future. Perhaps I was a natural fatalist from the start, instinctively gambling that life's outcome was not the result of endeavour and effort. Or perhaps I was just lazy and a bit stupid.

I drifted from job to job. Some I liked, others I hated. At times I was content to go with whichever current seemed to take me. But more often, I was restless and euphorically impatient, gripped with the belief that, at any moment, some calling would make itself known to me and that my life would change for ever.

You can't have belief without doubt, though. They are two sides of the same coin. As my friends moved on to the universities that I had failed to get into, and as they began to graduate with degrees and get good jobs, I started to struggle with panic and depression. Hadn't I been foolish and arrogant to think that I could get by without qualifications? Why did I think that anyone, least of all me, could beat the system, could squander every opportunity to learn and improve myself and then, somehow, be rewarded with an enjoyable life?

Gradually, I suppose I adapted to the highs and lows of living like this. Tried to enjoy the ecstatic hope of being young and learnt that it could quickly be followed by periods of despair. But it always felt like a journey, like moving forward. Sometimes, that feeling alone was the thing that kept me going.

It was a journey that was to lead me on to the stage for the first time ever at the Comedy Store in Leicester Square, London, in September 1986.

Until that precise point I had never thought of my sense of humour as anything but an unfortunate affliction. At school it prevented me from being able to concentrate and as an adult it would nag at me like an impossible toddler, constantly berating me for not paying it enough attention.

Although aware of comedians like Bob Newhart, Dave Allen and Peter Sellers, I didn't ever stop to think that comedy was their 'job' as such. I didn't wonder how they got to do what they now did, I just assumed that comedy had been their pre-ordained role, another of those things that happens to other people. But that was typical of my world view. My take on life was almost completely literal, as I think it is for most young children.

I'm in my classroom at primary school. A teacher is instructing us what to write on the front cover of our new exercise books. She tells us to copy the example that she has neatly chalked on the blackboard. I am proud of my effort. It looks exactly as she has written, but I still wonder why underneath 'Subject: SPELLING' I had to write the words: 'YOUR NAME'.

Lacking the perspective of experience or a scientific understanding of life, I was able to convince myself of the most improbable theories.

If my brother and sister and I pooled our pocket money, we could buy the latest single of our choice. And so a small collection of 45s began. Mostly, of course, we bought The Beatles, whom I idolized only slightly less than Pinky and Perky. For me, those two pigs were the real deal and when they covered a Beatles song in their speeded-up squeaky voices, I reckoned it sounded better. We had one of those old Bush record-players that look like a hard square suitcase. You opened the lid and could put five or six records on top of the stem in the centre of the turntable. One by one, the discs would drop down, and the stylus arm would swing across and land carefully on its spinning ridge.

I still love the crackle you get on vinyl before the song starts. It makes you feel like you're entering a different reality. I was intrigued by the little holes on the side of the record-player and loved to spy into them. I could just make out the internal glow of its valves. With my face pressed against the case, I could close one eye, shutting out the real world, and almost feel that I was inside the record-player itself. It was like a vast power station but at the same time in miniature. I was desperate to be able to shrink to the size of a pinhead, climb in and have a good look around. If I could, I was in no doubt at all that I would encounter The Beatles. There they would be, tiny John, Paul, George and Ringo, with their little instruments, waiting to start whatever song the chosen record requested. I could stick around, hang out with them, maybe have a go on the drums if Ringo would let me. Of course he would.

Sometimes the frustration of not being able to climb inside my record-player was unbearable.

When I recall that vivid memory, the thing that interests me most is not the conviction that I was right, or even the very notion of microscopic people living inside appliances. What I am drawn to is how my theory was not threatened by its massive chasms of logic. Leaving aside the difficulties of living in a record-player, even if you were small enough, how was it that my friends The Beatles could suddenly become the Dave Clark Five, Herman's Hermits, Tommy Steele (it was my mother's) or Petula Clark (my sister's), for that matter?

However, I never believed the same to be true of the television – that there were little people inside it. That would have been stupid.

The Virginian was my favourite programme. Most

people seemed to prefer *The High Chaparral* but I knew where my loyalties lay. I always thought of myself as Trampas and could hardly watch an entire episode to the end, such was my need to dress up as a cowboy, go into the garden and act out that week's story. I particularly loved it when they made camp and slept by a fire underneath the stars. I liked nothing more than to put on my waistcoat, hat and gun, roll up a blanket and stomp off into the Wild West. Imagining I was on a horse never quite worked for me, but a garden table and chairs could easily be arranged to form a wagon. With a flick of the reins I was making my way through the same canyon that my heroes had just negotiated, Winchester rifle by my side to shoot any Indians who tried to attack. Sorry to sound racist, but they were a nuisance and they always attacked me first. It's not like I was some nut on a killing spree.

If it wasn't *The Virginian*, then it was *The Man from U.N.C.L.E.*

Do you know what U.N.C.L.E. stands for? No? Well, I do. It stands for United Network Command for Law and Enforcement. Try to remember that in future if you don't want to be thought of as completely sad.

I decided that I was Illya Kuryakin. I liked his quiet, considered manner and cool Russian accent. Also, he was fair-haired as, at the time, was I. Yes, the similarities were endless. For this role I had a replica Luger – OK, a toy gun – which was similar in shape to the standard-issue U.N.C.L.E. P38 pistol. I lacked the accoutrements that could convert it into a rifle like Illya and Napoleon Solo had and was desperate to acquire the authentic set.

I would dress in a white shirt and a tie with black trousers and jacket for my assignments, which invariably involved orders given on a self-destruct cassette that had somehow escaped from *Mission Impossible*. Then to the garden, where I would have a hand-to-hand fight with a tree before hiding in a bush to assassinate my target, the old lady next door, who I knew to be Agent Salamander. It was always the same tree that I fought. One that had sufficiently spongy bark to absorb my punches without it hurting too much.

The great thing about working for U.N.C.L.E. was that anything could be a gadget. A fountain pen, a Smartie tube, even your shoes could take on a double purpose.

Through all this, it never occurred to me that the characters on the screen were actors. Up until the age of ten or so, I don't remember ever questioning the reality of what I was watching. At least not until *Star Trek* came along. That I knew was made up and, love it as I did, it rarely featured in my games of make-believe. Granted, the uniform was fairly simple to replicate. Just a T-shirt and wellington boots would pretty well get you there, but for me the show had too many restrictions to allow total imaginary escapism.

For one thing, teleporting is hard to fake. Just standing there and pretending that you are in the transporter room one minute and on another planet the next was highly unsatisfactory. It wasn't going to fool anyone. I also discovered that friends were reluctant to acknowledge my Spock-like powers. I made it quite clear that if I squeezed them with my fingers and thumb at the base of the neck, they were expected to collapse unconscious. And yet time and time again this failed to happen. I hated that. Once one element of power has been undermined everything else becomes pointless. If you ignore my Vulcan neck pinch, why should I even acknowledge your phaser?

Whether it was *Star Trek*, *The Virginian*, *High Chaparral*, *Doctor Who*, *The Man from U.N.C.L.E.* or any of the other programmes that I loved, they all had a common theme. Good prevails over evil: in the end the baddies get what's coming to them, and if man cannot intervene, then the universe itself ultimately delivers its own natural justice.

All of which helps to explain why the last thing you want is for your child to become a traffic warden.

3

DOWN IN MY CELLAR, I keep something very nasty indeed. The kids certainly don't know about it and if Jane has ever seen it she has kept quiet about it. Probably through shock and disgust.

When I became a grown-up and suddenly realized that I owned a house, it dawned on me that domestic maintenance can be a costly and sometimes embarrassing affair. A blocked lavatory is never a pretty sight, but the ordeal of enlisting outside help to deal with the offending article is too much to bear.

If this is becoming uncomfortable for you to read, please feel at liberty to skip this section. I won't be upset. If it's any solace, I might quickly add that loos don't always get blocked by turds, I've heard tell of quite unlikely items being recovered from stuffed-up drains. Mobile phones, shoes, hats – yes, hats – as well as teacups and other miscellaneous things like peppermills are all surprisingly common finds.

It is just about imaginable how you might lose your shoe or phone down the lav. A hat would take more doing and suggests to me a degree of malice, that the flusher was not necessarily the wearer.

You know the sort of thing: 'I'm going to an art exhibition, has anyone seen my beret?'

'No, 'fraid not. Try the cesspit at the end of the garden.'

'Sorry?'

'Oh, nothing.'

Less easy to picture is the pepper-mill. Perhaps an unwanted gift at Christmas when all the family are staying and it's hard to throw things in the bin without someone saying, 'Are you throwing that away?'

Even more difficult to understand is the butter wrapper that was found in our system one time. It's not even worth trying to work that one out.

So anyway, back to this particular blockage. The normal course of action would be to phone a plumber. As you know by now, I've got nothing against plumbers. They're smashing people who do a difficult job for very little thanks. So why didn't I call one? Well, because I couldn't face opening the front door and saying, 'Ah, hello plumber, do come in. There's a whole load of crap stuck down my toilet, let me show you.' Maybe I'm a prude, but I find that a bit awkward.

So I took the brave decision to look into the possibilities of dealing with this problem myself. Having made enquiries, I was persuaded that the best tool for the job (sorry) was a four-foot length of coiled steel. A great long wobbly spring designed specifically for its dexterity around U-bends.

I bravely confronted the shame of having to take it to the counter and pay. She knew what it was for, the cashier, glancing hatefully at me as she scanned it. Like it was her toilet I'd blocked. I knew she knew. And she knew that I knew that she . . . anyway I bought it.

When I got home I released (I wish it had a name) 'it' from the packaging. With a snip of the scissors it whipped round and round from its sleeping-snake position, jumped from my hands and fell to the bathroom floor. It wasn't long, however, before I was punishing the beast by pushing its head far, far down into the murky waters that were now so high they threatened to burst their porcelain banks.

When I had got it as far as I could get it, I began a to-and-fro action. At first, nothing seemed to happen, except for a grating sound as the spring's metal vertebrae grated against the pipework. But then, quite dramatically, the water subsided to its correct level, emitting a few bubbles as if Bog Python was exhaling his last. I pulled him out from the ghastly hole and pressed down on the toilet handle, releasing a cistern of fresh water to clean and refill the pan.

It had worked. Something I bought had actually

done what it was supposed to do. The only problem now was what to do with it.

To be honest, I didn't fancy handling it, not the wet part anyway. I ran down to the kitchen and returned wearing the washing-up gloves. With these on I felt OK about coiling it back into its dormant state. It even had a pleasing clip to keep it like that. But I have to say, Bog Python had lost some of its lustre. Mind you, after an experience like that, wouldn't you?

So down to the cellar it went, where it lies in hibernation until its talents are next needed.

In case it's worrying you, I threw the washing-up gloves away.

Why is this story so remarkable to me that I decided to share it with you? Well, because, as I have already stated, it is a story about buying something that actually did the job it was supposed to do. This apparently is so rare that the item in question doesn't even have a name.

By contrast, I bought a pencil the other day. It wasn't just any pencil. I paid a premium to go a cut above and acquire one with an eraser on top of it.

I always use a pencil for writing in my diary. It's an old habit from the days in the eighties when I did a lot of gigs for cash and wanted to be able to remove the evidence in case the tax inspector called. As it happens, he never did, and anyway I paid all my taxes because I'm weirdly conscientious like that.

The previous pencil had performed well, but had

got to that stage in a pencil's life when the lead keeps breaking no matter how much you sharpen it. I'm a patient man but after a week of being messed around like that I flew into a rage and snapped the damn thing. No one fools with me and gets away with it. Not even a pencil.

In the stationer's I looked at some of the propelling pencils. You know, thought about treating my diary to a smart Stabilo, but remembered that I had had a disappointing experience with one once before and chose not to. I could have gone for an exact copy of the one I'd just smashed over the corner of my desk, but today I was in the business of raising the bar, upping my circumstances, improving my life. So I chose one with an eraser and left.

I have used erasers before. It's not as if they are new or a gimmick to me. Nevertheless, when I got home I made a deliberate mark in my diary just to check it out.

And of course this is the point of the story. The eraser did not work. It did not erase. What it did was smear. With one wave of my hand, the neat but unwanted pencil-mark was blurred across the page in a dirty pink smudge of rubber-waste. Which, needless to say, not even a proper eraser could remove.

I started to think about the economics of this. The new pencil cost me 45p as opposed to 32p for the model without an eraser. So I paid 13p for a tiny one-centimetre cylinder of rubber substance that doesn't even work. I cannot believe that the profit margin on those little rubbers is anything other than enormous, so who made the decision to make them so that they don't work? Was it voted on at a board-meeting?

'Who's in favour of changing the perfectly good eraser on the end of our pencils for one that is slightly cheaper to manufacture but doesn't do anything other than make a mess on the page when you use it? Thank you, gentlemen, that's almost unanimous. Jenkins, may I ask what your objection is?'

Jenkins: 'Sir, won't that annoy our customers and damage our reputation?' (Everyone around the table laughs.)

Cut to: me with the new pencil and its eraser that smears instead of rubbing out.

Thanks for nothing, you bastards.

4

I SUSPECT THE REASON why so few book groups are populated by men is that there's only so much you can say about the *Guinness Book of Records*.

Not that it wouldn't be fun to meet up over a bottle of Chardonnay and a tub of taramasalata (plus, of course, the raw-carrot dippers to give the illusion of healthiness) and take it in turns to argue the merits of the 2009 edition versus all the previous ones. Perhaps there could be some concessions to the masculine preference for beer and nuts, and a farting competition at the end, but you get my drift.

I can almost hear the sparkling conversation:

'I felt that Guinness '09 was a beautifully woven saga of separate yet somehow connected achievements. I loved the way that athletic prowess rolled effortlessly from track and field to the more obscure records, always drawing the reader on to the next extraordinary feat. A remarkable piece of writing.'

'Never mind that. Did you see that picture of the heaviest man in the world? God, he was a fat bastard. Pass the crisps.'

OK, I don't have any statistics at hand, but I'd bet my laptop that book groups are overwhelmingly attended by women. Nothing wrong with that. Many women reach a point where, if they get stuck in another conversation about natural childbirth or how well little Ajax or whatever his stupid name is is doing at school, they'll go completely mad. You know, do something crazy like suddenly kick old Mr Lennox the lollipop man in the nuts next time they see him or go into Lakeland and scream, 'Why don't you stick your Tupperware up your arse?'

In fairness, if you reach that state, a civilized chat about literature probably does serve as a good sedative. At the very least, it spares you the disgrace of community service for attacking a helpful pensioner, or the ignominy of being sectioned.

So as not to cause offence to male members of book groups, let me acknowledge here and now that erudite conversation is not confined to women. Nor would it be fair to suggest that the type of men who attend book groups are those who labour under the illusion that intellectual drippiness and a fondness for Dido are the way to a woman's heart. So I won't suggest it. I'll come out and state it as a fact.

While I'm on the subject, I might as well throw in

my idea for a children's book group in which five- and six-year-olds discuss *Burglar Bill* while getting high on a bumper bag of Haribos. It would give children a chance to get together under a tacit agreement that nobody talks about their birth or how brilliantly Mummy and Daddy are doing at work.

I was not a great reader as a child. Only a handful of books really grabbed my attention. My favourites were *Swallows and Amazons*, *The Adventures of Huckleberry Finn*, *The Thirty-Nine Steps* and *Rogue Male*. There were curricular books as well, of course, most of which I dismissed on the grounds that any book forced upon me should not easily gain my approval. Jane Austen and J. B. Priestley bored me to the point of utter despair and Thomas Hardy depressed me more than anything I knew. I can remember pulling my own hair whilst reading *Tess of the d'Urbervilles* to distract myself from the numbing dullness of Hardy's prose. As an adult I can review my attitude towards such distinguished works, but like someone who never eats cabbage because of school dinners, I think I'll never really come round to liking them.

One book that did captivate me at that time was the story of Raffles, the gentleman thief. It took my fancy one day in the school library, so – somewhat aptly, I think – I slipped it inside my jacket and promptly left. I had seen Sherlock Holmes in films and instantly loved that era and the fantasy of a debonair sleuth, but Raffles was a character who really fired my imagination. What a wonderful life. Top hat and tails, rooms in Albany, go to a society ball, slip out unnoticed and crack the host's safe, making off with a near-priceless diamond necklace. Excellent.

I remember improvising the outfit, including cloak and white gloves, and making a cane from a piece of garden bamboo. Then I would clamber on to our garage roof, from where, with the correct pick chosen from a selection of Allen keys wrapped in a chamois leather, I would expertly open my bedroom window and climb in. For me, the challenge was to execute the plan with grace and elegance.

Once inside, I would draw the curtains shut, produce a box of matches and light a candle so that I could go about my daring heist without fear of the flickering light attracting unwanted attention. I could almost hear the muffled chamber music from the ballroom below. Moments later, I was quietly closing the window behind me, leaving no trace of my visit, save the wisp of extinguished candle smoke and a newly emptied safe. OK, cupboard.

Mostly, however, I was a prolific reader of first chapters. I'm not much reformed from the habit now, but as a child, if a book hadn't pulled me in by page five, then I'd give up on it without a second thought.

A common problem I encounter when reading novels is my inability to enter into the author's conceit. It's as if I'm conducting an argument with

41

him/her as I read. Typically, it goes something like this:

I read '. . . Edward placed the lid back on the pen, slipped it into his breast pocket and sat back in the chair as he remembered the sequence of events that had brought him to this moment: the train journey, the old woman who sat opposite him, her face so sad, the cold gush of air when he slid open the carriage window as they pulled into Paddington reminding him of the woman he had left behind . . .' And I think, 'How do you know that? Fair enough, he puts his pen away, but how do you know about all the other stuff? How do you know that's what he was thinking about? The train journey and all that? You're just putting words in his mouth. For all you know, Edward sat back in his chair and thought "I fancy a Cadbury's miniroll now" or "I wonder if I'm missing *Countdown*"'.

The other hurdle that I always stumble at is description. Alright, you have to have some of it, I know, otherwise your epic reduces quickly down to one or two paragraphs. Not even I would want books to debase themselves to that extent, but for the love of God, can't these writers rein it in a bit?

Don't get me interested in the plot and then stupefy me with a seven-page indulgence about the lovely countryside. I know what trees and fields look like, I've seen several, so I really don't need to wade through reams of turgid description just so you feel you've done your job as an author properly.

Somewhat to my surprise, I've recently discovered that in my case it was the sheer physical effort required to read that was the stumbling block.

My literary saviour has been the downloadable audiobook. All the classics from *War and Peace* to *Crime and Punishment* are easily available online and can be zapped on to your iPod in a matter of moments. There probably aren't many people who jog to the strains of Tolstoy and Dostoyevsky, but I'm one of them. I don't know, maybe I should just lighten up.

And when it comes to gadgets, the world of literature is not immune to their revolutionizing influence. The e-reader is with us. Perhaps you're ahead of the game and are reading these very words on an e-reader. But for those of you who aren't, it's an electronic tablet with a screen that you can read just like the pages of a book. It's about the size of a thin Penguin (paperback that is, not flightless bird) and can store in its memory the entire contents of 160 books, including, I'm told, the *Encyclopaedia Britannica and the Oxford Dictionary*. If it were a human it would undoubtedly be Stephen Fry.

I haven't bought an e-reader yet, but I expect I will because they sound so great. And also because I have a long record of being attracted to the inevitable crushing disappointment that such investments deliver.

So at the moment I am in the most enjoyable phase of the gadget-purchase cycle: the excited expectation that here is something that actually will change my life for the better, making it happier and more fulfilling. I'm still able to believe that I will look back upon my book-reading days and not know how I survived the ordeal of having to carry an actual book about all day long. To think that I went to bookshops and bought real paper books and put them on my bookshelves. Well, I can laugh about it now, but at the time it was a living nightmare.

When I get my e-reader I will be able to walk around with a veritable library in my pocket. I'll be able to quickly look up a random fact of astonishing interest and drop it into the conversation just to pep things up.

'Did you know,' I'll say nonchalantly, 'that during his lifetime Vincent Van Gogh only sold one of his paintings? Steve told me that . . . sorry, Stephen Fry, he's a really good mate of mine.'

The dreary reality is that the most useful aspect of my new electronic book will be that people won't be able to see what it is that I am reading. I will be able to sit in a crowded bar with my downloaded Andy McNab novel, free of the anxiety of title-sneer from my fellow drinkers. Equally, I will at last be able to read *Living with Piles* on the train without it provoking the usual smirking nudges. Instead, other passengers will observe my pained expression and wonder, with envy, what literary masterpiece has gripped me in such a way.

So for now I'll stick to the tried-and-tested paper

version. After all, what can replace the warm sense of altruistic satisfaction achieved by taking a box of thoroughly enjoyed novels to the charity shop for others to read? Or the secret thrill of knowing that I've torn the last two pages out of each and every one?

5

LET ME TELL YOU how the iPod changed my life for ever. This is not an endorsement for Apple products, but, let's face it, they make the best MP3 players.

If you don't agree, it's because you're one of those who went against their better judgement and purchased one of the many other types that exist out there in gadget-land. And you disagree that iPods rule not because your experience of the non-Apple MP3 player has convinced you that you are right. Quite the opposite. At best, your little music player is only as good as the real thing, and was probably no cheaper. Even if it was cheaper, what price not having to explain to everyone why you didn't just buy an iPod and be done with it? What wouldn't you give not to have to justify your clearly wrong decision? How nice not to feel obliged to trot out the same flimsy case that you have built in defence of your sub-standard player. A case that even you don't really believe.

You made a duff purchase, that's all. Don't feel too bad, everybody does it sometimes. I once stopped at a supermarket in Frome on my way back from holidaying in Devon, bought some bits and pieces, including some eggs, and when I finally got back to London and unpacked my shopping, guess what, two of the eggs were broken. I know. I couldn't take them back because the shop was miles away. I was lumbered with the knowledge that I was out of pocket by – what? – at least 80p.

Admittedly, you wasted a hell of a lot more than that on your loser's version of an iPod. I'm only telling you to show that I know how you feel about it. Let's just leave it at that.

Besides, there's no shame in it. Well, there is a bit.

If I were you I'd come clean about it. Gather your friends and family and tell them all at once, 'Mum, Dad, everybody, I screwed up.' No doubt there will be a lot of crying before you're finished, but I can guarantee you'll feel better afterwards and it'll be nothing but a relief to the people you tell. Almost certainly they will have been concerned for your well-being the minute they heard that you'd taken the Tandy Highway to Twatville. They never did believe you when you said, 'Anyway, all the circuitry inside is the same,' that 'It's not the unit that matters, it's the headphones.' Why would they? Beneath the smile you looked sad when you were saying it, like a black person laughing at a racist joke.

And think of this: once you've owned up you won't have to lie any more. All the fake alibis and phoney excuses, they'll all be a thing of the past. Throw away your gut-wrenchingly disappointing Korean impostor, buy yourself an iPod, a real one this time, and start living your life like you're part of Team Humanity going for gold and not just a wistful spectator.

So, how the iPod changed my life for ever:

In the telling of this story it's only right to credit the iPod's predecessors: the Sony Walkman and the Discman. We should be grateful to them for being sufficiently crap to necessitate the iPod's invention.

And don't leap to their defence. The first Walkman I owned treated most of my cherished tapes with as much care as a drunk treats dental-floss. Within weeks my collection of cassettes had been decimated. A happy community of albums all but wiped out by Walkman Fever, reduced to a clot of useless gnarled ribbon. I even came close to admiring its knack of chewing up only the music that I really liked. Bob Dylan and Jimi Hendrix invariably got mangled, and yet when I was forced to resort to the C-list, I found that Fleetwood Mac and Supertramp emerged unscathed.

But then, along came the CD and its hopelessly sized Discman. The early ones were like having a cake-tin hanging from your belt. Even once they'd slimmed down, they were always going to have to obey the dimensions of their contents. The fact is that nobody other than clowns had pockets big enough to house them.

'The Compact Disc is virtually indestructible,' I remember people saying, unaware, as were they, that they were lying. With good old vinyl, a scratch was a scratch, you could angle the record to the light and see it. The scratch itself produced nothing worse than a hypnotic repetition of a word, phrase or chord. Quite relaxing if it hit just the right note. But when a CD is scratched the damage is invisible, so you don't know until your speakers suddenly sound like they're travelling through a time-warp. The kind of noise that they used in cheap science-fiction films when everyone clutched their heads in agony and fell to the ground.

It was Nobutoshi Kihara, inventor of the original Walkman, who first gave us the notion that it would be fun to listen to music whenever and wherever. Although, of course, in many ways I was thinking very much along the same lines in my childhood when I was dreaming of being able to walk around inside my record-player. It's pretty obvious to me that it would only have required a small tweak to arrive at the idea of walking around actually wearing the record-player/cassette-player, call it what you will.

But fair play to Nobutoshi for running with the idea that I would have had anyway.

Putting aside the matter of who technically invented the Walkman, in some ways at least it was an advance.

Previously we'd had to put a record on or listen to the radio and hope it would play something we liked. That was always a compromise, the radio, hoping for Deep Purple but having to make do with Mud. Leaving your musical needs in the hands of a disc-jockey can only lead to frustration. Somebody playing records from a padded room in Broadcasting House was never going to be in tune with everybody's requirements. Not all the time. What if you'd just heard some bad news? The chances of the DJ playing something appropriate at that moment were incredibly slim. If I was a DJ I'd play gloomy stuff all the time in case one of my listeners had just found out he had only months to live. I'd hate to think that I'd made things worse by playing Cliff Richard's 'Congratulations' just as he was driving away from the doctor's.

At first I thought that investing in a Walkman would mean that I could keep abreast of popular culture. I'd spend every spare moment listening to music and that, in turn, would lead to a new lifestyle which would involve browsing in record shops for increasingly obscure music to record and listen to while I walked. I would amass an enviable collection of little-known singles and LPs. People would come round to my place and think it was cool. They'd hear my cool music and ask what it was, at the same time wishing they could be like me. Cool.

I might specialize in a genre that nobody really

wants to listen to but won't admit it, like jazz or fifties rock'n'roll, and probably become a recognized expert in the field, writing occasionally on the subject. Long articles without that many pictures. For the *Observer*, I expect. I'd be the type of person who is asked for his views when some musician you've never heard of passes away. Then I would speak on the news, by telephone, succinctly, knowledgeably. Something like 'He really was a pioneer of the electric lute and led the way for what came to be known as baroque/reggae fusion.'

The reality is that I listen to less music these days, thanks to my iPod. The conditions of me being on my own, out of the house, wanting to listen to music and actually having my iPod charged up, rarely converge. In any case, the theoretical ready availability of my favourite tracks at any given moment is not how the iPod changed my life for ever. Its true value is in what it represents rather than what it does. If you carry an iPod you have headphones that you can legitimately wear, regardless of the fact that the iPod itself hasn't played a note since Christmas when you last remembered to charge it. And the really great thing about wearing headphones is that you are excused from conversation with anybody you encounter on your travels. Most especially taxi-drivers.

The bigoted taxi-driver is a well-established stereotype: driving around, ranting on about other well-established stereotypes. We all have our own examples and they're all very similar so I'm not going to add mine. If you think this bit simply isn't complete without a bigoted-taxi-driver story then I'm sorry, I just don't see the point in putting mine in. It was a tough call, but one that needed to be made and I'm sticking to it.

Anyway, it's alright for you, you only have to read it. I'm the writer; it's very different. I could get blacklisted and never be able to hail a cab again and that's too high a price to pay. So if it's all the same to you, I'd like to leave it at that and move on.

If it's becoming a bit of an issue for you that I haven't included an example, then maybe type one yourself, Sellotape it in and reread it, pretending that I wrote it. It might help you realize how much we have in common.

In any case, it isn't the bigotry that I am trying to deafen myself from. Bigotry doesn't often offend me. I usually find it laughable. That taxi-driver you keep banging on about harbours views which are so utterly stupid that laughter is the only sensible response. Because if you give words the authority to offend you, they always will. What I really don't want to listen to, and the reason I wear headphones, is sport. For me the true, revolutionary, life-changing impact of the iPod is that I need never again be trapped in a taxi, humouring some haemorrhoidal driver while he tells me about his useless football team.

6

I DON'T KNOW WHICH sex you are. Maybe you don't either, none of my business, but I am a man. One of the many attributes expected of me, besides being able to mend cars and punch people to the pavement with one hand whilst holding a pint of lager in the other, is to talk endlessly with anybody about matters relating to sport.

I'm not going to tell you that I hate sport. This is no deliberate attempt to be contrary. It isn't that simple. For the most part I resent sport – its bloated sense of self-importance and the undeserved awe that it's held in. But the matter is complicated by my own inconsistencies. For instance, a football tournament like the World Cup can attract my attention, sometimes for an entire game.

It's partly the excitement factor. I get caught up in the event. I find myself remembering little football facts: a player's name, a goalkeeper's record on penalties or a manager's tendency to favour the 4-4-2 formation. With stuff like this up my sleeve I might be able to hold my own for hours in a conversation about our national game, should the need arise.

Five or six snippets is all it would take to encourage any genuine football fanatic to talk and talk and bloody talk. All I'd need to do is throw in the occasional 'absolutely' and he'd be hard to stop anyway, but to really get him foaming at the mouth with joy I'd offer the more informed version, such as: 'Well, it's like Scolari, isn't it?' That's all. No elaboration. It won't be needed, just sit back and listen to the rubbish that pours from him. If no name comes to mind then you just have to be tangential and say 'Well, it's like the FA itself, isn't it?' That's usually a good one because, if challenged, you can provide generic evidence that would fit any corporation, like 'No one knows what's going on, it's antiquated, they've lost everyone's trust' and so on.

Notice how those two words 'It's like' are invaluable. You can link any two subjects in the universe with that phrase. Example: he says, 'I mean, look at Fulham last season, lost practically every match, now you can't beat them.' And you say, 'Exactly. [Here it comes.] It's like when Pete Best left the Beatles and Ringo joined.' Obviously what you've said is nonsense but I guarantee that it will be greeted with an 'Exactly,' or at worst a slightly hesitant 'Yeah, no, it is like that, now you mention it.' That's your key. 'It's like' implies an indisputable link that only the dumb would not be able to notice and agree with.

It will come as little surprise to you, then, that I do not attend football matches. My default position is that if I want to watch a bunch of violent retards running around a pitch for ninety minutes then I'll apply for a job in the PE department at Parkhurst.

Alright, alright, calm down. I take it back. All footballers are not violent. I know. And the few that are hardly ever get done for it.

I live near enough to a large premiership stadium to be inconvenienced by the traffic when there's a match. I usually remember not to go near the place on a Saturday afternoon but still occasionally get caught up in the hordes of fans making their way to their blessed footy.

Don't get me wrong. I can see the point of going to watch a football match. I bet it's quite fun. I just can't get as excited about the subject as I'm obviously supposed to. I might learn the manager's name and the captain's, but the rest of them? Who cares? The only thing I know about footballers is they're not as intelligent as they look. And I include Wayne Rooney in that.

The nearest I come to watching live football is seeing the groups of men who meet to play on Sundays on the common where I walk my dogs. I know women play as well, but it is much rarer, and anyway, I'm not talking about that.

Sunday League football is the closest you can get to the perfect spectator-sport. I say that because, for me, the perfect spectator-sport would actually be two teams of over-fed camels chasing a Space Hopper around a field. Until the happy day arrives when that becomes a common sight, I'll make do with Sunday League despite the subtle differences.

One difference is that camels wouldn't leave behind a wake of discarded Lucozade bottles, KitKat wrappers, gnawed orange quarters and empty spray-cans of Deep Heat. Another is that camels probably wouldn't have older, even fatter camels on the sidelines, breaking wind with excitement and shouting instructional swear-words at them. Yet another difference, if you want one, is that watching a camel have a seizure and collapsing isn't secretly funny. Although, come to think of it . . .

I would love Britain to become a truly classless society, but until that day arrives I think it might be better if the classes we have in our existing structure stopped trying to be like each other. Let's be honest, it's confusing when working-class people send their children to private schools or when posh people retrain and become electricians. Worst of all is when a born-and-bred middle-class fellow declares his love for football. It turns the stomach.

Politicians, novelists, smarmy lawyers and advertising execs – every profession, every corner of middle-class life is now crawling with pseudo footy fans, the Johnny Come Latelys for whom a season ticket should only ever be for the 08:20 from Woking to Waterloo.

It feels as though football has become everyone's surrogate mother. Through football, all the ups and downs, the thrills and spills, dramas and disappointments of real life can be experienced in a safe context, without the actual pain of living. Football is a metaphor that you can piggy-back ride through your life. There's nothing wrong with it, except I don't get it. Many of us create a fantasy in which we can shelter from life. For some it's dressing up as a Cavalier or Roundhead and re-enacting the Civil War in front of bemused holiday-makers. Others claim sanctuary in train timetables or on the observation deck at Gatwick, counting the planes, noting their numbers. Some collect: comics, cars, clocks and all manner of things that don't begin with C. The difference is that none of these innocent hobbyists form a massive overwhelming majority in our society. They don't expect me to be one of them, to care about the Will's Tobacco Fighting Vessel cards from 1935, or to know which trains left Paddington on time that day. Much less do they imagine that a mere hint is all that is needed for me to know precisely to which misdemeanour in which match they are referring. A random clue like 'Ttt, penalty or what?' is meant to rile me into a frenzy of abuse towards a referee somewhere who evidently made a decision that conflicted with the crowd's opinion.

Think about it. It would be incredibly unlikely that your newsagent would cryptically refer to a Sealed Knot gathering that he had attended in Epping Forest and expect you to know what he was talking about. 'What about that on Saturday then?' he'd say, shaking his head solemnly, and you'd be obliged to confirm your manly credentials with an informed 'I know. That bloke with the pike, what was his problem?'

With football, the assumption is always that I too scurried off to the big match along with all the other lemmings and now want to talk ceaselessly about it until the next one. Well, I didn't and I don't.

Ignorance, betrayed by a casual 'What game?' or 'Who won?' is greeted with open-mouthed astonishment that gives way to McCarthy-like suspicion. Word will get back that I didn't watch the Everton–West Ham play-off and didn't even know the score. I could be shunned, spurned by colleagues, rejected by my friends. And yes, I'm aware that Everton probably haven't played West Ham in a play-off. I picked those two teams at random. Get over it.

But if I had to choose between watching football and listening to footballers talk about it, I would choose the former every time. Listening to footballers speak is not a rewarding experience.

It would be nice just for once to hear a player who talks with some intonation, some variation in his voice. I don't imagine for a minute that it would improve the content of his narrative, it might even highlight how vacant it is, but at least it wouldn't give me nightmares about being stuck in a doomed submarine with him while he drones on about 'the lads doing great early doors'.

I liked it in the old days, before I was born, when people did sport and then shut up about it. Scratchy footage of grey Olympics, plucky athletes sprinting to the line before the television screen twirled into a cheery commercial for Player's cigarettes. No need for the post-race analysis then. The sport was everything, but thankfully everything wasn't sport. The track-side interview is an unwelcome addition made in the modern era. Nowadays no televised sporting event is allowed to pass without the puffed-out competitors explaining in detail how they performed, whether they won, lost, broke the Commonwealth record or merely collapsed in a pool of their own diarrhoea on the side of the road.

Sometimes words are not needed.

The black American athlete Jesse Owens won so many golds at the 1936 Berlin Olympics that Hitler went into a prolonged sulk (arguably about nine years) and refused to watch any more of the Games. Like a spoilt child, stomping off and hiding because someone else won pass-the-parcel at his party.

Did we have to hear the magnificent Owens talk about his achievements afterwards? No need. His prowess on track and field had shown the world, without a single word, that the Führer's theory of white supremacy was completely ridiculous and that it was everybody's party, not just his. Of course, a more reasonable, nicer, better-brought-up Führer might have taken stock at this point, apologized for his tantrum and abandoned his bonkers Aryan fantasy, but there's no telling some people.

7

MY OWN GIFT FOR athletics was gauged accurately at school a week or so before Sports Day when I was about nine. As one of a large gaggle of boys straining to read the schedule that had just been pinned up, I watched my classmates break away in twos and threes, happily proclaiming their allotted fixture. The corridors echoed with delighted cries of 'Hundred yards', 'High jump', 'Long distance' and 'Hurdles' until I was left alone in front of the noticeboard. I had been selected for two events: shot put and another sport that I hadn't yet heard of called 'Rake'.

'Rake' – perhaps you've guessed, it isn't difficult – was not really an event or sport as such. More a responsibility. Mine was the task of preparing the sand-pit for the long jump and ensuring that after each attempt the sand was repaired to its original blank state. It had to be done swiftly, mind. There was no time for dawdling or making patterns. 'Next. Busher.' On the teacher's instruction, Busher prepares. He moves into position like a plane taxiing at the end of its runway as I cultivate the sand and stand back, enjoying the result of my work.

In the school library I had once seen in a *National Geographic* magazine (that reliable source of nude-women pictures) a feature about Japanese gardens. Miniature ploughed lines of pure Zen that swept round obstacles like the contour lines of a map. Given the opportunity I would create a design worthy of the front cover. It would be a first. From then on 'Rake' would be a recognized art form – no, more than that, a creed, a way of life, with me as its principal, founding, child-genius practitioner, travelling the world, teaching its intricate skills to admiring novices.

Different types of rake would be developed, most of them named after me, but the one in my hand right now would become, in time, a near-sacred artefact, the sandpit itself a Mecca for robed pilgrims, journeying humbly to the birthplace of their faith, carrying with them only a few simple provisions and, of course, their own rake. In a few hundred years from now, people would wear little jewellery rakes on chains around their necks and I would be known as—

'Come on, Dee, we haven't got all day. Rake the pit or someone else can do it.'

I quickly brush the sand over, covering the impression left by Busher's hopeless crash-landing.

'Next. Dixon Senior. Go.' The run-up, the plimsoll on the board, Dixon Senior hurls himself several feet through the air and lands, destroying Busher's score and my peace garden.

My idea of starting a major new religion with a rusty garden tool had to be put on hold as I handed over to Busher so that I could participate in the shot put.

In the week that I had known of my new status as shot-putter I had come to view shot put as probably the most important sport in the athletic arena. Running fast and jumping long or high are all very well, but the ability to throw a cannonball at least your own body-length was not only a mark of physical and mental strength but also, potentially, a genuinely useful skill to have, should you ever be in a situation in which throwing a cannonball away from you suddenly becomes a priority. So that was to be my incentive. I imagined that I was throwing one of those Tom & Jerry-type bombs with a hissing fuse off a ship, thus saving many lives.

Plus, I was not surprised to have been picked to do shot put, having done it twice before. This time, with added atmosphere, I was bound to do fairly well.

In fact there was very little atmosphere to speak of. From different areas of the field, five of us approached the giant slice of cake that had been painted on the grass for us. Waiting with her clipboard was the French teacher (I forget her name) and Cookson, a weedy girl-boy of a child who hung around with a teacher whenever possible, and today was self-appointed to help with measuring duties.

Cookson was, as the French teacher might have said, *un collaborateur*, who quietly garnered information about all of our underground activities and streamed it back to the staff room. As the result of this intelligence two boarders once got the slipper for venturing into the attic of their dorm for a dare. More to the point, Cookson let it be known – to the headmaster, no less – that I had used a slide-rule under the desk to solve a maths test question. For this I was barred from the play-ground for two weeks and had to spend every break during that period polishing cutlery in the dining room.

So, not to put too fine a point on it, Cookson was a real tit, and to make matters worse, I harboured a secret grudge that he had been trusted with the tape measure, but tried to set it aside in order to concentrate on my sport.

And that was it. Mme Frenchy and her little court eunuch Cookson. There were no spectators. I don't remember parents being present, at least not the way they are now when they turn out for Sports Day, tearing around the games field from heat to heat, camcording every second of it, cheering their offspring, desperate for any slight sign that could possibly be read as evidence of prodigy – a freak time recorded on the two hundred metres or a fine bit of hurdling – to oxygenate the hope that their child is the bearer of life's golden ticket: talent.

Certainly, there was no parents' race. Please. These were the days when grown-ups knew how to behave like grown-ups; when the door between childhood and adulthood did not swing both ways. We children endeavoured to emulate our parents. They were the mould and we the clay.

So, five boys – the heavy and the slow, the oddly shaped and the lethargic of our year group – assembled at the apex of the giant cake to do battle, ready to strain over every hard-earned inch.

I was not a fat child, just a bit chubby – or well-covered, as I was sometimes described. In 1970 it was unusual for a child to be overweight, but obviously it did occur. Every school had at least one and at my school he was called Simon Rothman. 'Rothers' and I were good friends. He called me Deezy and we were bound by a hatred of hard work, unbridled loathing of the same teachers and pupils, and the need to make each other laugh.

One by one we sombrely stepped into the circle and took our throw. Watching from the side as each school-mate took the dead weight and nestled it in his neck, it was impossible, even at that age when you accept most things in your life without question, not to marvel at the gob-smacking pointlessness of what we were doing: throwing a twelve-pound metal lump about four feet and then going to pick it up while weedy Cookson drew his tape measure out to the dent that had been made and declared the distance.

Cookson gained in confidence as each boy made his lumbering, impotent throw. He began to behave like a real AAA official, like the ones who wear blazers and act all nonchalant about the javelins being thrown in their direction.

Cookson's assumption that he needed to stand only five feet in front of us as we threw began to grate on me. I'm not proud that this incentivized me. But none-theless, I decided to confound Cookson's estimation in a way that he would regret. Possibly for ever.

The more I considered it, the more the horrible idea appealed. This was a perfect chance to maim the traitor Cookson, and it would all be his fault. I silently rehearsed my concerned 'Oh God, sorry, Cookers. That's really bad. Here, let me help you stem the blood. Hope you manage to walk again one day . . .'

And Miss Whateverhernamewas would say, 'Stop screaming, Cookson. Help is on the way. Don't worry, Dee. It's not your fault that you're so brilliant at shot put.'

'I know, Miss. I suppose he shouldn't have been standing so close. Just wrong place, wrong time, Miss.'

We were fond at the time of stories that charted the extremes of human achievement: Neil Armstrong, Sir Edmund Hillary, Cassius Clay and so many other heroes of playground banter. One story that intrigued me was of a woman who, having heard what sounded like a traffic accident, ran out of her house only to discover her small daughter underneath the wheel of a crashed car. Without a thought she simply lifted the front of the vehicle with one arm and removed her child using her free hand, thus saving her life. Like the Bionic woman. Except she wasn't Bionic. She was normal. When the ambulance crew arrived, they noted that the mother hadn't so much as pulled a muscle and nobody could explain her moment of superhuman strength.

I stepped into the chalk ring, heaved the put into place between my chin and shoulder and slowly began to swing my body in the rhythmic motion that would build to an explosive alchemy of technique and raw power. As I gyrated I took a look at Cookson standing there, merrily unaware that he was doing so for the last time. The last time without assistance, at any rate.

As my arm moved slowly upward, there did indeed seem to be an unknown force running through my body, a surge of strength that I had never before experienced. I could still sense the weight of the put, but it was as if my hand was being pushed through it, unhindered by the laws of physics. As my arm reached its straightened state, the leaden ball felt quite weightless.

Cookson didn't have a chance. I will always remember him looking up as a trapped rabbit would stare, misty-eyed, into the barrel of the farmer's gun. But I like to think that he saw nothing as the iron boulder descended from some eight or nine feet on to his head.

He fell without a sound and lay there, the tape measure tangled around his motionless torso.

Much of what followed is too distressing for the likes of these pages. Suffice to say that when poor old Cookers finally emerged from unconsciousness three days later he found that there was a silver shot-put cup by his hospital bedside. Silly, I know, but I wanted him to have it, even though it now had my name freshly engraved upon it. I visited him two or three times after that, hoping that the accident might in some way bond us, but conversation was limited to what his 'grade two permanent retardation', as the doctor called it, could cope with. I seem to recall that my visits excited in him a need to talk about farmyard animals, marbles and aeroplanes. All very random. In any event it was tragic for Cookers, who now weaves coasters for a 'living'.

Knowing that in reality it simply wasn't my fault at all, everyone was incredibly supportive and helped me through the guilt that I nonetheless felt.

Oh alright . . . it may have been more like this:

As my arm moved slowly upward, there did indeed seem to be an unknown force running through my body, a surge of strength that I had never before experienced. I could still sense the weight of the put, but it was as if my hand was being pushed through it, unhindered by the laws of physics. As my arm reached its straightened state, the leaden ball felt quite weightless.

And unhindered it was, for the great round lump had unbalanced itself from my cupped hand, rolled unstoppably past the tips of my fingers and plummeted directly to the piece of turf that was currently occupied by my foot.

I fell without a sound other than that of Cookson's laughter as I writhed on the grass, clenching my crushed toe.

8

THERE ARE SOME PEOPLE who think it's clever that they don't watch much television. It's as if it implies a higher degree of intelligence; that they're having a better, busier time of it, more friends than you've got, an altogether cooler existence that rides above the average bovine drudgery of everybody else's lives.

So when I say that I don't watch much television, it's not presented to you as a virtue. I am consciously making an effort to watch more. I should. I need to, especially as I work in the industry a lot of the time and could well benefit from seeing more programmes. It can be embarrassing, having to admit to acquaintances the woeful gaps in my TV knowledge.

Usually if I like a programme, I'll buy the box-set on DVD so that I can watch it at my convenience. Why should I wait around until a channel finally decides to air the show that I want to watch? Whenever I buy a DVD like that, I don't see it as a waste of money. Alright,

I admit, there have been a few that turned out to be less entertaining than I had hoped. Come to think of it, they were rubbish. I'm far too professional to use these pages to name and embarrass the culprits. More to the point, they might retaliate by attacking me in their books. Some people might call that cowardice. In fact I'm one of them. I hate myself for it, but you'd be the same if you were shallow like me.

No, when I buy a DVD like that, I see it as clawing back some control of my life. I don't have to be at the behest of some faceless corporate giant, obediently switching on the set when it wants me to. Nor do I have to fumble nervously through the *Radio Times* with a marker pen, planning my week's viewing in careful stripes of day-glo. And you know what? I'm glad. I never want to be like that, just like I never want to wear Marks & Spencer clothes or live in a bungalow.

I swim most mornings at a private health-club and in the changing room there is a television. Two televisions, in fact. Sounds great, doesn't it? Well, it's not, because one is digital and the other isn't, which means that there is a sound delay between the two, like an echo. It drives me bloody mad, especially as nobody else seems bothered. I've complained several times, in person, but nothing has come of it. Now I'm thinking that I'll write a letter and then retype the exact same letter over it with a three-letter delay, just to give management a visual concept of what I have to endure.

JACK DEE

The reason for me telling you this, however, is that when I'm getting dried and dressed at the club I watch the TV, which gives me a fair, if audibly unpleasant, taste of morning television.

Sometimes it's Jeremy Kyle, spitting and cursing at some poor chav who got his girlfriend pregnant and then decided not to hang around. In fairness, she was jolly ugly, but Jeremy was looking at the bigger picture: moral responsibility, the family, social cohesion and the chance to taunt an unemployed nineteen-year-old who was being held down in his seat by security.

Other times it's a show about people who are thinking of moving to Australia. You get to know the family and their budget, then follow them on a re-connaissance trip down under, where they're shown the type of life they could have if they made the big move. They look around some possible houses, the kind of thing that they could end up living in. Usually there's a swimming pool, if not a sea-view, and a fantastic open-plan interior that they always love. They'd have a really nice four-wheel-drive car and the husband would be able to join the nearby golf club, plus he'd actually be earning more. It's all so much better than where they live in Northampton or Staines or wherever. Then they have to sit down and watch a video of people they know back in England, like their gran, who are missing them. This makes the teenage daughter cry a bit and they all have second thoughts. By then I'm usually dressed so I never find out if they stay or go home.

But there was one programme in particular that interested me. It was another relocation-type thing, along the same lines as the Australian show, but it seemed to be all about couples who wanted to move to a bigger house and were prepared to run it as a B&B or even a small hotel in order to afford it. This strikes me as a bizarre strategy. Like buying the car of your dreams, but you can only afford it if you spend all your free time minicabbing in it.

One of the better aspects of this particular pro-gramme is that it revisits previous participants to see how they are getting on. Naturally, they all say that it's much harder work than they had expected and when asked if they'd do it again there's a loaded silence followed by a change of subject. But occasionally the adventure is a rewarding one and the couple are able to say that they have indeed pursued and achieved their goal and have loved every minute of creating their very individual boutique hotel. When that happens it always makes me feel guilty about what I once did in a very similar place.

I was doing a gig in Brighton and was put up in a quaint old Regency townhouse that had been lovingly restored and turned into a small, very luxurious hotel, run by a couple, Mark and Peter, who had done much of the work themselves. Mark, I remember, wore a long leather apron in which to conduct his housekeeping duties. Chattily, he showed me to the room, not long after which Jane arrived, having come from London by train to meet up with me.

Usually I hate being shown to my room in hotels. There is something insultingly unnecessary about having a mini-bar pointed out or being shown how to switch on the bedside lights, but Mark was a nice man, rightly proud of his and Peter's achievement. I have to say, however, that my heart sank when he introduced me to the en-suite bathroom, which was that most dreadful of inventions: a wet room.

I don't know what the official definition of a wet room is, but mine is 'a room in which everything ends up getting wet'. It surely is the invention of a builder who forgot to put a shower tray or screen in a bathroom and convinced his client that it was all the rage. That nowadays you just have a big hole in the middle of the floor for all the water to go down.

Mark asked us if we'd like anything brought to the room. He really was very thoughtful and took great delight in telling us all about how he and Peter had renovated the place, how long it had taken, who chose the fabric for the soft furnishings (Mark mostly, although the drawing-room curtains were Peter's idea) and how they'd been rushed off their feet ever since it opened.

Anyway, that night, after the show, I decide to try the shower. As I predicted, everything gets soaked. The toilet paper, towels, my clothes, the entire floor. Everything. To make matters worse, it is very slow to drain and Jane's annoyed because she can't get in there to brush her teeth without getting her feet wet, and somehow that's my fault.

Mark rings up to ask if there's anything we require. No thanks, we're fine, I say, thinking I can't really ask him to come up and fit a proper bathroom.

In bed I realize that the air-conditioning is a bit loud, but I can't figure out where to switch it off. I have to call Mark, who doesn't know but says that Peter will because he's a wizard at that sort of thing and was 'in on the electrical design', so he'll ask him.

Mark (I don't know why people bother doing this) puts his hand over the receiver and so I hear a muffled version of my question being asked, followed by a fainter and even more muffled answer from Peter.

Mark interprets and so I look where I'm instructed to. Peter the electrical wizard had decided that the switch for the air-conditioning should be located behind the bed.

Not without effort, I pull the bed away from the wall so that I can squeeze my arm in and reach the control with the tip of my finger.

Having turned it off I get back into bed and lie there. The lack of hum from the AC is nice, but it has revealed a second, underlying noise. Jane says that it sounds like a running tap. 'Go and look,' she says.

Not wanting to get my feet wet, I peer into the wet room from the doorway and can see that neither the shower nor the taps are causing the noise. It appears to be coming from the lavatory, which is in that mood where the cistern won't shut up. I often find that if you flush it again, that seems to placate it and all becomes quiet. So I tiptoe in.

'What are you doing?' asks Jane.

'I'm going to . . . oh, it doesn't matter,' I explain as I flush the lever.

'That's made it noisier,' decides Jane.

'I know, but once it's filled up again it should—'

'We can't have it like that all night. You'd better call Mark again,' she says.

'No,' I insist. 'Because it should stop again in a minute, when the cistern fills.'

Two competitive minutes pass, the tension of right or wrong rising like the water in the cistern.

I was wrong.

'It hasn't stopped.'

'I know,' I say.

'Call Mark.'

But I really don't want to.

'I really don't want to,' I say. 'I've already called him about the air-conditioner, he's going to think I'm some sort of pain.'

Jane called Mark anyway. Thankfully there was no answer, so I was spared from that humiliation.

And then I uttered the words that should be confined to professional tradesmen and lame sitcom scripts: 'I'll try and fix it.'

The trouble with this particular cistern is that it was a very bad design. The stopcock was inaccessible because the porcelain lid that concealed it was glued on. Madness. It's lucky that I'm quite practical. And strong.

With force, I could feel the lid begin to give. It was partially recessed into the wall and still wet from my all-encompassing shower, which made it hard to get a grip. I called out to Jane, asking her to pass me a dry towel from the bedroom. But there was no reply. She must have gone to sleep.

Still straining at the cistern cover, I reached for the bathrobe on the back of the door to use instead. At that moment the cover came loose. Well, more than loose. It sort of took off. The seal that was holding it stuck just gave way and the cover launched itself with all the force that I was exerting upon it. It literally flew up into the air like a piece of paper caught by the wind, this heavy white lump of china.

I so nearly caught it as well, but, as I said, it was wet and slippery (which is why I was reaching for the bathrobe in the first place) and it evaded my fingers, took a sizeable chunk out of the adjacent basin, and smashed into small pieces on the stone-tiled floor.

Luckily Jane hadn't stirred, although I'm sorry to

report that I said a few things that in this day and age could get you suspended from the Beeb.

Things got worse as I realized that damage had also been done to the bowl of the lavatory, which appeared to have suffered a crack. Better not use it just yet, I thought. Which was a pity, because, what with all the excitement and the two pints I'd had earlier trickling their way through my system, I was bursting for the loo. But, as I said, the cistern cover had cracked it and I didn't want to add to the problem by filling it further and causing it to leak.

My other worry was the shards of porcelain that I was increasingly aware of and trying to avoid. The best thing, I decided, was to stand where I was and try to aim at the hole in the floor which served as a drain for the shower; it was about a metre away.

I'd say that the first pint went to plan. I doubt McDonald's had this in mind when they came up with their marketing idea of a golden arch, but that's what it reminded me of. However, as the pressure in my bladder diminished, so too did the manly force of my stream, until I was left trying to calculate which part of the floor would best create a downward path for the remaining flow.

Inevitably this necessitated a degree of trial and error and to an onlooker, I admit, this could very well have appeared as though I was deliberately, casually urinating all over the broken pieces of lavatory.

Well, here's the thing. It turned out that Jane hadn't been asleep at all. In fact she wasn't even in the bedroom. She had taken it upon herself to go downstairs and fetch Mark.

I heard a small cough behind me and, still peeing on the floor, turned to see Mark, Peter and Jane watching.

It's fair to say that the next morning, there was a bit of an atmosphere at breakfast. Mark, though still tearful, was reasonably accepting of my explanation. It was Peter who was all put out. I'm the first to admit, fully and without trying to avoid blame, that what happened was simply a freak accident which (and I pointed this out) only occurred because we hadn't been able to get them on the phone in the first place, which in turn sort of makes it partly their fault.

Peter didn't follow my reasoning. His loss, not mine, if he doesn't want to look at the truth.

Anyway, please don't think that their business has suffered as a result of my misfortune. I tried to book a room there recently and Peter told me they were fully booked. For ever.

9

HAVING STATED MY DISDAIN for almost all sport, I acknowledge that it is a contradiction in my personality that I have nearly always tried to stay fit. I have jogged or cycled, swum or lifted weights on a regular basis for long periods of my adult life.

I enjoy the endorphin rush after a session in the gym. It can feel like quite a high for an hour or so, although side effects can include muscle stiffness, aching joints and an inability not to mention to people that I went to the gym that morning.

But the true barrier that we face in exercise is not the battle to continue when every cell and sinew of our being is screaming at us to stop. The battle is with the mind-shrivelling boredom that sets in after about four minutes.

Nothing can counteract it. Sure you can buy yourself any amount of new kit and gadgets to alleviate the tedium, but they are all merely painkiller remedies that can only ever address the symptom and never the cause.

Music is all very well, but by my tenth session on the running machine in a week, I don't mind admitting I hate every song that's ever been written.

You can buy elaborate wrist-watches that read your heart rate while you exercise by computing signals emitted from a thin strap that you wear across your chest underneath your shirt. Some of the guys at the gym I go to have them. You have to really want to know your heart rate to go to that much trouble. And you have to not mind it looking like you're wearing a sports bra. Such a 'guy' would argue that it doesn't look like he is wearing a bra under his shirt, but that's only because he didn't think it through when he rashly purchased it. He might also argue that it isn't just the heart rate that matters, it's your recovery time from exertion that counts, the differential between resting heart rate and training bpm.

There really are quite a few different ways to be bored by the workings of the heart. If you want to experience the ultimate in gymnasium dullness, that feeling of stagnating monotony that returns to you in horrid flashbacks where you find yourself shouting at the kids or taking a coin to the side of your own car for no reason, then I recommend you get a trainer.

Living in London, I get to witness all the latest fitness fads that the rest of the country sensibly eschews. For example, in Hyde Park one Sunday I saw a race that was comprised of men and women on bicycles that had no pedals. In other words, there was no chain, so their only means of propulsion was by scooting the ground with their feet.

I know. That's what I thought.

We're both right – that *is* what the first bikes were like before someone came up with the idea of a chain-drive.

They were wearing modern Lycra and helmets, so it wasn't some stupid vintage revival day that I'd walked into, just a bunch of men and women who thought they had a better way of cycling, but in fact didn't. For me, if you have a bike without pedals, don't go around on it thinking you're clever. Effectively, all you've done, apart from wasting your money, is gone back in time by some two hundred years. You may as well strip your house of all its electrics and then boast to everyone how great your candles are. And while you're at it, why not hitch a couple of shire horses to the front of your car?

On the common near my house, a group of people about my age (I can't be sure. Anyway, old enough to know better) have been lulled into the craze known as Nordic walking. This is walking with ski-poles, or skiing without skis – or snow, for that matter – whichever picture you prefer. Either way, they look completely ridiculous and it should be banned.

OK, sorry. That was uncalled for. Nordic walkers have never harmed anyone, least of all me. In fact, many of my best friends are Nordic walkers. Come to think of it, my life was once saved by a group of Nordic walkers who chanced upon me on Clapham Common after I had fallen down a ravine and broken my leg in three places. Well, what happened next was amazing. They used their poles and North Face anoraks to make a stretcher for me. No, I tell a lie, they're tossers.

Another of the latest fads in this area is a group of army instructors who, obviously not content just to goad recruits at Deepcut Barracks to hang themselves, have branched out into personal training. Commissioned or not, these instructors come dressed in army kit: camouflage fatigues, shining black boots and tight white T-shirts. Battle-ready, hard, fit and camp as a leotard.

Presumably they are soldiers who have left the army, unless it is now in the MOD's remit to help new mothers lose their stretch-marks. Perhaps I missed that in the Queen's speech. 'In addition to defending the realm and protecting our interests abroad, Her Majesty's forces will lead Mummy-Tummy classes twice a week.' Anyway, each Wednesday evening and Saturday morning there they are, the Special Arse Service, running effortlessly all around the common, followed by a herd of panting, red-faced women and one or two sweaty men, obeying every instruction. From a distance it looks like one of the Village People being mobbed by groupies. Closer up you can hear the terse nature of those barked instructions.

'Red Team: twenty sit-ups. NOW.'

'Blue Team: squat-thrusts, ten. GO.'

Then 'Everyone, sprint to the tree and back. Last one to complete, their team does twenty push-ups each. MOVE.'

In fairness, Karen is probably the most recent of all of them to have given birth and therefore found the sprint particularly difficult. In unfairness, Karen's a fat lazy cow who didn't try hard enough and caused all of Blue Team to have to do twenty push-ups. Between their exertions I guarantee each member of Blue Team is thinking, 'Next-week-I'll-watch-to-see-what-colour-bib-Karen-picks-and-then-I'll-pick-the-other-colour-Fat-lazy-cow.'

Team punishment for an individual's failing. That's how you get everyone to pull their weight, try their damnedest, gel as a group and turn on the weakling. It is bullying that is franchised out: get others to do the hating and punishing for you.

So what is it in the psyche of an otherwise sane person that makes her or him want to be shouted at in public by a skinhead with a fetish for military regalia?

It is not a sustainable way of exercising. Nobody taking part in this ludicrous spectacle will be involved in it in three years' time. Few of them will experience any benefit other than the knowledge that paying a body-squaddie to embarrass you doesn't get you fit and should probably remain in S&M clubs where it belongs.

The answer lies, I think, in that uncomfortable feeling that comes with the onset of middle age. As sure as the adorable toddler who once tugged on your heart-strings is now nicking fivers from your wallet to pay for condoms and lager, a voice within is calling. And it is saying, 'Your youth is over.'

The Dalai Llama recently said that one of the root causes of our unhappiness in life is that we are unable to accept the Buddha's words which state that nothing is permanent. Health deteriorates, looks wither, relationships break down, beliefs dwindle and, of course, ultimately we all die. As best-man speeches go, it was a bit of a downer, but he does have a point.

By way of evidence, he suggests that the reason why so many marriages fail is that people do not acknowledge that every relationship is fluid, always in a state of change. For example, you are unlikely to feel the same about your partner now as you did, say, five years ago when you met. The disparity in that feeling is what some people mistake for no longer loving each other any more (the irony being that without realizing it, they may actually love each other more).

Perhaps a more obvious example of this inability to accept that nothing is permanent is the way that some people attempt to defy the ageing process by surgically removing its evidence. And I think that obsessive physical exercise belongs somewhere in this category.

There is, of course, nothing wrong with exercise. I'd

argue that we are morally obliged to do what we can to remain fit and well. We should stay active and eat the right things, not just to avoid paying the ultimate congestion charge of a blocked aorta, but to be able to make the most of life. Certainly, the desire to stay fit isn't the problem. It's the desire to stay young that is our undoing.

A word of support is due to that exceptional group of people that I call the champion slimmers. These are men and women who courageously do battle with their 'before' photos and lose so much weight that they could hold a celebration party inside a pair of their old trousers. Among this group you get no thyroid-blaming self-pity. Just the determination to eat less, do more and shed a phenomenal amount of excess baggage. I would, however, be surprised if any such slimmer would give much credit to a hectoring commando wannabe.

It won't cause too much astonishment if I now tell you that I didn't sign up for the sergeant major's military fitness regime. But it won't do for me to point the finger and have fun at the expense of others if I am not going to be honest about what I *have* done.

I have had a personal trainer in the past, but it didn't work out.

'No way. How so?' I hear you say. I will try to explain.

The first thing I should say is that I don't have a good track-record when it comes to being taught anything. All my life, through infancy to school days, from adolescence and early adult life all the way to now, I have suffered from a hatred of being taught that perfectly outweighs my thirst for learning. In other words, I'm curious about things but too stupid to listen when people are trying to tell me about them.

Having said that, Mervin, the personal trainer in question, was particularly annoying, so it's not all my fault that things didn't work out.

I booked the session at my gym for ten a.m. Which is exactly when I turned up, ready to make a start on my new life of physical rigour and discipline. I have always set my watch to run fast so that I can be punctual even if I'm late. Which I wasn't.

Mervin was. Mervin was – how can I describe it? – not there. Absent. Mervin was there, not. Mervin was somewhere that wasn't the gym.

I didn't overreact to this slight snag in the paid-for arrangement that I had made with Mervin. Maybe he was delayed. These things happen. Admittedly that's why I set my watch fast, so that if these things *do* happen, I'll still be on time. But hey, let's not get into point-scoring over this.

The best thing for me to do now was warm up and get ready for when Mervin did arrive. The fact that I am paying £40 for this hour with Mervin (or rather without him, so far) shouldn't affect my motivation at all.

After five minutes on the elliptical, that strange

machine that allows you to run without your feet leaving its little rotating platforms, I work out that I have now paid Mervin about £3.30 for not being here. Not that that matters at all. He probably has a perfectly good reason for not being here. I decide I should ask if Mervin is around, maybe in the back-room having an energy drink or something.

'He should be on his way in,' I am told by another of the trainers, called Sean, according to his badge.

I don't lose it, but I do say, 'Not really, he shouldn't.' Which puzzles Sean. 'He should be here,' I explain.

Some conversations are a lost cause before they've even started and this was one of them. If I was Sean, I would have then said to me, 'Oh, is Mervin late for your session? I'm really sorry. I'll call him right now.'

But Sean wasn't like that. He just said, 'Oh, right,' and then, because the phone was ringing, he answered it. It wasn't Mervin. Back to the treadmill.

There were five TVs in the gym, each showing a different channel. Unlike in the changing-room that I told you about earlier, these televisions were mute, so the problem here was not synchronization but a total lack of sound. Luckily, I had the foresight to bring headphones so that I could hook into the system and watch one of the programmes on offer while I exercised. The choices were *Ready Steady Cook*, MTV, Sky News, golf or the inevitable Jeremy Kyle.

As everybody secretly knows, golf is a tragic waste of

time, a game invented for people who don't mind looking as if their mums dressed them that morning. It's
often said that golf is antisocial, but for me that is its
one saving grace, because it means the people who play
it stay away from the rest of us for long periods of time.
Hitting a tiny ball with an expensive stick and then
walking to where it landed, only to repeat the process
until the ball finally drops into a little hole, is not a
sport. It's a refusal to admit that you are very depressed.
Like snooker and darts, golf is more of a pastime than a
sport. Golfers will tell you that the walking does them a
lot of good. But when they tell you that, try to remember that they are not talking about a three-mile hike
around the green with a hundred weight of irons on
their back. What they are talking about is the fifteen-
yard stroll from their Lexus to the golf buggy.

I once sat next to a golf pro on a flight from Dublin
to Heathrow. Thank God it wasn't long-haul. If I'd
had to listen to him droning on about the US Open any
longer than I did, I would have felt an urge to tie something red round my head, jump up, shout 'I have a
sharp object' and run for the cockpit door in the vague
hope that there would be an air-marshal on board who
would obligingly shoot me dead.

MTV was the obvious choice for a workout, but it
was playing predominantly American rap music which
I couldn't cope with. And I wasn't interested in Jeremy
Kyle's latest sobbing guest or who the real father of her

child was. So I kept my spirits up on the cross-trainer with *Ready Steady Cook*, watching someone try to make something nice out of a tin of tomatoes, a vanilla pod, some black olives and a pork chop. The other team had brought some fish.

Just as that was getting interesting, guess who showed up? That's right. Mervin. Except instead of rushing over and apologizing, he was quite relaxed.

'Jack, hi.'

All through *Ready Steady Cook* I'd been mentally rehearsing my opening line under my breath, which was 'What the fuck are you playing at, Mervin, you prick? Twenty minutes late. Fuck you and your clipboard.' Which translated to: 'Oh hi, Mervin. I was beginning to wonder if I'd got the wrong day.'

I still wish I'd managed the rude version.

Instead, there I was, agreeing that the traffic was hellish, adding, 'Don't worry, that's fine, it gave me a chance to warm up properly. I like to do at least half an hour running before I get into the more serious exercise.' Lies, lies, lies. Why so many lies?

So instead of an apology, I get from Mervin, 'Oh, fair play. I'll leave you to it for another ten and then we'll get started.'

Now I'm knackered, but am having to keep running because I said that that is what I usually do and so I feel I have to prove it.

The ten minutes pass, by which time I'm hoping

that Mervin will forget all about me and I can leave the gym unnoticed, but he comes over and starts chatting to me about my goals.

I hadn't thought of it in these terms, but mutter that I just want to get generally fit. He stands me on some scales to weigh me, then he pretends to be a doctor and does my blood pressure. Then he takes a large U-shaped gauge that looks like the kind of thing a mason would use and measures the fat on my waist. Mervin mentions something about my BMI as if I know what it stands for.

Mervin is all of twenty-two years old. He probably has a degree, which admittedly I don't, but it'll be a degree in Sports Science. Or PE, as it used to be known. And frankly, I'm glad I haven't got one of those. Yes, he is fit, but so he should be. He went to Press-up University and he lives in a gymnasium. Something would be wrong if he wasn't fit.

We move around the room and I try out different fixed-weight machines. Each time, Mervin says something like 'Ten reps, rest up, ten more reps.' And then he notes it on his clipboard. Pathetic really.

As we do this, he asks me if I saw any of the golf yesterday. In fairness, Mervin wasn't to know that I hate golf, so I just say that I didn't, which prompts Mervin to tell me all about it. That made the workout really fly by. Thanks, Mervin.

Glancing at the bank of TVs, I notice that the pork chop wins on *Ready Steady Cook* against a fish stew made with coconut milk and chick-peas which, if I'm honest, looks like a plate of sick and didn't have a hope of winning.

I start to wonder if Mervin is timing my session from when I arrived or from when he arrived. I am pretty worn out, but can't decide whether I want my money's worth, i.e. the full hour of being bossed about, or whether I'd prefer him to call it a day after half an hour and go home feeling ripped off.

I'd much prefer the latter, I decide, as that way I won't have to do so much and I'll have a real grievance to go away with.

Half an hour passes, and it would seem that diligent Mervin is making up for lost time and continuing so that I get the full session. I'm feeling the pain, but no gain.

On a different machine I squeeze my legs together against two padded resistance bars. It looks like a special device you might sit on to give birth. On my last 'rep' the clock on the wall marks 11:30. I can go.

Thanks, Mervin. No, that was great. I'll call you to make another appointment. Mental note: delete Mervin from mobile phone and cancel gym membership so as to avoid embarrassment of bumping into him again when he knows that I didn't re-book.

Instead of which, Mervin suggests we carry on over the hour as (amazingly) he feels bad about being late. A freebie on him, he says. I say that's great, as I am in no way ready to tell someone half my age that, well, that he's half my age and I'm shattered.

By the end of the session I assure Mervin that I will call to book another session, knowing that I'll do nothing of the sort.

Having a personal trainer makes everything worse. It isn't just the tedium of exercise that has no purpose beyond the physical effort that it requires, it's the inane conversation that wears you down. Frankly, if I want lifestyle tips from a single, childless, 'living with the folks at present' twenty-two-year-old 'graduate' from a jumped-up polytechnic, then I'll start going to All Bar One, subscribing to *Nuts* magazine and hanging around with blokes who think it's cool to have Maori tribal tattoos all over their arms.

10

JOHN, A FRIEND OF MINE, once had a rescue dog called Tyson. He was a cross between most dog breeds that you can name and was very sweet, obliging and affectionate. Obviously Tyson was the name that he came with. Battersea Dogs Home suggested that it would be better not to give him a new middle-class name in case it confused him.

Sadly, Tyson hailed from a rough estate where people often named their dogs after professional fighters who've been to prison, and, worse still, called their children things like, well, Tyson.

It's a class thing. In Britain you're as unlikely to find a Pit Bull with a name like Pickles as you are to meet a Golden Retriever called Asbo. That's just the way it is. Anyway, Tyson's favourite pastime was to fetch an old tennis ball, which he could do for as long as you were prepared to throw it for him. Then one day, during his walk, he lost his tennis ball and looked forlornly at his owner. Wishing only to entertain the disappointed dog, John picked up a stick and attempted to throw it, whereupon Tyson bit him on the leg and ran away.

After a fruitless search, John contacted the police to report him missing. The policeman's voice shifted very slightly towards a less friendly tone when John said that the dog was called Tyson, but generally he was helpful and suggested calling the RSPCA.

Tyson was indeed being looked after at the nearby RSPCA centre and so John went along to collect him. They told John that rescue dogs often have a trigger that can make them behave aggressively without warning and he quickly realized that it had been the stick which had caused little Tyson – well, big Tyson, actually – to turn. Quite possibly, said the man at the RSPCA, it ignited in him the memory of being hit by somebody with a stick, and his reaction of biting John and legging it was a subconscious response to this.

And so, my friend learnt that Tyson would have to go through life being protected from the sight of such objects if a similar scene was to be avoided. The only alternative would have been to spend heaps of cash on one of those ridiculous pet psychologists to come up with exactly what he knew in the first place: that Tyson is a bit of a bastard when it comes to sticks. You and I know that sticks are not bad things, but for this particular dog they provoked an unfortunate reaction that he was unable to control or understand.

So what does this have to do with you, Jack? I hear you ask.

Well, it may surprise you to learn that I too have a raft of irrational, petty prejudices about people and things which, over the years, I have come to trust. On the surface, these prejudices may not seem fair, but then they wouldn't qualify as prejudices if they did. I've come to trust them because, fair or not, they invariably turn out to be reliable.

Time, then, to define these grievances that I adhere to.

OK. I don't like men who blow-dry their hair. There, I've said it. I can't get over it, I've tried, and if you are a man and you blow-dry your hair, then I don't like you and that's all there is to it. I acknowledge that it's a bit tough on those among you who bought this book in good faith only to discover halfway through that you are a prat, but let's face it, someone had to say it.

It shouldn't matter (and Lord knows I tried to warn you that these prejudices are petty and irrational), but it does to me. Very much.

Mervin, that personal trainer I told you about, he blow-dries his hair. It's probably why he was late. I know this because I have seen him in the changing-room giving himself a good seeing-to with the Revlon, shaping the flow of his shampooed and conditioned locks just like a girl would. I mention this because had I noticed Mervin preening himself at an earlier stage, I could have invoked my deep-rooted antipathy and avoided him altogether. Mervin had a good reason to be disliked long before he flounced into the gym looking like that other one from Wham! Had I known it, I could have saved myself quite a lot of money. It may seem to you like an odd thing to do, but I don't think it's unreasonable to ask men outright if they blow-dry their hair. That way you can forewarn yourself of the likelihood of despising them.

It won't come to that, of course, partly because I'm developing the ability to tell at first glance whether a man does the unspeakable. The sign is a carefully flicked, wispy wave of hair across the top of the forehead. Hair that has been persuaded by a preening current of fanned heat to defy its true nature and obey the sculpting comb. Hair that makes a chap look as though he should be in a commercial for toothpaste – probably one of those American ones where they've dubbed the voice with an English accent but you still know he's American because of the type of car and house in the background, not to mention his lantern-jawed wife and television kids. Hair that is too kempt. Hair that is fussed and fiddled, gently patted, mirror-checked and, who knows, possibly even sprayed into place. But let's not go there.

No. Let's. Hairspray is fine for teenagers of both sexes to play around with before they go out with their mates. You'd almost be suspicious if they didn't. And it's alright for older ladies who like to maintain a bit of volume up top. But for your average middle-aged male, hairspray is a very nasty finishing touch.

The same goes for hair gel. Again, gel is the prerogative of your average teenager, and, let's face it, any attempt they make to look good, no matter how hopelessly misguided, should be viewed with compassion. Otherwise, hair gel is worn by low-grade sports personalities and all the idiots who work in PC World under the misnomer of 'assistant'. If that sounds sweeping, it is – as should they be.

I also dislike anyone who holds his or her knife like a pen. Why? Because it's twee, affected, naff and tacky.

'But it shouldn't matter,' I hear you say. You just haven't been paying attention, have you? The nature of a good prejudice is that it is essentially unreasonable. Just like Tyson when a stick is waved in front of him, I immediately feel like attacking when I see a pen-knifer. To me, holding your knife like that illustrates pretension, a sort of smug allusion to refinement and life's niceties. As a posture of etiquette, its closest sibling must be the cocked little finger when drinking from a teacup, or possibly the downright unpleasant habit of nibbling the chocolate away from the sides of a KitKat, leaving a gnawed wafer that under any other circumstances would make you suspect a rat had been at it.

And as I said, I've learnt to trust these prejudices. So much can be gathered from the small-print of another's character, the subtle and not-so-subtle nuances of their behaviour.

The man-bag. Another example. So tantalizingly practical and yet, I don't know, it just won't do, will it?

In recent years, the man-bag has evolved from the clutch variety, for which, if I'm honest, I harbour a secret longing, to the over-your-shoulder model that is halfway between a woman's handbag and a rather effeminate briefcase. It's a worrying development and there are signs that it won't be long before this evolves into a full-on unashamed unisex handbag that anyone can dance around.

Again, I admit, I have had pangs of envy whenever I've seen the man-bag in use. But, as I see it, it's every gentleman's duty to resist such cravings and damn well get on with the business of being a bloke. Yes, I could keep my wallet and whatever in it and not have to spoil the line of my suit with bulging pockets, but I'd also look like a twat. In Mediterranean countries menfolk often have a small clutch-bag, but somehow they don't look so bad. Maybe it's the contents. A packet of Gauloises, a Bic lighter and keys to the Lambretta, which stands casually outside the café while you finish your Ricard with double espresso; how could that offend?

Mind you, the Italians and French have an annoying

knack of getting away with all manner of fashion offences. For instance, they somehow look quite good in shorts and Nike flip-flops, unlike the standard British male who always manages to look like a sex-tourist as soon as the weather hots up. Something to do with the podgy white skin offset by a cheery summer shirt by George at Asda. Add a man-bag to that combo and don't be surprised if you get met at the airport by Interpol.

All of which deepens my sense of unease when I'm around a male bag-user. It's not right and you know it. Or at least I do. There's something disconcerting about that degree of orderliness, of always knowing where everything is without having to frisk oneself.

And this leads me to another prejudice. I tend not to trust people who live in very tidy houses.

I know that on the surface of it there is nothing wrong at all with a person being well ordered and disciplined. Nothing, except that it leaves the impression of that person having lived in the confines of a stark institution which, although he or she has long since left, still remains within.

I live in a Victorian semi-detached house with my wife, four children and two standard smooth-haired dachshunds. Let me say straight away that I do not consider untidiness to be a particularly good thing. It's not big and it's not clever, but it is better than the joyless minimalism that glossy lifestyle magazines and some, usually very thin, people would have us believe to be desirable.

I'm not talking about when your kids have grown up and left home. When that happens it's your business how you choose to celebrate. It may be a necessary healing process, once you've packed them off to university, to clear their stuff out and turn your home into a temple of unadorned, clutter-free emptiness for a few years. What I am talking about is the modern urban ascetics. The pristine couples whose houses are like show-homes. Any sign of life is expunged or at least reduced to a merely academic reference. Cooking utensils, toys, coats – nothing is displayed. In a large kitchen drawer wedding-gift saucepans still glisten, and in a cupboard a child's mudless wellies stand, ignored. This is an unnatural way to live and I can't ever fully like its practitioners.

At its most extreme, tidiness is a form of mental illness. I knew a woman whose passion for tidiness developed into an obsession with cleanliness and, eventually, a phobia of germs. She became so inhibited that she was housebound, intent on protecting her space from the filthy interference of outsiders such as her husband and children. An ornate fireplace had to be boarded over and sealed in case specks of soot should fall from the chimney, and a new set of armchairs and sofa were left in their plastic wrapping for fear of dust.

If I'm pushed, I'd also have to admit I don't like people with allergies. They just annoy me. There seems to be something far too self-centred about it.

'No thanks, I'm allergic.' Why not just say 'No thanks'? I wasn't asking for your medical history, I was just passing the nuts around. Trying to be friendly, that's all.

Obviously there are one or two allergies that should be taken seriously and are definitely real. I, for instance, am allergic to penicillin. It's a fact that I've had to live with, stoically and without fuss, for many years. I was given some when I was seven and came out in quite a nasty rash. And a temperature. So obviously that is a proper allergy that actually does exist and isn't just a thing that's been made up by someone who's simply embarrassed to say that they are a fussy eater.

I accept that there have been occasional cases of people having a fatal allergy to – well, alright then – nuts. But does that really mean that nuts have to be banned from schools?

I wouldn't dream of asking my local hospital to make sure that they don't have any penicillin in the building in case I have to come in for treatment one day. Although there is a lot of sense in it.

Why wouldn't I dream of it? Because I'm a realist, and deep down, extremely reasonable. I can see that despite the fact that I can never take advantage of the healing qualities of penicillin, some people can. Hypochondriacs, most of them, admittedly, but at least they go away feeling they got some attention.

11

NOW MIGHT BE AS good a moment as any to tell you about the time when I decided to start attacking people.

Pilgrims' School, which I attended until the age of thirteen, was and still is a prep school that lies between Winchester's great cathedral and the college. Boys were either in the cathedral choir or the Winchester College choir. The latter, being called Quiristers, were distinguishable by their different uniform. If you weren't in any choir, you were referred to as 'a commoner', which is what I was.

The school smelt of lockers and wood polish and some of the classrooms were in a medieval priory, giving the place an atmosphere of history and tradition that you couldn't ignore. Some of the beams had graffiti that went back hundreds of years. I can remember the view from the window of almost every classroom I ever sat in. During Scripture I would count the bikes lined up in their racks. Mostly teachers' bikes; unmistakable with their sensible wicker baskets. In Science I could see right across the school yard into the cathedral square, with the Dean's garden over to the right. Ancient History was taught by the aptly aged, army-whiskered Mr Whickes. From his classroom, in a house that was loaned to the school, I could see into College Street.

Mr Whickes was a mere new boy next to Mr Patan (it rhymes with Satan, which naturally was his nickname), who taught us Maths and was probably there when algebra was invented. Satan looked exactly like that teacher in the Giles cartoons. I'm being genuine when I say that I consider myself lucky to have had a teacher who actually smoked in class. Even in those days, that surely must have been considered a bad thing among the staff, but who was going to tell him? Aged ten, I thought it was excellent.

There were younger teachers as well, most of whom will be forever associated in my mind with one vista or another.

I was a very low-achieving pupil. The educational term at the time was 'thick'. I never did get the hang of paying attention and felt almost compelled to mis-behave. It doesn't take long for a reputation to print itself on to your identity and for the two to become inseparable. Give a dog a bad name, etc. Ask Tyson.

After two or three years of struggling and sliding behind, messing around and generally idling, I was becoming thought of as the school dunce. I wasn't without friends, but when my name cropped up in their end-of-term reports, cited as the cause of so much distraction, they began to fall away one by one. By the time I left, I was really only friendly with the two or three boys in my year who had a lively sense of humour, who could create funny characters and comic scenarios with me.

Most of the teachers were professional enough to tolerate me, but a few were less kind. One man in particular really hated me, and the feeling was mutual. I wouldn't have the school photo in the house until I'd obliterated his face with black biro and drawn horns on his head. Childish? Yes, he was. And funnily enough, he held his knife like a pen.

I nicknamed him Punk and it was perhaps my greatest school achievement that the name stuck, passed from generation to generation until he retired some ten years after I'd left.

Punk liked to belittle me. When I got a bad grade for an essay (in fact, I don't remember a good one), I'd have to stand on my chair in front of the class while he said something like 'Dee by name, D by nature.' I didn't care so much after this had happened a few times, but what started to hurt was that the rest of the class would laugh, and, encouraged by Punk, taunt me. That betrayal was far worse than anything and began to really eat away at me. I started to take note of who was laughing.

Then one day – I suppose I was twelve and soon to

leave the school – I accidentally set off the fire-alarm. A few of us had been larking about in the corner of a class-room, I got pushed and my head cracked against the little red box, breaking the glass and triggering a screeching chorus of bells around the school.

Wishing to avoid the fire brigade being called out on what I knew to be a false alarm, I sprinted across the yard to the headmaster's office to own up. Unfortunately, I was greeted by his wife, who was busily evacuating the building. My hasty explanation was dismissed with a triumphant 'It's too late for that. The fire brigade have been called.' I felt like screaming at her. All it would have taken was a phone call to cancel them. But no. That would have involved going back into the burning building, even though we had established that it wasn't in fact burning.

With the entire school assembled on the lawn in the cathedral square, one of the senior teachers barked out a roll-call as two fire-trucks pulled up. I was marched by the ruddy-faced headmaster (for legal reasons, let's just say he was called Mr Briggs because, well, that was his name) up to the firemen to explain. Naturally I was petrified, but managed to say that it was my fault as good old Mr Briggs shook me and cursed me.

I'll always remember how calm the fireman was. It was as if he felt sorry for me at that moment and was a little puzzled by the head's mad, aggressive manner towards me. I was truly grateful to him for not joining in.

The fire crew left and everyone was ordered into the assembly hall so that the school could be informed about why they had been so inconvenienced. I was made to stand before everybody for what I expected to be a severe reprimand.

What followed seemed like an unending rant about my extraordinarily low IQ and the fact that no school would be stupid enough to accept me when I left at the end of the year. Just like when Punk humiliated me in class, I looked around and saw the same faces smirking at me.

Something changed in me at that moment. Like in the film *Carrie* when they pour the pig's blood over her, I made a decision to get them. Every one of the treacherous bastards.

After a couple of weeks, when all the fuss had died down, I began my vendetta. As one of the shortest in my year, I don't suppose anybody considered me in the least bit dangerous, but I think at that point I actually was.

I would walk into a classroom during break, for example, and if one of the boys from my little blacklist was there, unattended by any members of staff, I'd simply walk up to him and, before he could say 'What do you want?', punch him in the face. Sometimes that would be that; sometimes a second or third punch might be called for. At other times they'd hit back and a full fight would ensue. Because many of them were bigger than me, I was occasionally overwhelmed and beaten, but it didn't stop me continuing down that list.

The more people I attacked, the angrier and more isolated I became. It was like a fire that had started inside me. I really hated fighting people and hurting them, but felt unable to stop. I was on a mission. Deep down I knew that it was wrong and that punching them wasn't the answer. It was almost worse that I didn't get caught or reported.

Of course, the irony of this is not lost on me. The cliché of becoming a comedian to avoid being bullied was, in effect, turned on its head. I was going around picking fights with people because they had laughed at me. Having said that, to categorize my behaviour (inexcusable as it was) as bullying is to miss the point of the story. I was on a quest for retribution. It was me against all of them, as far as I was concerned.

How this campaign of violence ended is as odd as the way it started.

Being in the shadow of Winchester Cathedral, and Pilgrims' being the school of its world class choir, the Christmas carol service was always of an incredibly high standard. I loved visiting the cathedral. It had a powerful atmosphere that was hard to ignore. Perhaps it was the deliberately awe-inspiring architecture at work or the visible history of worn stone steps, tombs and plaques. Perhaps it was something else.

That year as we filed into the pews for the service, I

felt completely wretched and friendless. I had a horrible feeling of not belonging, of being in some way unworthy to be there in the cathedral. Even the carols, written to lift the heart with good news, had the effect of deepening my despondency.

During one of the readings, my mind wandered and I started to stare at a large statue of Christ on the cross. I remember wanting to look away but being unable to. At the same time I became aware of a sensation of complete tranquillity, a feeling that I was cherished by God and that everything would be alright.

I can't account for why that should have happened other than to say that's what happened. The fighting stopped after that.

12

I KNOW AN INCREASING number of people who Twitter. This, in case you are not as hip as me and consequently don't know, is a way of conversing via the web, with a community of invited 'friends'. It's the same as a blog but your entries are much briefer (a maximum of 140 characters) and more frequent.

And if you don't know what a blog is then this bit of the book isn't for you. I'm not going to waste time going through simple stuff that you really should know by now, because I'd end up having to trudge further and further back, explaining what emails, mobile phones and texts are. Much better that I just exclude you so that I can get on with what I want to say and you can tear this bit out and use the pages to make paper aeroplanes or something.

Good. Thank God they've gone. Now where was I? That's right, Twitter. Twitter allows you to give an ongoing commentary of your life by updating your entries as often as you like. Most Twitterers assume a pseudonym because . . . well, because they like that kind of thing, although if it was me, it would be due to the eviscerating shame that I'd be feeling.

Twittering is, as I understand it, simpler and quicker than emailing and is ideal for filling in everybody you know on the smaller details of your day-to-day life. The thinking behind this is that it's nice to know what your 'friends' are doing when you're not with them and, correspondingly, it's great fun to tell them what you are doing.

Notice that's the second time now that I've placed the word 'friends' in inverted commas. That's because I think it is helpful to stay reminded of the fact that these are not friends in the traditional sense. That's not a judgement, it's just true. Many of them are people that the Twitterer (if that's the noun: obviously there are more tempting ones, but I'm trying to be impartial) has never met and never will meet in person. In the event of a life crisis, it's questionable whether you would turn to Twitter-World and interrupt the general chit-chat in order to type in and send off your breaking news.

Dizzy@ Just ordered a pizza.

Ratking234@ Lucky you. I'm ice-skating with Leona and Emily.

Dynamic@ I like ice-skating. I went last week.

Shopaholic@ Hiya everyone, am at the airport. Just looking round Accessorize.

Spacecadet@ Isn't new Girls Allowed single awesome?

Topgeeza@ Hey you guys, just ran someone over in the car and legged it. How bad is that? Probably have to go to jail. Seeyas.

My suspicion is that Topgeeza is more likely to be in hysterics on the phone to his/her parents. That, or on the run, hiding somewhere until sobriety returns and the decision to hand oneself in at the nearest police station becomes preferable to spending the night cowering under a hedge by the A3.

All of which supports my theory that the people on your Twitter list should not realistically be counted as friends.

Perhaps by now you are thinking that this is a bit of a soft target, a needless attack on the harmless and enjoyable hobby of sharing the ordinary, humdrum details of your day with others. All manner of people, you may argue, gain confidence by knowing that someone else is interested in their choice of sandwich for lunch. Moreover, you continue, the frustrations of a normal existence can be alleviated by Twittering about them. It's great if you're stuck in traffic to be able to vent by texting everybody in your address book in one hit. Or if you go to Homebase to look for a specific washer for your dripping bath tap and they don't have it, all that anger can be dissipated through the keypad on your mobile as sympathetic responses come chiming in, one after another, from all over the world. Messages of support like 'Poor you. I hope you find your washer! Try B&Q!!!'

All that may be the case, but I still think it's a waste of time and energy that belies a serious deficiency in the participant's ability to process dross in a normal way. If you don't agree, then I would urge you to think about the people that you have known personally who talk too much. Unless you are determined to deceive yourself in order to prove me wrong, you will admit that they are nearly all bores. A stroke-by-stroke description of a game of golf or a detailed account of a recent holiday can be deathly enough in the spoken form, but appearing in text on your phone or computer screen would be enough to make you want to throw yourself down a stairwell.

But much more importantly, Twittering reduces the consequential to the same level as that dross, allowing significant thoughts to bounce unnoticed into the general ping-pong of banal exchanges.

How different would history have been had the great thinkers of our past been tempted to Twitter instead of formulating their views with paper and quill?

What if Darwin had had a mobile phone on the Galapagos Islands? He might very well never have given himself sufficient time to contemplate the profound meaning of his observations. The frustrations of such crass limitations and the constant pandering to lesser mortals would kill the keenest intellect eventually:

BeagleBoy@ Am on the Galapagos Islands and have just seen the most splendid giant tortoises.

Ratking234@ Lucky you. I'm ice-skating with Leona and Emily.

Dynamic@ I like tortoises. I saw one last week.

BeagleBoy@ No, but seriously, the extraordinary thing is that the species vary from one island to another.

Spacecadet@ No way. That is so random.

BeagleBoy@ Well, quite. Is it random? Or could it not be a response to environmental and genetic influences? Might it be that this variability within the tortoise population has been . . . [Error: Twitter entry has exceeded 140 characters].

Spacecadet@ Eh? What you on about? Sounds freaky'n'mental to me.

BeagleBoy@ Yeah, you're right. Forget it. I'm just talking bollocks. Sorry everyone. Any yous heard from Topgeeza btw?

The fact is, it's impossible to sum up anything worthwhile in 140 characters. Although, admittedly, Einstein managed to reduce the complexities of the space-time continuum to $E=MC^2$. And he still had 135 characters left. But that doesn't count because it's just showing off.

The more advanced our technology becomes, the more we are forced to confront the extent to which it helps and hinders us. Let me state here and now that I am no Luddite. Whilst it is true that I have had some difficult and challenging scrapes with IT, on the whole I am pretty OK with computers. Yes, I pay a guy to provide 24-hour technical support so that I can ring him in the event of a problem, but that's just sensible.

Why should I automatically know, for instance, how to set up an Internet connection in my house? That is advanced stuff that needs a trained IT consultant to come round, fiddle with it for three hours and then say, 'Mmm. That's funny. Why's it doing that?'

I got my printer working on my own. That wasn't entirely straightforward. I had to put a disc in, drag icons around, do some nifty double-clicking and all sorts. The kind of thing that would confuse and defeat a normal person.

But it all went well. Plain sailing. Easy-peasy lemon squeezy.

Until a few weeks later, when the ink cartridges needed replacing. I removed them and took them with me to the computer store so that there would be no confusion in the shop and thus no possibility of being sold the wrong replacements. It's good to think ahead like that. The last thing I wanted was to end up having to describe, in loose terms, more or less the kind of thingy that I needed. That way lies disaster.

I could have just made a note of the make and model of the printer, but they always try and trick you with other questions. You could go in and say you need ink for, let's suppose, an HP Laserjet 1200 and they'd say 'Which 1200 is it?' And you'd say 'I don't know' and they'd say 'There should be a letter after the 1200. It's impossible to tell what cartridges it takes unless I know the full model number with the letter.'

And that is precisely the kind of situation in which I tell lies.

I would know that she is right, that there is a letter after the 1200, but that I didn't think it mattered for some reason so didn't make a note of it. However, that is a lot to admit, especially to somebody I don't know, so I would then claim that there was no letter after the number and she would say that that was not possible and I'd end up leaving the store claiming to be disappointed.

Then, outside in the car park, I would ring Jane and ask her to look at the front of the printer and tell me what the letter is.

'It doesn't matter why. Just look at it and tell me what it says after Laserjet 1200.'

And she might take issue with my tone of voice, thinking that I'm cross, which I would be, but not with her, and decide not to tell me, so then I'd be forced to drive to a different shop and hope that they have in stock the exact same printer as mine so that I can point dumbly at it and ask for the correct ink cartridges.

I don't need that kind of hassle. No way.

Much better to walk into the original store where I had imagined all that trouble taking place, produce the empty cartridges and simply ask for new ones. By doing that, there is no room for error.

That is what I call 'anticipatory planning'.

What I don't call 'anticipatory planning' is approaching the assistant, producing the cartridges and only then discovering that, despite the printer's adamant warning light, they hadn't been quite so empty after all, and my hand and the inside of my pocket are covered in sticky shades of Cyan, Magenta, Yellow and Black.

I had no option but to exit the store and somehow find a way of getting cleaned up. This involved going to a chemist's (on foot so as not to smear ink all over the car interior) and buying, with my unsullied hand, a packet of nappy wipes, so that for the rest of the day I smelt like a baby.

When I finally got home with the new cartridges, I followed the instructions and inserted them into my printer. A simple test-run then established that it didn't work. I took the cartridges out, reinserted them and tried again to print a short document, nothing too challenging – a short letter of complaint, if you must know. But still not a word appeared.

So I took them out again, made sure that the nozzles were unblocked and that the sliding brackets in which they sat were not compromised by any foreign matter. Yet again came the perplexing blank sheet of paper, snaking its way through the machine and emerging without a blemish.

If you want to know what the problem was, in case this happens to you one day, then I'm afraid that you are reading the wrong book, my friend, because what I did next was to unplug the printer, quite calmly, put it in the back of the car and drive it to the tip.

This might sound extreme, but believe me, sometimes it is the only way. That printer was given no fewer than three chances to sort itself out and it failed to do so.

My local tip stands next to the Thames at Wandsworth and is a busy maze of cursory recycling. There are colour-coded mammoth skips for different types of rubbish. Garden waste, cardboard, metal and 'household' (if that isn't a catch-all name, I don't know what is). You have to park up next to the appropriate container and unload your waste, pretending, for the sake of your eco-conscience, that it doesn't all get dumped together on a barge and shipped off to a land-fill site in China, or just sunk somewhere in the Channel while nobody's looking.

On previous visits I have found myself being too nice to the men who work at the tip. For example, eagerly asking them where an old bicycle should go, knowing full well that once I had gone, they would descend upon it to add it to the collection of relatively useful spoils that they place like garden ornaments all around their little shed in the middle of the site. They just said 'Leave it there' with no hint of gladness or, frankly, gratitude. Next time I won't bother trying to be helpful, I thought. I'll just throw-and-go like everybody else.

In addition to the skips there is a designated area for old paint pots, a cemetery for dead washing machines and a giant replica oil can, obviously for pouring unwanted motor oil into. At least I hope that's its purpose, because that's what I've used it for in the past.

Finally, there is a huge lockable cage for redundant monitors, computers, fax machines, copiers and so forth. A sort of detention centre where recalcitrant office equipment is held before being transported to North Africa to be used in schools. But only after any hard drives that they might contain have been hacked into for personal bank details, NHS records and Ministry of Defence files, that kind of thing.

If I felt any remorse as I left my printer at the mercy of all those bored, beige, electronic old-timers with their amputated plugs, it was fleeting. No good getting sentimental about an appliance. Especially one that resisted every opportunity to change for the better. Given a good home and countless (well, three) chances to prove that it could make a go of things, it had flunked. Well, now it was on its own. Like I said, I'm no Luddite. Quite the opposite: my objection to progress only surfaces when that progress falters.

All of which demonstrates the extent to which technology can and does hinder us. Its modus operandi is to make us dependent on the service it provides (in this case, printing), and then, suddenly and without explanation, withdraw that service. It's brutal and unethical, like a drug dealer giving out freebies to teenagers until they're hooked and then leading them into a life of crime and vice so that they can pay for their habit.

If you think that's too strong an example, OK, you're probably right; not all that many people become rent boys because their printer packs up. I certainly didn't, I'll have you know, but I think you can see what I'm saying. In the modern age we are developing a dangerous addiction to the technology that flaunts itself before us.

A new and rapidly growing trend is Second Life, an online 'game' in which you create your own visual alter-ego, or avatar, who interacts in a cyber-world inhabited by a huge population of different avatars, all of which are controlled by other people. So, it didn't entirely-surprise me when Amy Taylor and David Pollard in the United States got divorced because Amy's avatar walked in on David's avatar having sex with an avatar prostitute. Just to recap then: nobody was actually doing anything more than sitting at a computer, alone, tapping keys and pushing a mouse around, and yet the ramifications were catastrophic. A couple are now divorced because, for the first time in human history, we have a way of seeing each other's thoughts, and when we do, just as I always suspected, it isn't very nice.

I was fascinated to discover, when I researched this story, that David Pollard, in order to actually have sex online, not only had to go to the trouble of paying the virtual prozzie, but first had to buy himself some virtual genitals. When a technology obliges you to go to an imaginary shop and say, 'Hello, I'd like some balls. Oh, and a penis. Massive, please,' then you need to take a good long look at whether you are actually benefiting from that technology. Or not.

13

THE IDEA OF LIVING your life in a strange, parallel version of the real world is not as new as it seems. When I was thirteen a Japanese soldier, Hiroo Onoda, emerged from a jungle island in the Philippines and finally surrendered from his World War Two mission to conduct guerrilla and intelligence duties in the area. I remember being very excited to learn of this as I felt it gave me a direct link to the Second World War. I've since read that leaflets were dropped straight after the Japanese surrender, asking him to give up his struggle against the local population, but he dismissed the copies that he found as US propaganda and persisted with his campaign of random crop-burning and cow-killing.

Even from his hideout, signs that things had moved on must have been all around. Clues that peace prevailed were surely everywhere. Gaudy cruise-liners now frequented the nearby waters where, previously, menacing battleships had patrolled, and the sky was laced with the vapour trails of modern jet aeroplanes that passed silently, dropping nothing more than the frozen contents of their toilets. Yet Hiroo was adamant that he was still at war.

In the end, it took a chance encounter with a teenage backpacker from Tokyo to convince him that it was the Emperor's wish that he should end hostilities. And so he agreed that he would surrender, but only on the condition that the order came, in person, from his commanding officer.

The officer in question was summoned and some weeks later a meeting took place in the hills of Lubang Island between an unkempt Hiroo and a very confused, retired old bookseller by the name of Taniguchi. It was three p.m. on 10 March 1974, and as far as I was concerned, the real end of the Second World War.

I was proud of this connection with modern history, a history that at the time was taught by our parents and grandparents more than by our teachers. War was central to my understanding of the world, and its recentness was a source of fascination to me. As a child at primary school, playtime had been spent gathering friends and walking arm in arm in an increasingly long chain, rhythmically chanting 'Who wants to play Commandos?' If the answer was yes, you hooked on to the end and joined in the singsong invitation until enough of us had been conscripted for a battle.

I'm told by my children that this activity is unheard of nowadays. Well, they didn't actually tell me, they just looked confused and asked if they could leave the table. But Jane, who has more successful conversations with them, tells me that nowadays they prefer to play Ball or It. Anyway, I'm fond of the idea that at a small school somewhere in Japan a teacher is patiently trying to dissuade her pupil from just such a game: 'Now, Hiroo, you know we don't play War any more.'

'But Miss, Grandad said I could . . .'

At just about exactly the same time as the good people of Lubang Island were wondering why their cattle were disappearing and how it was that their barns kept burning down and, for that matter, why live rounds were occasionally fired at them from the trees, I was encountering real Red Indians. Obviously I am enlightened now and know that they are really called goddamn Apaches. My introduction was via an American neighbour whose elderly Bostonian mother came to stay most summers. Mrs Olney must have been at least eighty-four, and when she was over here on holiday I was at liberty to visit her whenever I liked, which I did, mostly after school.

Let's be realistic here. Like most thirteen-year-olds, in an ideal world I would have had friends my own age to play with, but with one or two exceptions, I really didn't like the kids in my village and I can confidently say that the feeling was mutual. So, hearing the distant noises of a cricket game commencing across the fields, I would make my own way and call in on Mrs Olney.

She didn't fuss like so many old people. Didn't obsess that I should have a biscuit or a glass of milk. She just got on with talking, which I loved. She could tell a story from her childhood and make you think that you were right there with her when it happened. Stories about her father's ranch, about rustlers and real sheriffs, men with guns and boys with horses. She told me all about the ranch-hands (cowboys as far as I was concerned, though she never did call them that). Quite frequently, a group of itinerant 'Red Indians' would timidly visit the house with goods that they hoped to sell: beads, hand-made tools, animal hides and so on. The reality was that they were considered a nuisance and the ranch-hands would always refer to them as 'those pesky A-rabs' for some reason that nobody in her family understood.

I was astounded to talk to someone who had known such people. Her childhood was spent in the same landscape as all the Westerns that I loved to watch. Talking to her was like peering through a window into history, but she was also wise and witty and as interested in my life as I was in hers. And it wasn't just history that she talked about. She told me that in America, right now, boys not so very much older than me were being drafted into the Army to fight in Vietnam. I didn't know why that was so bad. All the news footage that I'd seen was of huge planes showering bombs on tiny villages. It didn't seem that risky to me. Quite cool, really.

Mrs Olney described how on the ground it was a different story of innocent civilians being killed and American boys coming home in zip-up bags. I learnt that when you turned eighteen in the US at that time, your name was put into a kind of lottery and if it was picked you went to Vietnam. It made me imagine my older brother, himself about to reach that age, having to go to war and how horrible that would feel.

Happily, the most dangerous thing my brother and I were asked to do at that time in our lives was to take part in an evening of Edwardian entertainment at the village hall, organized by the Parish Council to bring in the New Year.

Rehearsals began and I quickly took a dislike to all those variety songs like 'Daisy Bell', 'Down At The Old Bull And Bush' and 'I'm Henery The Eighth, I Am'. I found myself sullenly opposed to the extrovert, hearty good fun of it all and was dreading the night. A thirteen-year-old's natural response to the grown-ups' idea of amusement, I suppose – although in my case, I've never managed to evolve from that attitude.

But then my brother Dave had the idea that he and I should come up with our own act for the night. Dave was always brilliantly, effortlessly funny, so I was very happy to go along with this, especially as it would excuse me from much of the singing. We decided that we would do a ventriloquist act, with me as the dummy. Gathering jokes from our parents, grandparents and *The Good Old Days* on television, we had enough material to devise a five-minute routine.

'I say, I say, I say, my dog ain't got no nose,' I'd exclaim, sitting lifelessly on Dave's knee, his hand behind my back, my head twisting to and fro, my mouth opening and closing mechanically as I spoke.

'Your dog ain't got no nose?' Dave would ask in the benevolent tone of the ventriloquist.

'I just said that,' I'd say.

'Yes, I know. How does he smell?'

'Awful.'

And so it continued. The great thing was that the jokes actually had to be old for them to work, but the beauty of it was (not that I realized this at the time) that the real comedy was generated by the situation: a boy pretending to be a ventriloquist operating a dummy that was clearly another boy.

Naturally, it was a supportive audience, but our turn went down incredibly well and the thing that I remember most about the night was that one man in the front row almost literally choked to death from laughing so much. I was thrilled. Afterwards his family apologized on his behalf and took him home to recover. Perhaps it seems strange that that wasn't an epiphanal moment in my life, considering what I went on to do much later. But a bit like when a real ventriloquist's dummy is put away in a suitcase until the next show, I isolated the moment and shut it in a box, where it would have no real relevance to me for a few years yet.

14

GROWING UP IN A SMALL Hampshire village in the sixties and seventies was a bit like being given books for Christmas: it's something you don't appreciate until much later. When we first moved there, when I was four, Easton had two pubs, a post-office, a log man, a garage, a baker and (I'm told, though I don't remember this) a cobbler. In the heart of the Itchen valley, we were surrounded by farmland on which a good few of the village's inhabitants worked.

This, I can now see, was a near-perfect example of rural England. Though undergoing enormous change that would see the village transform over the following thirty years, at the time it felt as though it would be like that for ever.

Today the pubs and the small garage remain, but the post-office and bakery are now both prefixed with 'old' and enjoyed as cottages. St Mary's Church is on the perimeter of the village and, like all village churches throughout Britain, bears witness to the price that was paid by its small community during both World Wars, with its buffed brass lists of men who waved their families goodbye, never to return.

Many who belonged to those generations still lived in the village when I was there. The log man and Mr Passingham the baker would surely have served in the First World War, though as a boy who only knew them in their quiet rural existences, it never occurred to me. In addition, there were several ageing spinsters whose stories I didn't know and now, long after their eventual deaths, can only imagine.

Though he was not from Easton, there was one old soldier, however, whose story I did know a little bit about.

My grandfather, Thomas Dee, occasionally came to stay. Born in 1893 in Gloucester but brought up in Suffolk, he finished his schooling when he was fourteen, left home and followed his father's trade, becoming an apprentice gardener. When war broke out in 1914, Thomas Dee enlisted with the London Irish Rifles and more or less immediately found himself at Ypres.

Rising to the rank of sergeant, his fighting career took in the battles of the Somme and Passchendaele. During one of many typically horrific assaults, now commanding a trench mortar detachment, he defied orders and opened fire. Presumably he had been unable to watch such an appalling massacre of his comrades without retaliating. It's likely that the order not to fire had been given so as to protect the mortar unit's position, but this now seemed irrelevant to the young soldier and, rightly or wrongly, Sergeant Dee's action saved lives while endangering his own. Possibly fearing a court martial for his improvisation, he must have been surprised instead to be awarded the Military Medal for gallantry, the Military Cross being reserved exclusively for officers, though technically the same medal.

In October 1918, Thomas Dee was very seriously wounded by shrapnel and shipped home, where he remained in hospital for a considerable time. His injury entitled him to a small pension, but this was later reneged upon by a parsimonious peacetime government. He married my grandmother, Beatrice May Earl, whom I never knew, in 1922 at another St Mary's Church, this one in Lambeth. Her father, William Earl, was a glass-blower with a fondness for rum. He died before my dad was born and left an estate of fourpence and a comb. I never did find out what happened to the money, but my brother and I have frequent arguments about who'll get the comb.

Easton has swelled greatly in population since I left, a fact that I like to put down to coincidence and natural demographic trends rather than my departure. Land was sold and large gardens divided up to accommodate new houses for the incoming families. It's tempting to

romanticize the countryside and regret such development, but a village is really about people, not just
thatched cottages and quaint lanes. Fields are, in their
own way, industrial. Whether used for crops or pasture,
they belong to a harsh process of manufacturing, as of
course do the unsuspecting livestock.

Having said that, I find myself careering headlong
into the cliché that as a small child I had a freedom
hardly imaginable today. I hate to say it, but I really did
know the streams, paths, trees and hedgerows as my
playground.

But occasionally my mum took me to London. I
found it the most exciting place I'd ever seen. Everything
enchanted me, from the enormous echoing glass cavern
of Waterloo Station to the frantic bustle of the shops
and the traffic. I knew that I wanted to live there one
day. Now I do and the novelty has never worn off.

Having said that, Jane and I suffer from Summer
Fever every August, when we fantasize that a move to
some tranquil idyll in the Home Counties would make
life easier. The only effective cure is to take a trip out of
town to exorcize the thought of it and remind ourselves
that we love the countryside because it's there and we
don't have to be. Many friends have made the move.
Some have loved it, but others have raced back with
stories of gloom and depression brought on by the
drudgery of quietness and the isolating presence of
unseen neighbours.

I have known too many country-dwellers who waste no time listing their reasons for hating London. They loathe its pollution and violence, its lack of space and rude inhabitants. As one of the latter, I listen politely and suggest it can be quite nice to have a café to head to when walking the dogs, or a ready choice of cinemas, shops, parks and restaurants to use. Sorry, but no one's going to persuade me to trade all that in for a load of cow-pats and a Londis.

But none of this is heard by the likes of Neil, an accidental acquaintance of mine. Neil is a gloating neo-bumpkin who lives in a converted barn, which is great because it's only ten minutes by car from the Dog and Duck, with its ruddy-faced landlord and his brassy wife.

'It's fine to drive back,' says Neil. 'Anyway the police are very relaxed about that sort of thing round here. I mean it's different if you're not from round these parts and you don't know the lanes . . .' he continues.

In Neil's defence, and don't try this in court, the reason why Neil and his chums drive around pissed is that the only form of public transport available in the country is a bus. Yes, there's a bloke from the next village who does 'a spot of minicabbing', but quite frankly, you'd be safer driving yourself home after ten pints having forgotten to switch the headlights on.

Rural buses are God's way of telling you to stay in your cottage and starve to death. I know this, because like many bastards, I have a second home in the country. Sometimes, when we are there, I become nostalgically pious and convince my wife that we should use public transport more often, for instance to travel into the nearby (six miles away) town. And to her credit, she doesn't entirely disagree, meaning that I walk on my own to the bus stop while she and the kids jump in the Discovery and zoom off.

I don't know whether I've just missed a bus or am soon to be relieved by the happy sight of one making its way lethargically up the road. The timetable is behind a thick plastic screen on the side of the 'shelter'. But I can't read it because it's been scratched and scratched and scratched by somebody, probably with a small coin. This is a nuisance, but after ten minutes of standing there, my hopes raised and then dashed by every distant mechanical rumble that turns out to be a lorry, I am beginning to enjoy the thought of further defacing it. I might even try to get some battery acid to pour over it. I've often seen the results of that at bus stops in the country. It's very effective and causes a melting effect on the Perspex.

A bit later, the bus coming back from town stops on the other side of the road and a Humpty-Dumpty-shaped man with grey NHS crutches gets off, holding a carrier bag of shopping. His left foot appears to be in plaster, probably broken. I imagine he tripped on a way-ward paving stone and is suing. Or he's diabetic and his foot isn't broken but slowly rotting from the toes upwards. I've heard that can happen. Or maybe he really is Humpty Dumpty and really did fall off a wall.

The bus pulls away as its doors hiss and close, leaving its hobbling passenger to tackle the rest of his difficult journey home.

Nothing more to report about my wait. I'm left wondering if that will be my bus, once it has reached its final stop and turned around again. A round trip could easily take forty-five minutes, especially if the driver decides to have a cup of tea and one of his wretched sandwiches before setting off again. Surely there is another bus already on its way which will be here sooner.

But then again, why would there be? To cope with the rush? I am the only person in the entire poxy parish waiting to go anywhere.

Jane calls to say they are just parking and do I want to meet them at Pizza Express in, say, half an hour, for lunch? She is surprised that I am not yet on my way and am still standing where she last saw me.

'It's not funny,' I say and she denies laughing.

As I shuffle my feet, looking up from time to time, I feel like the teenager I once was, waiting for the 214 from the end of Easton Lane. Sometimes if you stared for long enough at the bend in the road where all the traffic emerged, the hedges and the tarmac would momentarily conspire to form a cat's face, smirking as it teased you with an approaching diesel purr that would finally reveal itself to be nothing but a truck.

Bored with the endlessness of it, the lazy kicking of grit and the plucking of long grasses from the verge to suck the tiny sweetness from each stem, I would hold my thumb out to passing cars. Sometimes one would stop and I'd get a ride into Winchester, making cursory conversation along the way. Other times that bend would eventually yield a bus. Once or twice, nothing at all happened and I'd give up and wander home.

So thirty years later I'm drawn back to this ridiculous and unnecessary waste of time. An inexplicable impulse to relive some of the dullest moments of my youth. I suppose I just thought it might be nice to get the bus. Who knows, maybe it would have been, had it turned up. I can't hitch-hike now, people will think I'm an escaped loon and report me to the police, or recognize me and report me to the tabloids. I give up and walk away from the shelter as my family order pizza and the bus quietly approaches and flashes by in a sudden billow of warm engine air.

15

AFTER PREP SCHOOL, I was sent to one of the comprehensive schools in Winchester. I had failed my Common Entrance aged thirteen, annoyingly in very much the way that had been predicted by Mr Briggs on the day that I set off the fire alarm. The original plan had been that I should follow the academically dull from Pilgrims' to one of England's third-division public schools so typical of the 1970s. The type of place whose prospectus boasted of a large pottery department, a well-equipped woodwork room and a heavily subscribed 'Television Club'. Those schools were alluring, make no mistake. With their long drives and great old houses, they promised tradition, parenting by proxy and a clutch of exam results that might just get your teenager into an equally rubbish university, followed, after five gap years, by an unrelated career in bee-keeping.

One school that we looked at was little more than a

working farm with the odd spelling test thrown in, a mixture between Ford Open Prison and a really nice residential centre for the mentally impaired. Displaced youths wandered around in overalls and wellingtons, carrying buckets or pulling hay bales around the place. This was an establishment for posh delinquents who defied both nature and nurture to become mumbling, shuffling zombies.

It is an obligation of any Head when showing prospective parents around his school to casually interrupt his patter with a friendly word to a passing pupil in order to demonstrate that a) he knows the child's name and b) he is the kind of Head who always stops for a friendly word with passing pupils. Such exchanges are usually brief, but watermarked with an in-depth knowledge of the pupil's activities to further demonstrate the Head's dynamic, hands-on approach.

'. . . and this is our Science block, completely renovated since the incident . . . Ah, hello, Robert, how was the rugby?'

'We beat them, Sir, 48–0.'

'Excellent,' says the Head, as if he didn't know, then turns to the parents. 'Robert came here on a fencing scholarship, but he's a real all-rounder, sports-wise.'

Having looked at the choices available, in the end my parents wisely decided that it would be better to make a bonfire and put their money on it.

On a bleak, wind-swept hill to the west of

Winchester, a new comprehensive school had been established on the grounds of a failing secondary modern. Montgomery of Alamein, named after the Headmaster's greatest hero, was in fairness becoming a pretty decent school when I joined it in 1974. Dennis Beacham and his deputy Roy Starkie were committed educationalists determined to rid Romsey Road (as it was previously called) of its notorious reputation.

After being reopened with Monty himself there to cut the ribbon, they did just that, and for the following twenty-odd years Montgomery enjoyed an improving reputation. In the year that those two teachers retired, somebody very high up in the Department of Meddling decided that it should be merged with the nearby girl's school, Danemark, and renamed King's School. Some of the buildings were bulldozed and the remaining ones are now, I'm told, used as offices, where concerned district councillors no doubt discuss what to do about the area's ever-growing educational needs, perhaps in the very classroom where I learnt the meaning of the word 'irony'.

There were some fine and dedicated teachers at Montgomery, but I suspect my desire to learn had already been stymied by the time I got there. Certainly, I soon found out how easy it was to go unnoticed if I sat at the back of the class. My concerns were more in the area of establishing myself socially. I did get into a number of fights at Monty's, some of my own making, but most were to do with my plummy prep-school accent not pleasing the rougher types. Entire days of utter joylessness could be spent merely trying to avoid being picked on. At times it seemed impossible to find a kindred spirit in the stark warren of iron-windowed buildings and bleak 'playgrounds' that spread across the hill like concrete eczema.

I soon discovered that at state school, by crikey, the Queensberry rules of gentlemanly fisticuffs were generally ignored in favour of wild flailing and vicious kicking, often with the assistance of a friend or two. Effective, to be sure, but not at all the kind of thing that I wanted to be involved in.

The other disadvantage was that grievances in school could easily spill over and become an issue out of school and vice versa. Much of the bullying that I witnessed couldn't be reported to a teacher, because it was an issue way beyond the jurisdiction of Sir. It's no good reporting someone for attacking you in the play-ground when he walks the same route home as you do, or lives on your estate.

Friendships developed, however, and I realized the value of conversation and, in particular, humour. There were one or two boys with whom I could share the fun of improvising and creating characters that would make us laugh. But when those boys were not in school (truancy was common), I felt totally lost and bewildered in that place.

Occasionally I would bunk off as well and go to a friend's empty house to hang around, smoke and raid his parents' drinks cupboard. But it was a glum way to pass the day and strategically hard to get back into the school in time to catch the bus home, smelling of ill-gotten sherry and Silk Cut. So, somewhat meekly, I abandoned the practice.

I had begun to learn the guitar and before long this led to the formation of a band with a handful of friends. Teej, our bassist, suggested that we call ourselves Greekart, after the title of a book in his front room, where we were all sitting listlessly one afternoon. Punk was at its anarchic height, but we were determined to continue flying the tattered flag of hippydom. Hawkwind, Pink Floyd, Sabbath (of course), Free and Dylan (my insistence) all had songs covered by us, as I'm sure they will be chuffed to know.

We played a number of gigs – five, I think it was – before deciding to pursue solo recording careers. Of all the members, I was the one who stood out musically. I was the one who was useless. If Teej, Bri, Rache, Steve and Simon didn't know it then, I certainly did. A possible clue that they did know it was that after we 'split, man' they suddenly decided not to go solo and re-formed under a similar name. Alright, the same one, but without me. That's showbiz.

In school, my academic effort was almost non-existent, so I was stunned to pass my English Language

O level a year early. Mr Thompson was a gentle Scotsman whose great joy in life it was to inspire young people. I remember still the pleasure in his voice when he told me that I'd got a B.

A good start, and one that I should have built upon. But it was as if I'd been taken over by an uncontrollable urge not to succeed. History, Geography, languages and all the sciences, I treated them with a kind of disdain. Having done no work for two years, my prospects were awful. I was downgraded in nearly all subjects to CSE standard, the now-scrapped lesser qualification for those pupils who would struggle to achieve a pass at O level. The CSE was generally accepted among school-boys and employers alike as a mark of stupidity.

Such was my indignation that I refused to do the exams, judging that no qualifications would be prefer-able to a list of CSEs. I hate to say this, but I still think that was a good call. I left with four O levels.

The careers-advice teacher, Mr Grant, spoke to me briefly about what I might do at sixteen. He suggested a job at the postal depot, but considering that his own son was the full-time trolley collector at Sainsbury's, I came to the conclusion that Mr Grant, as he himself might put it, must try harder.

On a form, we were expected to outline our career plan. Naturally, I had no idea what to put, so wrote that my ambition was to reform the Church of England. Clearly this was meant as a joke, but it wasn't taken as such. I incurred the wrath of Mr Beacham and was informed that my stupid response to such a serious matter would jeopardize my future. For weeks after that reprimand all I could think about was Mr Grant knocking on Mr Beacham's door, sliding into his office and explaining the nature of my offence.

'He wants to *what* the Church of England?'

'Reform it, Mr Beacham. Look, it says it here, in his own hand, on this piece of paper.'

'Good God.'

'I know. Shall I bring him to you, Mr Beacham?'

'Yes. And send this career form on to the authorities to warn them.'

It would be a few years later, in the Winchester job centre, sitting in front of a puzzled-looking clerk with a form in her hand, that I was to discover that that is exactly what he did. If nothing else, it cost me a possibly very satisfying career at the cathedral gift-shop.

16

AS MAY BE CLEAR by now, I like gadgets. I enjoy the hope of an improved life that they suggest. I don't believe that I am a sucker, however. Those little magazines that drop out of your Sunday papers very rarely excite me. I can see that there is no point in a system of plastic compartmentalizers to organize my underwear drawer, and I know for a fact that anything remotely connected to the idea of a foot-spa is going to be a waste of time, effort and money. Even if you enjoy the experience of having your feet in a vibrating washing-up bowl while you watch re-runs of *Countdown*, you still have to lift the thing up to the kitchen sink to empty it. Waddling with bare, wet feet across a tiled surface holding an electrical appliance containing two gallons of slopping water isn't ever going to be a good idea.

If there is a place in the Afterlife for people who died in ridiculous accidents, I imagine it might well be run by somebody who came to grief using a foot-spa.

For that matter, St Peter probably has an entire department devoted to electrical-appliance-related deaths, with extra staff on Boxing Day to cope with the rush. Think of the queue. People lined up holding Black & Deckers, comparing notes. 'I was putting up this CD rack we were given with my new drill here; first hole was perfect, then next thing I knew I was flying through the air. Just a freak accident.'

Well, I don't mean to sound pedantic but that isn't, strictly speaking, a freak accident. A freak accident is something impossible to predict, that happens once and is unlikely ever to happen again. Like a sudden and completely unexpected gust of wind that brings a tree down on top of you during a picnic. Whereas what you did was to drill straight into a live cable which a) you could have predicted, as you were drilling directly above a light switch, and b) will always happen, because, unlike the picnic incident, piercing a live cable with a sharpened metal rod will have the same catastrophic result every time you try it. Much as it pains me to point it out, you are literally dead wrong.

One gadget that I was given for my last birthday is a device that you swipe across a wall before you go anywhere near it with a power-tool. The idea is that it emits a shrill noise if it detects an electric current or pipework beneath the plaster. The way that I tested it was to see if it would detect a stainless-steel fountain pen (another birthday present) underneath my sleeve. It did. Hooray.

Never again will I have to endure the buttock-clenching anxiety of drilling deeper and deeper, millimetres at a time, into the chalky plaster that spews its white powder, eventually turning red as I reach brick, which always makes me feel as though I've made the house bleed. From now on I can scan the designated spot and bore into it, unafraid of the consequences.

'Look,' I said to the kids as I pushed the pen back up my sleeve. 'Look what this does.' But this time the little scanner didn't work and the children looked at me disappointedly, pityingly, as though I was a magician that nobody liked. I fiddled with the dial, but nothing would get it to beep consistently. Let's hope the same company doesn't make land-mine detectors.

Personally, I would prefer something that never works to something that can work but has an attitude problem and occasionally just doesn't give a toss.

So now I'm back to getting a handyman, called Gav, round to do odd jobs, and the underlying reason is that if one of us is to be killed by accidentally connecting himself up to the National Grid, on balance I'd much, much, much rather it was Gav. Besides, Gav sort of deserves to die, because about a year ago he fitted a dimmer switch in our bedroom that buzzed like a sub-station and eventually began to smoke. So, 999, fire brigade, everyone out of the house, even though it was past midnight and we had to be up at five thirty the next morning to go on holiday. You'd have to be a real hand-wringing liberal not to want to see him swing for that.

Hey ho, back to gadgets. The Holy Grail of gadgets for me is the electronic organizer. I have spent more money than I dare think about trying to get one that really is as good as paper and pencil. For varying reasons, they all fail just at that point when you've put all your dates into it and gone 'instruments only' for a couple of days, so that there is data on the gizmo about what you are supposed to be doing that doesn't exist anywhere else. Typically, that is when it crashes, losing the vital information that you've entrusted it with. So I call the helpline and, amazingly, get it all working again. Now I can sync it with my computer so that if I put something into the organizer it automatically tells my laptop about it, and my laptop in turn enters it into my main calendar, which I can then access anywhere in the world via the internet. This is truly incredible and only possible because I apparently have a main diary that is in a cloud or something. Anyway, I'm delighted by this and continue using the organizer for several more days until I suddenly realize that it and the laptop aren't speaking any more. I don't know how it happened, who said what, but there's an atmosphere when they are both in the room together.

Deliberately, Mrs Laptop is showing the same appointment four times on the same day. I try to find out why and, basically, according to Mrs Laptop, 'that bitch' Little Miss Organizer kept telling her the same thing, even though she'd already made a note of it. She is arguing that she is just a computer and it's not her job to say if something is right or wrong, just to store it, because that is what I asked her to do. I'm exasperated and try to persuade her to get on better with Little Miss Organizer, that she shouldn't see her as a threat but as a friend – a secretary, if you like – who will help me to arrange my schedule so that I can spend more time with Mrs Laptop. But she's having none of it. 'It's me or her,' she snaps.

I consider getting a trained IT consultant in to act as a mediator, a sort of Relate counsellor for computers, but what would be the point? Another £200 for him to fiddle about for hours on end, only to mumble, as ever, 'Mmm. That's funny. Why's it doing that?'

So I conceded, as I always do. Mrs Laptop got her way and I've told Little Miss Organizer that from now on her duties are restricted to answering the phone.

17

BACK IN THE SEVENTIES, technology was altogether more primitive. When I was fifteen I got a job in an artificial-leg factory called Digweed's, a name that Charles Dickens himself would have been proud of. In fact the whole place felt as if it should have belonged to one of his stories. It was a Saturday job to begin with, but come the summer holidays I worked there for a month or so to raise enough money to go camping in the Lake District with Brian, my best friend at that time.

It was more of a foundry really. You would approach it via a track that was banked by steep bramble bushes. My employment there must have trickled into the autumn as I remember eating the blackberries, each juicy mouthful, enjoyed in the morning sun, making my journey into the oily darkness of Digweed's a harder one. The foundry itself was like a large old garage with a couple of clapperboard extensions on either side, a corrugated-iron roof and windows that were opaque with grease on the inside and creeping moss on the outside.

Brian had got a job there first and had spent Saturdays making legs for as long as I knew him. It was steady employment and if there were news reports of civil war somewhere in the world, Brian always guessed that there would be overtime at Digweed's.

I don't know which particular conflict brought about the surge in demand that created an opening for me, and it sounds especially callous to say that I was grateful for the opportunity. I could make a glib joke about the camping trip costing me an arm and a leg, but the truth is that, indirectly, someone somewhere paid just such a price. So pretend you didn't read that bit.

Brian and I would meet in a nearby lane shortly before seven in the morning so that we could smoke a cigarette, walk our bikes up the track and chat before the monotony of work began. I hated smoking like that, outside on a clear morning, but it felt like the only way to get through the day. Your cigarettes were your way of punctuating the work. Even though Health & Safety hadn't yet been invented, smoking was not allowed in the foundry, apart from old-man Digweed himself, who was never without a pipe hanging from his long-bearded jaw. So the seven o'clock ciggie was a small act of defiance, a way of stretching out, puff by puff, the last few minutes of freedom.

Once inside, the aroma of smouldering tobacco

gave way to the acrid smells of metal filings and the filthy water that we used to cool the bits as they drilled their way repetitively through endless identical components.

At ten there was a break. Flasks out, tea poured and cigarettes lit. The first drag felt like coming up for air after swimming underwater. A quarter of the working day had passed and this smoke was my reward for tenacity, a trophy to mark another three hours' pay.

Perhaps it was the performer's instinct in me that steered me towards doing just as the others did in that place. I'd sugar my tea as they did and learnt the benefits of having that burst of energy to push you through to the next break. I switched from my preferred Marlboros to No. 6s and fancied that the smaller non-king-sized were better designed for the labourer's fag break, seeming to burn down to their grubby little filter precisely as we were beckoned back to our lathes by a yell from Digweed.

Most days involved the repetition of a single task. Typically this would be making your way through a large wooden crate of rectangular metal plates, about two inches by one. Each plate had to be set into a template on the lathe and drilled through in the corresponding holes. The completed box would then be passed on to Brian, who, because of his greater skill and experience, was entrusted to file down and countersink each hole so that the plate at least began to look like a component of something.

Brian and I would race each other, my aim being to overwhelm him with parts waiting to be finished so that I could make a show of tipping a crate of freshly tooled pieces into his box and then pretend to yawn and say, 'Wish I had something to do.' His aim was to be left redundant at his bench with an empty box so that he could feign boredom by whistling indiscreetly in my direction. He had a talent for staring at you until you had to look back, which inevitably produced fits of laughter. I guess you had to be there.

This was to be the first of many boring jobs in my life, but it was here that I learnt that the only way to deal with tedium in the workplace is to do whatever it is you are doing better, faster, more accurately.

The longer leg sections, those grey metal strips of vaguely tibial length, were machined by the full-time workers. Of these I remember bad-tempered Mike, who had joined as an apprentice and was now in his thirties. He wore steel-toed boots that were the colour of the dirt floor and his overalls could stand up without him wearing them. Once, when he wasn't there, we arranged them with his boots dangling out of the trousers so that it looked as though he'd vanished and left his clothes behind. And there was Steve, who was the same age as Mike but, I suspected, with fewer CSEs. At lunch, his duty was to bring in an urn of boiling water and a tub of Swarfega the size of a paint pot. The water would be poured into a grubby plastic bowl and we'd all line up in order of seniority to clean our hands. Mike, Steve and the others would take a fistful of the thick gloopy detergent, work it into their hands, wrists and forearms, then without flinching, rinse it off in the scorching hot water. By the time Brian and I got to it, the water was black but still too hot to put your hands into. I never did understand how they did it. We would grab some Swarfega and wash it off under the outside tap, swearing laddishly back at the others as they derided us.

Mike read the *Sun* and always had a Mars bar after his sandwiches and crisps. Steve didn't like to read. Instead he'd make child-like conversation with us.

'I seen a new combine last night. Over in Brown's field, look,' he'd say ('look' being a common suffix to the Hampshire sentence).

Brian and I would respond, giving him the confidence to continue.

'Yeah. Brand new,' he'd add. 'It must have been the first time it had been used, I expect.'

Everyone else had long since stopped bothering to chat to him. To be honest, had I gone full-time there, I might have had to as well, for my sanity.

'Nice,' Brian would say.

'Yeah, it was nice . . . brand new, I expect it was.'

'Must've been,' I'd say. Steve would think dreamily about the combine and Mike would roll his eyes.

'Brand new,' Steve repeated to nobody in particular.

'I wanted to see it go past again but that field is so big it took ages for it to come past again.'

'Did you wait?' I wanted to know.

'What for?' asked Steve. Mike turned the page of his paper, tutting at Steve's inability to follow even his own conversation.

'For the combine to come around again.'

'Yeah,' said Steve laughingly, as though I'd told him a joke. 'Must have cost him a fortune, though, look. A whole new combine harvester like that.'

'He's rented it,' mumbled Mike.

'Absolute fortune to buy that, new,' continued Steve.

Mike repeated impatiently that Brown would have rented rather than bought, because that's what farmers do, but Steve had got up and gone inside to tell Digweed all about it.

There was a brief silence as we ate and then Mike could restrain himself no longer.

'Fucking idiot,' he hissed, jerking his head towards the foundry door through which Steve had just gone. 'Why would a farmer go and buy a fucking great combine when he's only got 'bout five pissy little fields only need harvesting once a year?' With another more aggressive head-jerk in Steve's direction, 'Fucking twat, he is.'

It was difficult to know whether Mike wanted an answer, so I offered, 'Yes, I suppose you've got a point there. It makes sense to hire.'

After lunch, time seemed to go quickly until the very last hour, which dragged by like a bad play. That particular afternoon, Steve came over and spoke to Brian and me confidentially. Taking a handful of the rectangular pieces that were waiting to be drilled, he said, 'If you muck any of these up, just come and tell us, you won't get into trouble. But whatever you do, don't put it in your pocket and throw it over the hedge on your way home, look, 'cos one of these could do a lot of damage to Brown's new combine.'

The finished leg was a crude piece of engineering that really only resembled a leg in that it was about the same length and could be manipulated to 'break' halfway down, the way a leg bends at the knee. Those rectangular plates that I spent all day drilling formed part of the locking mechanism. The legs were adjustable and were fitted (presumably) with an appropriately sized foot elsewhere, before being shipped to some faraway war-torn land and issued to some newly crippled man, woman or child. It wasn't a thing that was ever mentioned. Except once, when Steve turned to me as we worked in the stifling dark heat one sunny afternoon and cheerfully announced, 'I'd rather make these than wear them.'

18

WHEN I LEFT SECONDARY school I was lucky enough to be given a place at Peter Symonds College to study English, French and Religious Studies at A level. Considering my poor school record, I have no idea how I got in. In retrospect, my guess is that I acquitted myself well enough in the entrance interview to convince them that I had within me some vast, unlocked academic potential. If that was the case, then it can't have been long before the staff were all scratching their heads and blaming each other in the common room.

In no time at all I had reverted to type, dropping French, daydreaming my way through RS and stubbornly refusing to read the set books in English. At the time I no doubt convinced myself that I was taking this stance because I should be free from the shackles of such a rigid and disciplined approach to literature. But the truth is, they were just bloody long books.

Worse still, I believed that exams were nothing more

than a test of one's salesmanship, one's ability to bluff and improvise. It had more or less worked in the past, but my tutors warned me that at A level the examiners would be looking for signs that the candidate had done some, if not all of the work described in the curriculum.

Instead of a place of study, then, Peter Symonds became for me a place of convalescence from my previous experiences of education. Socially, I started to enjoy life and the stimulating atmosphere that the college generated.

My English teacher, Sarah Hawkins, was keen that I should audition for *The Taming of the Shrew*, which she and Chris Cooper, the head of English, were planning to produce. There had been no drama productions at Montgomery, so this was an entirely new experience. One after another, the students got on stage and read their piece for the teachers to assess.

Although nervous, I could hardly wait to get up there and try for myself. Partly because I knew that this was something that I would be able to do quite instinctively, but, more importantly, because the concept appealed so strongly to me. That is, the hitherto overlooked possibility that my inclination to fantasize could have an authorized outlet. I felt the strongest urge that this was 'my thing' and that I belonged up there on the stage.

So I was cast. I got the lead part of Petruchio. Rehearsals were chaotic but, for me at least, intriguing.

Fellow student Nicola Duffett played Kate, the object of my wrath and affection. She has since enjoyed success as a professional actress and always had an infectious confidence that I benefited from hugely.

Not that any of that helps on the opening night. I remember sitting behind the curtain, being so numb with fear that I didn't think I could stand up, let alone go on and remember all those lines. Finally my cue came and I stepped into the light, discovering for the first time since my debut in the village hall with my brother that curious heightened level of existence that you enter on stage. You somehow walk on and somehow speak your first line and then the concentration, adrenalin, preparation and your character take over.

It would be wrong to romanticize this story as anything other than that of a competent schoolboy performance, yet for me the experience was significant. I sensed that here was something with which I had a special relationship. I didn't understand it; I just sensed it. I still have that feeling today when I walk on stage. I never take it for granted because it's so enigmatic, but I do know that I first became conscious of it that night at college. It was also, apart from christening Punk and that B at English O level, the only time in my thirteen years of school that I had done something that could reasonably be described as a success.

Perhaps I should have realized there and then that performing was what I wanted to do. But that would have been far too easy and sensible. And it would have made for a shorter book. My eventual journey to the stage is a lot more complicated. And besides, I did have an excuse for not pursuing it harder at the time.

I've always raised an eyebrow when people say of some particular trait that 'it's in the blood'. In my experience, sailors and equestrians are especially prone to this conceit. I knew a show-jumper who was fond of saying 'Horses are in my blood', a distasteful image for sure, but possibly less daft than an amateur yachtsman who once told me that he had the sea running through his veins.

Following my debut in *The Taming of the Shrew*, I did indeed consider the possibility of becoming an actor. But my mother, whilst happy for me to have that ambition, insisted that, were I to pursue it, I should first get a trade that I could fall back on. She didn't have any particular trade in mind, just something to sustain me during the long stretches of unemployment that I would encounter. I suppose I found her attitude a little dispiriting, but, as she reminded me, her caution was forged by experience. My mother's parents, Edna and Lionel, had both been actors in their younger days. Several years of repertory, digs, small-town shows and financial insecurity had finally convinced them to give it up, get regular jobs and provide a more settled home for their new daughter.

A generation before that, Edna's father, David

Howard Innes, had been a theatrical agent who went by the professional name of Will Gamble. When his health failed, Edna had to abandon her medical studies so that the money released could finance his treatment. So instead of becoming a doctor, she took on the stage name of Teddy Gamble and joined a touring company. A sacrifice certainly, but such a radical change of direction suggests to me a pre-existing ambition.

It was during one of their productions that she met Lionel, who had become an actor after having abandoned an ill-suited job in the City, which had been procured for him by his father, Frederick Pope Stamper. Lionel's change of career enraged his father, but not for the reason that you might expect from a Victorian patriarch. The fact is that Frederick too had been an actor for quite a few years. Some records remain of cast lists bearing his name. Most of his work was on Broadway, from what I can gather.

It was during these years that Frederick met Daisy Le Hay, a beautiful actress and chorus girl from Southern Ireland. My mother suggests that Le Hay was a fanciful corruption of Leahy and whilst I have no evidence to support it, that's as good a guess as anybody's. Anyway, Daisy and Frederick married and Lionel was born in 1906. The story goes that Daisy Le Hay was due to go to America, but cancelled at the last minute because her infant son Lionel had measles. 'So what?' you're thinking. Well, I'll tell you so what: she was going to go to America on the *Titanic*. That's right. She had a ticket for the *Titanic*. But fate had it that she wasn't to sail on board 'the ship that God himself couldn't sink', as they were fond of saying. Before it sank.

And no, we don't still have the ticket. But that doesn't make it an untrue story. I like to think she sold it when she knew she wouldn't be able to go, perhaps to a keen sailor who claimed to have the sea running through his veins. Well, he does now.

Ironically, having avoided that notorious iceberg, their marriage eventually hit the rocks and Daisy and Frederick divorced a few years later. Lionel went on to have a theatrical career which was faltering and un-remarkable. I knew him as a wonderful grandfather who would entertain me with card-tricks and shaggy-dog stories, which he had a great gift for telling. But none of that helped him in his stage career and he ended up in a succession of jobs which ranged from funeral director to working in a bank and running a pub.

All of which, I think, explains my mother's attitude to the acting profession. The mixed and mostly disappointing experiences of two generations before her had been enough to make her very wary of acting as anything other than a hobby.

Incidentally, while I'm on the subject of my ancestors, I am not the first actor in my family, nor, I'll have you know, am I the first author. That honour goes to Frederick's brother, Charles Pope Stamper.

Charles (always referred to as Uncle Charlie) worked for a large motor-car company that had its rather impressive showroom on Piccadilly. Their most prestigious customer was Edward VII, who was keen to avail himself of the delights of this newfangled trend of motoring. Uncle Charlie was duly summoned to the Palace to advise on the matter and was promptly employed to accompany the King on his drives into the countryside, an arrangement that lasted until Edward died in 1910.

Uncle Charlie decided that his experiences of travelling with His Majesty all over Britain and sometimes beyond should be shared with the nation in the form of a book. But the Palace requested that he refrain and for that reason most publishers were unwilling to get involved. However, Mills and Boon were more encouraging, providing him with a large cheque and a ghost-writer. Sounds perfect to me.

So it was that in 1912 *What I Know* was published, the account of one man's car journeys with the King. My mother has a copy which she describes as 'unreadable'. I've flicked through a few of its pages and reached the same conclusion. However, it's only fair to give you the chance to make up your own minds. This is one of the book's highlights, which was picked out in a review that appeared at the time:

On one occasion, the mayor of a small Welsh town confessed that he had left his carefully prepared speech in his office. His Majesty remarked as we drove on 'How awkward for the poor man'.

More excitingly:

Mr Stamper tells of his dash through the night across Europe at 50 mph to be in time to meet the King at Marienbad.

In fairness to Uncle Charlie, his raw material was limited because, as the review points out, 'He was never employed in any confidential capacity or had the slightest concern with affairs of weight, either State or social.'

In spite of its innocuous contents, the book caused quite a stir both here and in the US (where it was retitled *King Edward As I Knew Him*), the reason being that it was unheard of for a member of the royal staff to publish his memoirs. Think Paul Burrell, basically. Although, of course, Uncle Charlie didn't pinch stuff. And neither did Paul Burrell.

Uncle Charlie's book caused considerable displeasure in Court circles. As a result, the showroom in Piccadilly, where he had returned to work after the death of the King, fell out of favour amongst the wealthy and Charlie was shunned by all. My mother met him once or twice and recalled that he lived in a basement flat somewhere in central London with the manageress of a café. He apparently liked to collect cold tea in milk bottles, which he stored on a Welsh dresser, and was never known to wear socks, a description that sounds oddly like the lyrics of a Beatles song.

But the ancestor that excites me most of all is one that I only found out about when I was researching my heritage for this bit of the book. The name Thomas Pope appears on a sketchy family tree provided by my cousin Priscilla. Born in 1811, Pope would have been my great-great-great-grandfather. Using the most sophisticated resources at my disposal, I began to investigate the name Thomas Pope, which led me to the staggering discovery of one Thomas Pope who was a sixteenth-century actor, comedian and friend of William Shakespeare. I was quietly satisfied with this, feeling that, frankly, it made sense that the Tudor version of me would be in the same business and hanging out with none other than the Bard himself.

So it was that I emailed the information to a friend with an accompanying note, which on reflection might have had a faint air of 'stick that in your pipe and smoke it'. My friend, in response, took the trouble to read the rest of the Wikipedia article, including the boring bits that, in my excitement, I had overlooked. He emailed me back, saying that he doubted any connection as Thomas Pope died without issue, leaving his estate to two other actors. Adding, rather sarcastically, it has to be said, that 'If it wasn't for the fact that he was an actor, I'd almost say he was gay.' It's an ugly thing, jealousy.

19

I STILL CLING TO my theory that when it comes to A-level results, technically a 'U' is not a fail, because by definition it means that my paper was actually ungraded. There was no mark given. I therefore have no way of telling how I fared. Or how many A levels I have. Your guess is as good as mine. Sadly, the universities I had optimistically applied to took a less existential view and wasted few words in telling me that I wasn't wanted.

My parents suggested that I should go to live in France for a while. A second language might prove an advantage to me, just as not having me moping around at home would be an advantage to them.

In modern parlance, my time in France would be described as a 'gap year', except that a 'gap', strictly speaking, has something at the beginning and at the end of it. I travelled to Grenoble under the pretext of studying French, but soon made so many English and

Scandinavian friends that I hardly ever spoke it. Certainly, rather less still, once I had decided to be a permanent truant from the course that my parents had paid for me to attend.

My reasonably good ear for accents had the effect of making French people believe I was one of them. However, doubt would creep across their faces once they entered into conversation with me. Let down by my pitiful vocabulary and heinous grammar, locals started to regard me as mentally handicapped in some way.

With fellow 'students' Paul, Mark, John and Phil, a drive to Milan was planned, taking in the Riviera on the way back, funds allowing. We pooled our francs and, for the equivalent of about £100, bought a Renault 12, which Paul, a self-taught mechanic, got working.

And so began the adventure. After a tortuous, seemingly endless drive which included turning back after two hours to get Phil's forgotten passport, we arrived in northern Italy. None of us had enough money to survive properly on, so meals usually involved bread and/or a tin of something from the supermarkets that loomed on the edge of most towns, canned food being cheaper than its weighed, fresh counterpart.

Our downfall was that in these supermarkets the cheapest red wine cost less than bottled water. With little consideration for our health or sanity, it was decided that we would economize by drinking this instead of water and put the savings towards petrol for the car and non-alcoholic fluid for our designated driver. When the radiator started to fizz and steam and we were miles from anywhere, it was topped up with plonk. Likewise, when the screenwash expired it was replaced with a cheeky little number from the hills of Verona.

One of the advantages of drinking wine (and I use the term loosely) all day is that it enabled us to sleep quite well when we finally pulled up alongside a field. We'd take it in turns to have the back seat to stretch out on for the night, the rest of us bedding down on the grass, inebriated, numb and immune from discomfort of any kind. And so, occasionally squirting the windscreen with rancid red Valpolicella as we went, we drove down through northern Italy to Florence and Pisa before heading back, our money almost all gone, ten nights of alcoholic saturation, sleeping rough, without so much as a shower or change of clothes.

In Genoa, I cunningly suggested that we sought free parking in the poorer back-streets away from the town centre. On our return, we found that the Renault had been vandalized, graffitied with spray paint so badly that it was hard to recognize it. How was I to know that the Italians hate the French too?

In Monaco, we parked up on the harbour, in between a Bentley Continental and a Lamborghini, and gazed in awe at the yachts and the Bond-movie landscape behind them. Almost as if to invoke a scene from one of those films, within minutes we had been joined by four policemen in a large Citroën.

'What are you doing here in Monaco?' one of them asked, getting out of the car. Privately I congratulated myself for having understood, but then again, he was speaking English.

'We're just visiting, sightseeing,' we all explained in turns.

'Non,' said the more senior officer. Now he was speaking French.

'Pardon?' we asked. In French.

'Non,' he repeated with a dismissive wave of his hand, and then said that we had to go. Paul's French was better than the rest of ours so he asked if we were in a private car park.

'Non,' said the officer again. It wasn't the car park he was talking about. He was saying 'Non' to us being in Monaco generally.

I think I managed to say 'Mais pourquoi?'

And that's a classic example of where my French fails me: when I've asked a simple question and I get the answer shouted in my face by a moustached local, breathing his garlicky lunch all over me.

In the car, Paul explained that we had to leave Monaco because we were all 'arseholes', according to the policeman, and that it was unlikely that a return visit at any time in the future would be greeted favourably by the authorities there. They followed us to the border to make sure we left. The shame of it.

20

To OFFEND WITHOUT realizing that you have offended is said to be a sign of stupidity. I'm not so sure. There are a lot of very chippy people out there who are capable of being offended by more or less anything. So it's nothing to do with stupidity, it's just my bad luck that I keep running into them.

Soon after I returned from my travels, I got a job as a waiter in a French restaurant in Winchester. Ironically, and no doubt to my parents' annoyance, I actually did learn quite a lot of French there.

Not that all the staff were from France. Adolfo, another waiter, was Spanish. He was a petite man in his late forties with black hair slicked back across his head, Jack Nicholson style. Thinking about it (which I didn't at the time), he was probably one of the last people to have been named after Hitler, if that was his proud parents' intention. If it wasn't, then without realizing it they had instantly caused deep offence to millions of people throughout the world. That's quite an achievement, but it still doesn't make them stupid.

Maybe I just didn't put two and two together and Adolfo actually was the Führer in disguise. When I look back, he did have very piercing eyes and was incredibly persuasive when it came to selling the specials on the menu. But let's be realistic, changing your name from Adolf to Adolfo is such a lame effort at disguise that it can't have really been him. Still, makes you wonder.

On his first day, I was polishing cutlery in the prep-room and he walked in asking, 'Any coffee in dis house?' I immediately thought that here was someone I was going to get on with. That was until the next day, when he arrived and said exactly the same thing. And the next. 'Any coffee in dis house?' By the end of the week it was getting on my nerves to such an extent that I started deliberately not putting the coffee on when I arrived in the morning. This was because, implicit in Adolfo's question, I felt, was the assumption that I should have coffee ready for him at all times. So screw him, I thought.

Things came to a head after the lunchtime service one day. Adolfo had become quite surly and irritable with me. As I began to buff a tray load of wine glasses for evening service, he turned to me, incandescent with rage, and said in his thick Spanish accent, 'Never, never tell me what to do again.'

I was taken aback, so I asked him what he meant.

Before I could even finish the question he continued, shaking, 'Dis lady on table seven. I am known her from restaurant where I am work before dis, and in fron' of her you tell to me "Can you get bread for dis table?"'

I gave a good account of myself, coming back with 'Er, well, you know, I didn't mean to, you know, like . . .'

Unintimidated by my obviously superior command of the English language, he came straight back with a counter-argument.

'Because you are waiter,' he said, drawing heavily on a freshly lit cigarette, 'and I am waiter . . .'

'True,' I said, trying to sound reasonable, which wasn't hard because it was true.

'So you no tell me my job. You never tell me how do my job. Yes?'

'Fine,' I said magnanimously. 'I apologize.'

Another deep inhalation of Benson & Hedges. 'Because you are no my boss. Dis is no your restaurant.'

'I know, Adolfo. Coffee? I've just made some.'

He shook his cigarette at me, the exhaled fumes jumping around his mouth and nose as he spoke.

'I am been waiter since twenty-six years. I know my job. I no need you telling me how to do.'

'Point taken. Once again, I'm sorry.'

'Because you are waiter and I am waiter . . .'

'Gosh, now you really are starting to bore me,' I said, which was rude, but I intended it to offend so it doesn't count. In any case, what's the point of an argument if you don't shut up once you've received an apology?

So for the next couple of weeks we continued working together in a fairly tense atmosphere. It all came to a head when someone else gave Adolfo instructions in front of a customer. When the restaurant had emptied, Adolfo launched into the same line of undeniable logic, i.e. 'You are no my boss, dis is no your restaurant' (etc.). Except that this time it was deniable, because he was shouting at Bernard, the slick Frenchman whose restaurant it indeed was and who therefore was his boss. Within about three minutes, poor old Adolfo had his coat on and was walking up the road, cigarette glowing at full thrust, never to return.

Later that day I came across Adolfo's CV in the office. In twenty-six years the only places he had worked for more than a few weeks were cruise ships. Presumably nobody felt sure that they could throw him into the Atlantic and not be arrested at the next port. All of which goes to illustrate how easy it is to cause offence without knowing it. But a better example springs to mind which, coincidentally, also involves a waiter.

Some years ago, Jane and I decided to take ourselves off for a weekend break at a country-house hotel. We chose Cliveden, erstwhile home of the Astors and backdrop to the Profumo affair, nestled in a Berkshire hillside overlooking the Thames, which until our visit I had no idea was so beautiful.

From the moment we arrived, the car wheels

crunching majestically on the gravel drive, we were enchanted by the house and its staff. Well, most of them. Mind you, I gave up trying to impress at places like that a long time ago. We once stayed at Chewton Glen in the New Forest and – somewhat vainly, I know – I insisted that after the long journey down we pull up before arriving in order to lower the roof of my Saab convertible and thus be able to sweep along the drive in considerable style, so making a proper entrance.

As we approached the front of the hotel, hood down, I don't mind telling you I was pretty damn pleased with the effect. Several porters trotted respectfully on to the forecourt and waited.

'See?' I said to Jane. 'That's what happens when the staff realize you've got a bit of style. You get some respect.'

'Oh, I see,' she replied.

At which point a thunderous noise filled the air and my baseball cap flew away. The porters broke again into a quick trot and went straight past my car towards the private helicopter that was landing about a hundred yards behind us.

Luckily, we had packed light on that occasion and I managed the bags fairly easily on my own.

So anyway, we're at Cliveden. We have a room overlooking the river and its stunning valley, marred only at night when the orange glow of distant Maidenhead radiates into the sky. We had a drink, relaxed and then decided to go down for dinner.

Sitting in the drawing room, Jane and I ordered a cocktail and read the menus. Then the head waiter approached and informed me, graciously but firmly, that jeans were not allowed in the restaurant.

I've never been opposed to dress-code, which is why I rang in advance to enquire. All I was told was that a jacket and tie were required and trainers were not permitted.

'Good, quite right too,' I thought. After all, there's nothing worse than the atmosphere of a fine Georgian dining room being tarnished by the presence of some scaffolder from Slough in an Adidas shirt throwing his money about.

I was wearing jeans, perfectly respectable jeans (proper Levis, mind, not the type worn by politicians in casual mode). The point is, they were clean and present-able and didn't let the side down. However, rules are rules. Unfortunately, I hadn't packed any other trousers apart from a pair of tracksuit bottoms in case I wanted to make use of the gym in the morning. As a joke, I said I could put them on, but to my alarm the maître d' asked that I did just that.

Half an hour later I escorted my elegantly attired wife into the restaurant. For this I was wearing jacket and tie, black brogues and tracksuit bottoms. Adidas, I think they were.

I noticed that my fellow guests treated me with

disdain because of how I was dressed. What a pity that they have to base their assumptions about people on such superficial values. Pathetic really. I'm glad I'm not like that.

The next morning we enjoyed the ultimate luxury of waking naturally at about ten o'clock, as opposed to being woken by the noise of our children running around like crazed banshees from six onwards. We sat up in bed enjoying the late-August morning, everything bursting with life and colour for as far as the eye could see. Jane wasn't really hungry, but I insisted that we at least have some croissants with our coffee anyway. I picked up the phone and dialled room service. Life is good, let's enjoy it.

'Hello, could I order some breakfast, please?'

'Yes. I suppose it's possible,' agreed the sulky French voice.

'Sorry?' I asked, not quite understanding.

'If you are 'ungry this morning, then you can 'ave a breakfast.'

'Well, I am hungry so I would like to order,' I growled.

'Of course,' said the waiter in the same tone that he might be justified in using had I walked down to the kitchens in my pyjamas and slapped him hard around the face. 'One moment, please,' he continued. It was obvious the wretch didn't have a pen.

I turned to Jane. 'What the hell is it with these

waiters? You'd think no one had ever asked for breakfast before. The prices you pay at these places and they can't even answer the phone pleasantly.'

By now he'd found a pen, not that it had cheered him up any. 'Yes, what would you like to order?'

Borderline aggressive, that was. It just made me want to order more. I wasn't settling for croissants. Not after that. I reached for the room-service menu.

'Yeah, I'd like the fruit compote twice, two bowls of bran flakes with skimmed milk, one fried egg with bacon, black pudding, fresh field mushrooms and tomato, one kedgeree with chorizo, two freshly squeezed orange juices, coffee for two with hot milk, a basket of pastries with homemade jams and mixed toast, please.'

There was a silence, during which the bad-tempered waiter wrote and Jane gestured that this was not what she wanted at all. I covered the mouthpiece of the phone. 'Unbelievable attitude,' I said to her. 'You should hear this guy.'

'But I don't want any of that,' complained Jane.

'Don't worry, you don't have to eat it, it's the principle.'

'What princi—'

The waiter had finished scribbling and was back on, sounding even more miserable than before while he read the entire order back to me as if it was an affront to his very being. Then, in a voice that I can only describe

as sarcastic, he said, 'It's everything you require?'
Definitely sarcastic. I'll show him. The gloves are off now.

'I'll have a bottle of champagne to go with that.'

'Champagne?' asked the waiter and Jane
simultaneously.

'That's right. Champagne. I would like champagne.
If that's OK with you.'

A pause while the waiter composed himself. He'd
met his match with me. Nobody pushes me around and
gives me attitude.

'Yes. Will be with you before twenty minutes.'

I put the phone down and did a quick impression
for Jane's sake. ' "Will be with you before twenty
minutes." Unbelievable.'

'He's probably perfectly nice. Some people just
sound a bit like that on the phone.'

'Well, they shouldn't. Not when they're supposed to
sound helpful.'

The discussion continued until, 'before twenty
minutes', there was a knock at the door.

'Here we go,' I said, jumping up and looking
forward to seeing what this joyless man looked like.
And in he glided, silently pushing a trolley with two
silver-domed cloches.

'Your breakfast, Sir,' he said glumly. 'May I set it for
you here?'

'Please,' I said, making a point of smiling broadly,
which I could see unnerved him.

With a great flourish, like a corny magician, he threw a white tablecloth into the air and snapped it from its folds to rest perfectly on the table. Quickly and skilfully (I'll give him that), the table was made ready for my feast.

As I sat, I thanked him, maintaining my fixed grin.

Lastly, the waiter placed my newspaper on to the table with the words 'Ze Princess of Wales is dead. Enjoy your breakfast, if you can.'

It was the right-hook from nowhere that leaves you on the canvas wondering who it is you can hear counting to ten.

I staggered to my senses, mumbling. On the front page was mention of a car-smash in Paris. Jane found the remote, switched on the television and flicked through the channels, every one of them full of the story.

The truth began to sink in as the waiter asked, 'Would you like me to open the champagne for you now, Sir?'

21

FOR A FEW YEARS, in my early twenties, I settled into the world of restaurants believing that, in all probability, this would become my career.

I got a job in Covent Garden, at a kind of English brasserie specializing in pies. You could have shepherd's pie, fish pie, beef and oyster, lamb and apricot or vegetarian pie. It was successful, packed out most nights with a queue going into the street. On Sundays they served a roast, which was popular with American tourists who tipped well, so everyone was happy, not least the owner. His most annoying habit was ringing from his country home to check on us in the middle of a hectic service and then helpfully commenting that he thought the music was too loud.

I was a trainee manager, but within about a week I was asked to run the place on my own because one of the other duty managers had to leave suddenly due to a drug problem. From what I can gather, the drugs themselves didn't affect her work in any way except for when she was cashing up. When it came to counting money she seemed to count most of it as hers and so the poor girl had to go. Let's ask Jack to take her shifts. He seems reliable.

It was great having my own restaurant. The work was easy and the company good. To increase my enjoyment of the evening I had a large glass of red wine that the barman would constantly top up. Every time I returned to it from showing customers to a table, the glass was full.

By the end of the evening I was pleasingly inebriated, and most nights that didn't matter. How was I to know we were going to get raided by the police?

Almost without exception, the large basement kitchen was staffed by Moroccans at that time. It wasn't exactly cheffing, but they were skilled at what they did and were popular with everyone. Inevitably in an operation that size, people drop out or get sick and replacements are brought in, and one of the hardest parts of managing the staff was ensuring that each person was legally employed. Sometimes you had no option but to get somebody in at the last minute to wash up and pay them cash for their time.

I was happily sitting on my stool, sipping Rioja and chatting to the bartender when about seven uniformed policemen came in and asked to speak to the manager. I stepped up and the plain-clothed sergeant leading them showed me his ID and said that they had reason to believe that we had in our employ a number of illegal immigrants. I began to protest that this couldn't possibly be the case. For some reason the sequence of events is a bit fuzzy in my memory, but I am confident that some sort of warrant was produced. As I looked at it, several of the waitresses made their way down to the kitchen to warn any of the staff that might be affected.

The police trundled down the main stairs and barged into the kitchen as the small service lift made its way upstairs, carrying a contorted North African washer-up. The police found nobody that they could arrest in the kitchen, so decided to make their way up to the prep area, a room to the side of the restaurant where the service lift came up to. As they barged in, one of the waitresses hit the down button, the police looked round, asked a few questions, decided to take one more look downstairs (up went the lift) and then left.

In my own defence, I'd have to say that I wouldn't have lasted five minutes in that job if I wasn't fairly good at dealing with the customers. Queues of people barging through the doors for hours on end excited me. I enjoyed learning how to handle them by sharing a joke with them or talking to them in a way that would get them on your side. It was almost the best part of the job. As a waiter I had learnt how to deal one-to-one with people (which is invaluable as well), but this was proper crowd-control.

Most of the waitresses and bus-boys were at drama or art school, studying for degrees, or singing in a band, and were simply working at the restaurant to make ends meet. I liked their company. One girl was at RADA, another was raising funds to put on a play that she'd written. They were supporting themselves. They were supporting each other. The thing that they all had in common was that catering was not their ambition. We'd sometimes go for a drink after work and invariably I'd be asked what I 'did'. I'd say that this was what I 'did'. I was a trainee restaurant manager. Several of them insisted that I must be an out-of-work actor, saying that I had a knack for telling stories and entertaining. But I had long since buried any thoughts of a career on the stage. One thing they all agreed on was that they found it funny how I dealt with customers in such a deadpan manner and got away with it.

This was news to me. I genuinely thought I smiled the entire time. It goes to show how wrong you can be. I went back to the flat I was renting – a few drinks on board, I admit – stood in front of the bathroom mirror with my eyes closed, and when I was sure that my face was in its normal work mode, opened my eyes. Looking back was a miserable little guy who looked like he'd just sucked on a lemon. How nobody had punched me in the face as I walked up to them in the restaurant, I'll never know. I would have.

I'd say that this was the beginning of a long, slow

awakening, a realization that I wasn't doing what I was supposed to be doing with my life. It was the un-covering of a disquieting sense of destiny that was to cause great turmoil and confusion in me. I lived with the feeling you might have if you're on the wrong train and can't decide where to get off in order to change direction. The word 'destiny' is packed with gravitas, I know, and unless you are Nelson Mandela it's probably a little pompous to use it in the context of one's journey through life. Nevertheless, I was greatly agitated by a growing sense that there was a different path that I had to find and travel along.

My social life too revolved around the restaurant. I made some good friends, but my general mood was darkening and I found myself shunning their company in favour of solitude. The reason for this? As much as I liked the parties, what really interested me at that time was the drinking, and to be honest, that was easier to do alone.

Sometimes, when all the staff had gone home, I would carry on drinking as I counted up the night's takings and locked them in the safe. The trouble with that was that I would eventually get back to my flat and not be able to recall any of it. I'd pace around madly trying to remember whether or not I had locked up properly or if I'd even put the money in the safe. On more than one occasion I had to go all the way back to the restaurant and check that everything was in order, just to ease my anxiety. An obvious solution to this would have been not to drink, but that would have involved, well, not drinking, so a better idea had to be found. This came in the form of kneeling down in front of the safe after I had placed the money inside it and cracking my head against the thick steel door, so that the resulting bruise would later reassure me that I had conducted my duties responsibly. Brilliant.

I had always liked alcohol, but this was different. My drinking was out of control and I couldn't work out a way of stopping. Today I wonder why it was so hard for me to see the real problem, that whenever I wasn't fully occupied I became depressed and unmotivated. The likeliest answer is that the original solution I sought, namely Alcoholics Anonymous, did seem to remedy matters.

One Saturday morning in 1984, I walked into my first AA meeting and was immediately taken with the idea of their twelve-step programme. Nowadays there's a twelve-step programme of recovery for many addictions and conditions, but they all stem from this, the original one. Essentially, it is a series of suggested actions that an individual can take in order to find fulfilment and happiness without alcohol. These include an admission of powerlessness over alcohol, asking for help, taking personal inventory, making amends and so on. Many people take years to work through the programme completely and some, in fact, never reach the stage of 'finishing' it. I still think that it is the most effective path to spiritual growth and continuous sobriety that has been devised.

Its genius is twofold. Firstly, it exploits positively the idea that the best person to help a drunk get and stay sober is likely to be someone who has been there him or herself. At the same time, helping sufferers towards sobriety and away from relapsing is a highly effective way of guaranteeing your own continued recovery. This is a seemingly obvious fact that eluded mankind until the 1930s, when a newly sober chronic alcoholic felt the need to seek out and help another suffering alcoholic in order to prevent himself from drinking again. Secondly, alongside the twelve steps that emerged during the following years, twelve traditions were established, the most important of which is anonymity. Members are only ever known by their first name and the organization holds no personal records. In addition, members are urged not to discuss their involvement with AA in the public domain.

Some famous AAs have been outed by the press and thus are left with no option but to 'admit' their connection, but in the last few years I've noticed a willingness among some celebrities to offer up this information. It's a dangerous trend. After all, such a person is inevitably setting himself up as an example of what AA can do. Great, until he falls off the wagon and becomes an advert for what it can't do – namely, help you to drink normally.

For that reason alone, although my own involvement with Alcoholics Anonymous is already public knowledge, I am careful when talking about this time in my life. What I can say is that I'll always be grateful for the solace and peace that I found in those rooms and the friendship that I encountered there. I went to AA regularly for six years or so and only stopped going when I came to realize that my underlying problem was not genuine alcoholism, but depression.

It was to be a good many years before I tackled that problem really effectively, but for the time being, I attended meetings, abstained from alcohol and, crucially, stopped banging my head against hard objects.

22

ONE OF THE WORST things about working in a restaurant, be it the kitchen or front of house, is the split shift.

This, if you didn't know, is when you work lunch and dinner services with a token two or three hours off in between. Often the prospect of a busy evening is enough to keep a rookie chef diligently at his station throughout this 'rest', prepping garnishes and sauces, turning vegetables, boning joints of meat and filleting fish in dread of being caught unready for the onslaught of the hungry.

As a waiter, that brief afternoon furlough was frequently revoked by the presence of a late-sitter, that guest who enters the restaurant minutes before the kitchen closes expecting to order lunch. It was unheard of then to be paid by the hour – whether it is now I don't know, but it would explain the wearisome look from waiting staff when you walk through the door expecting a happy welcome at ten to three.

So it frequently happened that you could be held back, serving a table of four businessmen, their ties loosened, their wine drunk, as they asked for cigars and brandy, espressos and more brandy. The minutes would crawl past as you stood behind the bar, pretending to be occupied, polishing already polished glasses and pointlessly reorganizing the liqueurs. Under such circumstances, the only sport to be had was recommending the absurd. A vintage malt whisky at £30 a shot or a rare Cognac supposedly favoured by Napoleon (yeah, right) was too tempting for an inebriated executive to decline.

Wilton Reid, a customer in one restaurant where I worked, was in the habit of clicking his fingers at the staff to impress his colleagues with his casual command of us minions. At the end of each month he would reward his top-performing employees with a lunch at which they had to laugh at his feeble jokes and applaud his self-trumpeted achievements. Over coffee he would summon me and loudly demand champagne, whilst discreetly pointing with his sweaty finger at the house pop, so that kudos needn't cost.

At the end of one financial year, Mr Reid decided to 'treat' all his clients to lunch, which he did over two successive Fridays, a party of ten or so on the first occasion and thirty on the second.

On the first Friday he got very boozy and was as obnoxious as ever as he waved his credit card at me in order to pay. Tired of being detained all afternoon, unpaid, by Mr Reid's tedious lunches, his pompous, needy, drunken beckoning and consistent stiffing (failure to tip), I devised my revenge.

The second Friday with the much bigger party arrived and as I went around the table pouring coffee he snapped his fingers to draw my attention.

'Champagne, *garçon*,' he called, enjoying the reverence that his words seemed to evoke in his guests.

'Certainly, Sir,' I said in a loud hammy voice that sucked everyone present into the exchange. 'Dom Perignon?' I continued, half hoping that he'd choke at the thought.

'What?' gasped Reid, confused, his face reddening.

'The Dom Perignon, Sir? The same one you gave everybody last week? At your client lunch?' I enquired innocently, knowing full well that he had ordered the same cheap fizz as always.

One of his guests blurted merrily, "Ere, aren't we your clients, Wilt?' which got a big laugh, not least from myself, although naturally I didn't show it. Too professional.

I'm told that 1979 was a forgettable vintage for the Dom Perignon, but I beg to differ. I will always remember it, just as I will always remember rude Mr Reid's vascular face as I popped open the seventh bottle in order to fill the last glass. Those flutes were on the large side and the restaurant did have smaller ones, but I

Below: A postcard of my great-grandfather Frederick Pope Stamper. I should explain that he was an actor. And not a seaside resort.

My great-grandmother Daisy Le Hay, seen here on stage. At least, I presume so. I'd be surprised if she went around like that at home.

Above: Great-uncle Charlie was King Edward VII's motoring consultant. That makes me a minor royal in my book. Which this is.

Middle: My grandfather Lionel in his car. Lionel was actually much bigger by the time I knew him. As was his car.

Right: I didn't really know my grandmother Teddy. But this is definitely her.

Below: On holiday in Salcombe. Obviously the rest of the family were there too. I didn't just go on my own.

Above: The house in Easton where I grew up. Plenty of wall space for a nice blue plaque. As I frequently point out in my anonymous letters to the Council.

Below: Aged twelve with Flicker our Shetland sheepdog. She was a rescue dog. I don't know what happened to the sheep.

Left: My comedy debut, aged thirteen, sitting on my brother's knee. I was worried we'd be gottled off.

Peter Symonds Esq., His Players

Present

Will. Shakespeare's

THE TAMING OF THE SHREW

THE PLAYERS (in order of speaking).

LUCENTIO,	Son to Vincentio, in love with Bianca	RICHARD CROKER
TRANIO,	his Servant	ROSS BENDALL
BAPTISTA,	a rich gentleman of Padua	CAESAR SLATTERY
GREMIO,	suitor to Bianca	IAN CRAWFORD
KATHERINA,	the Shrew, daughter to Lucentio	
HORTENSIO,	suitor to Bianca	NICKI DUFFETT
BIANCA,	daughter to Lucentio	HENRY THOMAS
BIONDELLO,	servant to Lucentio	GEORGINA TISDALL
PETRUCHIO,	a Gentleman of Verona, suitor to Katherina	DAN WEISSELBERG
GRUMIO,	his Man	JACK DEE
BIANCA'S SERVANT		ANDY KEY
CURTIS,	Petruchio's Housekeeper	
PETRUCHIO'S other Servants		AMANDA STAPELEY

AMANDA STAPELEY
CAROLINE JONES
PETER CORNER
JON FORNI
ROB CHRISTIE
JOHN WELLS
NEIL FLETCHER
PIPPA WHEELER
KATE FIRTH
ROBIN PHILLIPS
TREVOR SMITH
JOHN WELLS
MARY LOUGHRAN

HABERDASHER
TAILOR
PEDANT
VINCENTIO, an old gentleman of Pisa
OFFICER
A WIDOW

Servants, Gentlemen and Ladies: JULIE BURT, RICHARD CLEMINSON, CHARLOTTE CLOW, EDWARD FINNIGAN, NICOLA GEBBIE, LOUISE GOODMAN, PENNY HAINES, PENNY HILLIER, NICOLA HUTCHINGS, LIZZIE TUCKER, ROGER TWEEDY, PHIL WARDLE AND LUCY WITCHER.

ACROBATS: under the direction of MANDY BERNSTONE: ANN BAKER, SIAN DUNSTAN, HELEN KINSLER, KAREN NEAL AND MARGARET SMALL.

The Play Directed by Sarah Hawkins and Christopher Cooper.

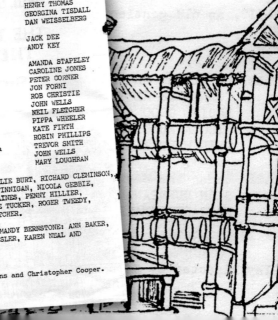

Left: My first ever dramatic role, with the cast listed in order of speaking. I would have been further up the bill, but I missed my cue.

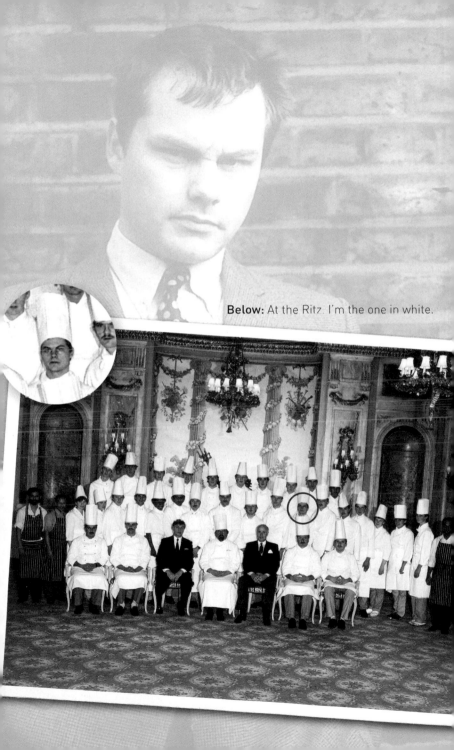

Below: At the Ritz. I'm the one in white.

Above: A recent photo. Alright, I recently found it in a drawer. If you must know, it's me in 1986, a few weeks before my first visit to the Comedy Store.

Below: My motorbike (Jane and her car in foreground).

Above: The love of my life. Seen here being hugged by Jane.

Happy at last. My first professional photo shoot.

Below: An early bill. 'Jack Dee' would have been printed a lot bigger, but Hattie Hayridge's unnecessarily long name took up all the space.

thought his guests might appreciate a decent-sized drink. With a wine bill alone that came to over £1,500, plus a service charge for tables of six or over, the episode was a resounding success in my opinion.

And on Mr Reid's subsequent visits to the restaurant, although they were admittedly much less frequent, I detected a small measure of cautiousness, even courtesy in his manner. Certainly, he never again clicked his fingers at me or called me *garçon*. I ventured to call him by his first name and it felt like I'd tamed him.

'Hello, Wilton,' I'd say, enjoying the temerity of it.

'Hello, Jack,' he'd reply politely.

After a while, I went to work in a different restaurant, called Bates. Alan, the owner, suggested that I get some kitchen experience as well as front of house and I was thankful, not least because it gave me refuge from working directly with alcohol for a while.

Although untrained, I got on reasonably well as a commis chef and became interested in the stories of all the chefs there who had worked in the big kitchens like the Savoy and the Dorchester. Coincidentally, I had just read George Orwell's *Down and Out in Paris and London*, in which he describes life behind the scenes of large restaurants. It struck me as an intriguing world and one that I wanted to learn more about.

I wondered if this might be the change in direction that I was seeking and decided that I too would work in a large kitchen. That way I could spend time in all the departments, acquiring detailed skills in everything from fish to patisserie. Once that had happened, I'd probably be made head chef, if they'd got any sense, whereupon I'd make a name for myself, leave and set up my own incredibly successful gastronomic establishment in Fulham – no, Chelsea – no, I know, Mayfair. People are loaded there.

The next thing really did happen just like this: I went to the staff entrance of the Ritz in Piccadilly and said that I had an interview with the head chef; obviously a lie. The man at the desk rang down, announced that I was there and then turned to me, saying, 'Chef says he doesn't know about any interview.'

'Oh, what? But I arranged it on the phone last week.'

'Who did you speak to?' asked the man.

'Personnel. I've had to come quite a long way as well,' I protested.

The man repeated my story on the phone. There was a pause and then he said, 'Chef will see you. If you'd like to make your way down to the kitchen.'

Bingo. I was in. Down I went. As I entered through the swing doors the kitchen seemed to stretch as far as I could see, each section a micro-climate of its own heat and industry.

Michael Quinn was the head chef and he didn't waste time with niceties. 'Personnel, my arse,' he mumbled. 'You haven't got a fucking interview. Who the fuck are you anyway?'

I came clean, instinctively knowing that was the best policy, explaining that I wanted a job in his kitchen and that I'd accept anything. He stopped me there and bluntly said that if I had the bottle to bullshit my way in as I had done, then he was prepared to give me a go.

The following week I began and soon realized that I had made a big mistake. Owing to the fact that I'd said I was trained, everybody assumed that I was, so I was given work to do that was way beyond my abilities. Each hour of each day spent there was a living nightmare. Nobody wanted me on their section because I was so useless and therefore increased the workload of whoever was landed with me.

As I had read in Orwell's book (despite this being some fifty years later), hierarchy in the kitchen was strictly adhered to. Commis chefs were expected to be clean-shaven, sous chefs tended to have moustaches, and the head chef wore the only beard in the place. The kitchen porters were mostly from Bangladesh and stoically put up with all manner of abuse, knowing as they did that work is hard to get when you don't speak good English and have no skills that pertain to your new environment.

For me, every day was an exercise in trying to remain unnoticed amid the busy clatter of prep and the shouting steamy mayhem of service. Somehow I was tolerated. Jokes make a good currency in situations such as that. Also, bit by bit, I had been relegated to the lowliest of jobs as a general realization of my ineptitude spread throughout the Ritz.

Maybe you are one of those who has been lucky enough to enjoy the decadent luxury of the world-famous tea at the Ritz. Well, I'm one of those who has been unlucky enough to have to prepare it.

What a palaver it was, poncing around with scones and Sachertorte. (Mind you, that is some cake: the number of times I'd deliberately shut myself in the walk-in patisserie fridge and ram a great slice of it into my mouth, then return to my work hoping not to be noticed as I all but passed out on the chocolate hit.) Then there were the finger-sandwiches to be made. Three hours of egg and cress, ham, cucumber, smoked salmon and cream cheese. Several trays of twenty-four-inch loaves that would arrive ready-sliced, horizontally, to be spread thinly with soft butter and the filling, stacked up like high-rise flats, de-crusted and sliced through to create the finger shape that looks so elegant on the three-tier stand. What a pain.

But the job was not without its bonuses. For the first time in my life I tried caviar. Being a simple but time-consuming dish to prepare, it often fell to me to put it together on a tray of crushed ice with little pots of chopped herbs and boiled egg. I quickly developed a taste for it and it was never difficult to prepare myself two or three little canapés to enjoy on the sly.

At any given time, a hotel of that size would have

thousands of pounds' worth of truffles, lobster, caviar and foie gras in its larders, not to mention turbot, fillet steak and rare charcuterie. With a little bit of guile, it was possible to eat well in the kitchen.

After a month or so, I had picked up enough to know how to keep busy and, more importantly, to give the impression – to most, at least – of being busy. But Michael Quinn was a formidable presence and was never fooled by such antics. I was glad that he was seldom in the kitchen itself and tended to stay in his office, a grotto of antique furniture and old photos that probably hadn't been moved since that great culinary icon Auguste Escoffier put them there at the turn of the century.

When Chef did venture out, he would usually reprimand me for something, throwing a plate of food that I had prepared on to the floor, his boozy crimson face swelling with rage. 'That, to me, is a fucking load of shit. Clear it up and fucking do it again.' (If you're ever in a similar situation, it's helpful to know that the correct answer to that is 'Yes, Chef.)

It came to be my turn to do the night shift. I didn't mind as it gave me the opportunity to work unsupervised. All I had to do was a few room-service orders and then, at about six a.m., start preparing the trays of bacon, sausages, mushrooms and tomatoes for breakfast.

On my first night I did fairly well, I thought. At

around midnight you'd start getting the odd order in for club sandwiches and other items from the small menu. Baffled by a request for cauliflower cheese, something that wasn't on the menu and that I hadn't cooked before, I somewhat pathetically covered some raw cauliflower with pancake mix from the larder and browned it under the grill. It looked the business, but was, I accept, essentially inedible. My plan for when it got sent back, as it surely would be, was to claim that it was a pre-made dish that I had re-heated on order and that it obviously couldn't have been made properly. I'll never know if that story would have fooled the waiter, because it wasn't sent back, something which puzzles me to this day.

I took preparing the breakfasts more seriously as I knew how busy it could get and didn't want to let down the breakfast chefs by leaving them an ill-equipped section. But some breakfast orders were more trouble than others. When Rex Harrison was staying he was on a special diet and his request would be read out by the sous chef. 'For Mr Rex Harrison, one bowl of rolled oats with Austrian granola, wild blueberries, warmed goats' milk, semi-skimmed, and a side order of Yemenese honey.'

'Aye, Chef' and 'Yes, Chef' came the responses from those charged with fetching the components for the great man's meal as they ran to various larders.

This became quite a ritual for a week or so. As

multiple orders for more conventional breakfasts echoed around the kitchen, suddenly would come 'For Mr Rex Harrison, one bowl of rolled oats with Austrian granola, wild blueberries, warmed goats' milk, semi-skimmed, and a side order of Yemenese honey,' until one day when Chef picked up the chit that had come through and announced, 'Oh fucking hell. Another bowl of porridge for Doctor Dolittle.' 'Aye, Chef.' 'Yes, Chef.'

But for the most part, every shift was an ordeal and increased my sense of confusion about what I should be doing with my life. One night, at about three in the morning, the doorman came down to the kitchen in his top hat and cloak, looking like a ghost from Victorian London, and asked if I would cook him his supper. I made him a steak and chips, which he took away to eat in the canteen. Half an hour later he returned. Taking his hand from his waistcoat pocket, he slid a fifty-pence piece across the counter towards me. 'Very nice, lad,' he said as he left.

I must have stood there for twenty minutes looking at that coin. All I could think was 'I have just been tipped by a doorman. My life is all wrong.'

One day, after six months at the Ritz, I was preparing some raw meat and managed to put a boning-knife through my finger. The wound required several stitches and the bulky bandaging prevented me from working. A week of convalescence brought me to my senses and I never went back.

23

DURING MY TIME IN the Ritz kitchen I had gained the habit of slipping out after service, not caring for an afternoon of sculpting carrots into perfect little barrels or getting involved in the dreaded afternoon teas.

There was a subterranean staff-room with a stained pool table, a cigarette machine and some worn-out hotel sofas where you could kip or sit around, smoking and talking shop. I hated it in there.

Then there was Piccadilly to wander down; Jermyn Street with its shop windows to look in; the Royal Academy if I was in the mood, which was hardly ever. These hours became hard to fill without a heaviness descending upon me.

I acquired the habit of visiting St James's Church on Piccadilly. There I would sit, read, pray or sleep, depending on how I felt.

In accordance with the emerging pattern of my life, any lull in activity usually ushered in a sense of numbing despair. I felt compelled to seek out spiritual answers, believing that maybe the sense of permanent restlessness I felt was a sign of some kind of metaphysical calling. When I had the time, I would go to bookshops and 'research' Christianity. My amateur theology extended to attending one or two talks at the same church, as well as occasional services.

The Church of England for me had always been like an elderly relative that I felt I should visit from time to time. I took religion much too seriously, however, and its overall effect, I have to say, was depressing. I would have really liked to discard it, but somehow I couldn't.

I found it harder and harder to lighten up and just enjoy life. I'd suddenly break off promising relationships for no good reason and neglect friends for weeks on end. I'd fall into a silent inertia that would only temporarily be resolved by an AA meeting. It was a despondency that wouldn't leave and could, at times, make me feel very panicky. I had a longing for ritual, something that I could cling to, a routine that, if adhered to, would make me feel well and contented.

I liked the idea of Catholicism. At least you get a rosary and some pleasingly convincing sacraments, like crossing yourself when you pray and regular Mass. Incense was another plus. Its authority, smothering you at the door like a cassock, could give a tangible feeling of the holy. But once again, I was in conflict with myself. Tradition and ritual make good hiding places for religious doubt, and for me that wouldn't do.

Instead, I wanted to do battle with it all, to wrestle with God and all the inadequate answers that surrounded Him. It sounds pretentious. Perhaps it was, but I suspect it was more the symptom of a malaise that felt as though it was destroying me, bit by bit. At times I didn't know if I was seeking God or trying to rid myself of the very notion of Him.

I continued to spend much of my spare time in bookshops, reading Bible commentaries and theological critiques, hoping they would nudge me closer to some kind of absolute that I could hold up as a torch to light my way. Combining this manic quest for the divine with my bizarre and ridiculous position at the Ritz, I think it was the closest I have come to being truly mad.

I can't explain the obsession. Atheism was, and still is, far more fashionable and would have been much more convenient. The most likely reason for it all is simply that I was depressed and was totally unable to escape the gloom that had descended upon me. In particular, I found praying very disturbing, like swimming with bricks tied to your feet. And yet I was drawn to it constantly. I just didn't know what else to do with myself.

I don't really remember how or why, but eventually, feeling increasingly anxious about everything, I made an appointment to meet with the Reverend Donald Reeves, then rector of St James's.

We sat in his office and he asked me about myself. I told him the story so far, and after an hour or so he suggested that we meet up on a regular basis so that I could talk – about whatever I wanted to. Quite matter-of-factly, he said he thought that might help.

Before very long, these conversations eased the pain of what I was going through. Donald's approach was pragmatic. He seemed to have fewer answers than I did, which slowly became rather reassuring. Sometimes I would ask him a question like 'Why do natural disasters happen?' And he'd shrug his shoulders, almost as if it were not germane to what he stood for. (I've since learnt to be wary of Christians with slick arguments, especially those who use the Bible to support their point.) In any case, our discussions were very helpful, particularly as he appeared quite unconcerned with proselytising or even encouraging me to attend church services. On one occasion, Donald described the resurrection as a good metaphor for what happens to people when they let go of their preconceived dogma and discover the freedom that that allows. It was a very liberating idea.

In the following weeks my lightening mood soared out of control and such was my relief that the depression was over that I was gripped with the conviction that I was somehow being called to serve God. I would look for signs in the most ridiculous ways. For instance, I might impulsively get off a bus miles before my destination, believing that some message would be revealed to me as I completed my journey on foot through the familiar streets. Of course, there was no message. Although, if truth be told, I did choose to disregard the offices of an overseas missionary that I passed in Buckingham Palace Road. I've never fancied Africa.

Nevertheless, my enthusiasm for ordination grew. I began to fantasize that my schooldays prank of stating my desire to reform the Church of England had been prophetic. I imagined that I must be being called to immerse myself in a life of devotion and service. This, I might add, was quite at odds with the reality of my conduct, which bore no resemblance to the persona that I was attempting to construct.

I told Donald that I felt I was destined for the Church and that I had to do something about it. Very patiently, he listened to what I had to say and suggested that I leave it a few weeks at least. But I was adamant, when I returned three days later, that this was the course I wanted to follow. And so, I'm sure with a degree of justified reluctance on his part, Donald put a call in on my behalf.

A week or so later, a letter arrived inviting me to meet with the Director of Ordinands for Westminster. The agreed morning arrived and I put on the tweed suit that I'd bought from one of the many second-hand clothes shops in the King's Road and made my way to the address in Lincoln's Inn Fields.

The suit detail is quite telling, I can admit to that

now. I was playing a part, creating a character. Emerging from the role-play was an angst-ridden intellectual. I'd been reading the works of Dietrich Bonhoeffer, the German theologian who had resisted Nazism, been imprisoned in a concentration camp and was subsequently executed just before the end of the war. His writing and his life had fascinated me and now I was trying to present myself in his quiet, 1940s image.

The Georgian house was, as I remember, in the corner of the great square that is Lincoln's Inn Fields. I arrived early and sat on a bench watching a group of barristers camping it up as they floated around the place in their gowns. Part of me envied that sense of purpose they had. That feeling of identity and belonging to the establishment that you must get with a profession.

I knocked on the door and an elderly secretary in a cardigan opened it. She showed me through to a dark, oak-panelled study and gestured for me to sit down in one of the two leather wing-back chairs, asked me if I would like tea or coffee and then left me on my own. All very nice, I thought. Like stepping through a time warp. A study like this suited my fantasy nicely.

I waited for several minutes, perusing the room, looking at the large, cluttered desk in front of me. A pile of paperwork sat to one side. Documents, letters and manilla A4 envelopes stuffed with more documents were piled high. How could a priest have so much paperwork, I wondered. Maybe there's a formal appeals process for sins that you don't find out about until you get your dog-collar. To one side was a window that seemed to have been precisely placed so as not to get any of the potential view of the square outside. Pinned behind a postcard of some quiet seaside cove was one of those crosses they give out at Easter, made of a folded reed.

The Reverend Graham Hayworth came in with a tray of tea. That's not his real name. I regret to say that circumstances prevent me from publishing that. The circumstances being that I've forgotten it. So I've had to make one up. Anyway, the Reverend Hayworth came in with the tea. I was glad of this down-to-earth entrance and stood to help him find space on his desk to put it down. He poured me a cup and then seated himself, moving several books from his chair before doing so.

With a few well-pitched questions, he drew all the information he wanted about my background from me. As he reciprocated with details of his own past, I began to wonder what the hell I was doing there. I realized, precisely at that moment, that I didn't want this. Me? A vicar? Who was I kidding?

'And you attend St James's? What is your involvement there?' he asked, jolting me from my brand-new decision not to become ordained.

'I just go along sometimes,' I said, thinking I'd better play it down in case he decided I fitted the bill and I had to spend three years stuck with a load of religious weirdos in some dreary seminary on the outskirts of Norwich. I'd be eating meals in silence and sleeping in a cell, and even though it's not Catholic, they'd still expect me to give up women as a token of good will.

He was a nice enough man, but as he outlined the process that leads to holy orders I felt a strong urge to blurt out something completely odd to make sure I got excommunicated before the farce went on any longer.

Asked what books I had been reading recently, I was able to talk about Bonhoeffer with a small amount of conviction. I could also recite a list of writers whose books I'd browsed, but my knowledge of them, when asked to enlarge, was pretty patchy. Despite having decided that I didn't want to train as a vicar, I now found myself competitively trying to win my interviewer's approval. God knows why.

The Reverend Hayworth must have seen through this floundering performance and brought the session to a gentle but unmistakable end with the suggestion that I read more and get properly involved in Church life and maybe come back in a couple of years' time. Feeling slightly piqued, but at the same time relieved by this outcome, I thanked the Director of Ordinands as he showed me to the door. As the elderly secretary in her cardigan looked on, I stepped out into the freedom of Lincoln's Inn Fields.

24

IT'S HARD TO EXPLAIN the feeling of powerlessness that overcomes me at the barber's. There is something paralysing about the nylon cape that saps my arms of all their energy. I sit there and watch the mirrored salt-and-pepper clumps tumbling off my shoulders and on to the lino.

Today I had a haircut and noticed that Ingrid shaved white fluff from the nape of my neck. It was as if she had dipped her hand into the dustpan by the seat while I wasn't looking and sprinkled the ashen snippets about me. Is that mine? I have hair that is white? The same colour that old people have? How did that happen?

I had no knowledge that my hair was approaching its autumn until a very camp hairdresser, Christophe, said some ten years ago, 'You've got nice hair, and hardly any grey.' Small-talk, I know, and probably a necessary alternative to asking where I would be holidaying this year, but that was how I learnt that, slowly, I was on the turn.

Sometimes I can see the back of my head. If you can too then it can only mean that you are hideously deformed or, like me, you appear on television enough to get a regular sighting of your crown. Mine is thinning just enough for the pink of my pate to glow through like the grass-covered footprint of an ancient building that can only be seen from the air.

Don't get me wrong. I'm not going under because of the state of my hair. It really isn't bad at all. I haven't booked appointments to waste vast amounts of money on useless remedies. I won't be taking hairs from my groin and planting them in clumps above my brow so that I look like a walking pubic paddy field. I am not yet pre-emptively growing one section of hair unusually long so that it can be combed over a more deprived area of scalp. There is certainly no intention to cover it, if it worsens, with a toupee that everyone has to be warned not to mention when I walk into the room. And if I lose all my hair I won't become so depressed that I'll have to finish off a nice day out canvassing for the Lib Dems with an obliging male escort defecating on me.

It really isn't that big a deal.

Anyway, back to Ingrid and this morning's haircut. She's an independent, spirited twenty-five-year-old East Berlin girl who now wants to train as a tattooist and live in Barcelona. And I have no doubt that that is exactly what she will do. Just like she ran the half marathon when she said she would. She's learning Spanish because it's more practical, but Catalan would have been her preferred choice.

Ingrid is quite an accomplished, though untrained artist. Already she has designed a floral tattoo for her friend Gerda, who works there too. Gerda (I think that's how you spell it) likes it so much that she's actually going to have it done in a week's time. Obviously not by Ingrid, as she is yet to learn the ropes and buy the equipment. Ingrid wants to go with Gerda to watch, but then there would be nobody left to open the shop, which is owned by Vincent, who is hardly ever there as he has a smart salon in West Kensington as well.

Ingrid prefers renting flats to buying, has had two – no, wait, three – bicycles stolen since she moved to London when she was twenty, and sometimes thinks it might have been better to live in Brighton, near the sea. But then again, Brighton's small and after a while that would have 'droven' her crazy. She likes to live in the kind of place where if you get fed up 'of' one club or street or shop you can just think, You know what? I'm going to check out this other place instead.

Sometimes her parents come over to stay from Berlin. Her dad's an artist as well, but trained originally as a telephone engineer. She's much closer to her dad than her mum. They run together and visit art galleries, but her mum isn't into that so she stays in

Ingrid's rented Bermondsey flat while they go out.

To Ingrid, it's 'totally not so interesting' that she was born and brought up in East Berlin. People ask her what it used to be like when it was Communist, forgetting that she was only five or something when the wall went down, which Ingrid thinks shows just how ignorant English people are when it comes to history or knowing about other countries. Alright, Ingrid. I was only trying to make conversation.

Anyway, her dad was a very relaxed Communist, it seems, allowing her to watch American cartoons but making her promise never to mention them at school. He had cool friends as well. Other artists mostly, but musicians and writers too. They were always getting into trouble with the authorities. Sometimes it was funny, but mostly it wasn't, if you know what I mean.

The tattoo training will take a year. Gerda would like to do it as well, but she isn't artistic. Not in that way at least. She sings in a band, sings really well, she has a great voice. But she can't draw.

It takes a year to train and during that time you practise on pig skin. I thought of saying that it's funny you don't see that many pigs running around with tattoos, but I tried a joke with her once before and she didn't get it, just kept talking. She doesn't know that I'm a comedian. All she really knows about me is how I like my hair cut.

I discovered Ingrid because I was looking for

someone like her. I used to go to an old-fashioned barber shop, but the guy in there, George, asked too many questions about what it's like to be on television. I don't blame him for being curious or just trying to make small-talk, the trouble was that it was the same small-talk every time. George cut hair the way a pensioner trims hedges. I don't even know why he went through the motions of asking customers how they'd like their hair. It was the same basic thing for everyone. Short, shaved at the back and over the ears, with a small amount to play with left on top. Depending on your age and head shape you ended up looking like Tin Tin, Hitler or one of the Pet Shop Boys.

'I'll tell you who I think's funny,' George would say every single time. 'It's that – oh, what's his name? I'm no good with names. The Irish one.'

'Frank Carson?' I'd suggest, knowing that it's Frank Carson because it always is Frank Carson and he can never remember his name. There's probably a Frank Carson fan club on the Web somewhere that nobody knows about, not even Frank, because it's run by George and called www.the-irish-one-oh-what's-his-name.com.

Then George explains why he likes Frank Carson so much. In essence, his reasoning is that 'He's just so funny, he cracks me up, he really does.'

If I'm completely honest, George's intonation always grated with me. Maybe I'm over-sensitive or in-secure, but 'I'll tell you who I think's funny' always came across as if George was actually thinking, 'I don't rate *you*, but . . .'

Then, one time, I decided I'd had enough of George's craftily veiled digs. So I gave him a dose of his own medicine. When he was holding the mirror up behind my head, asking if I wanted any wax, in that instant I realized that I hated George. So instead of saying what a great haircut he'd given me, I sort of shrugged and said, 'I'll tell you who does a really good hair cut, that bloke round the corner in Brewer Street.'

George didn't respond, just went to his dirty little till and asked me for eight pounds.

I paid and walked down the street, realizing that several years of festering resentment had just reached its dramatic climax. George's undermining comments may have amused him, but now he was nursing a meta phorical bleeding nose from someone who wasn't going to stand for it any more.

Looking back, I'm fairly certain that George had been at it since he started in the barber business; the slick sleight-of-hand insult that you're not even aware of until it's too late. Suddenly your confidence is drained and you can't think why. George's conversation is like drinking a cup of coffee that just so happens to be radioactive. Long after you've forgotten about the coffee you'll be wondering why you feel so dreadful.

I realize that it doesn't completely add up that I kept

going back to this loathsome barber. I don't understand it myself, but I think the answer might lie in my natural sense of curiosity. For whatever reason, I needed to find out how unpleasant a man George actually was.

The genius of George is that while he poisons you with his passive contempt, he's cutting your hair, making you look better, which is why he's never been suspected. Well, now his game is up.

I wouldn't be surprised if George had customers from every profession imaginable who have left his grubby shop tissueing stray cuttings from inside their collar, wondering just what he meant by that comment. Men from all walks of life who have felt to some extent diminished by George's spitefully harmless chitter-chat. And each has had to collude in his own insult by helping George with his faltering name recall.

To the MP: 'I tell you who's a good speaker, that – oh, what's his name? Gave up his title . . . ?'

'Tony Benn?'

'Tony Benn. Brilliant. Best speaker by far, he is. Anything on it for you, Sir?'

To the solicitor: 'I tell you who's a good lawyer though, that – oh, what's his name now? Always in those human-rights cases, silver-haired gentleman.'

'You mean Michael Mansfield?'

'That's him. Brilliant man, he is. Mind you, he's a barrister, isn't he? Hasn't just wasted his life shuffling papers around a desk. How's that looking for length, Sir?'

George retired not long after I stopped going to him for eight quid's worth of tidy-up and subliminal pummelling. He had mentioned once that he and his wife June planned to go and live in Spain, where they had an apartment. 'It's a lovely place to live because of the weather and the golf,' he had told me.

And now George's barber shop has been coiffured into a boutique hairdresser's called 'Scissor'. The two old leather adjustable seats have gone, replaced by a row of three rococo-style chairs in front of gilt mirrors on ironic crimson flock wallpaper. Loud music plays while a Goth girl and a very thin man charge £65 and upwards for giving you the hairstyle of your dreams, although you do know, don't you, that you'll never look as good as them?

When it was George's there were some faded black-and-white photos in the window of immaculate men who had recently had haircuts. The photos were printed on flat card and were possibly dispatched from the marketing department of some kind of hair product, although they had no logo and I never saw the same pictures in any other barber's window. In any case, those men were so devoid of personality that they appeared to be almost not human, like very well-groomed androids. Of course, it is possible that they were real photos of real customers that George had whittled down over the years with his toxic pleasantries, until their confidence and self-esteem were at such a low ebb that they agreed to pose for a series of utterly lifeless portraits that would remain in the window for decades.

An admission: I did go to Scissor soon after it opened. Partly my motive was vengeance. After all the times that George had chipped away at me with a comment here and a casually thrown-in remark there, I wanted to experience his little domain now that it had been stripped of his presence and refurbished in a way that he would have not liked. Pathetic, I know, but I'm being honest here. I didn't even need a haircut is the truth of it.

I'm not ashamed to say that it was a satisfying experience. I drank coffee and flicked through a GQ magazine while the Goth girl quietly snipped at my hair. I felt that I had triumphed after a prolonged battle of wits. Vile George was now in Spain, sunburnt and scissorless, left to live out his days on a parched golf course wandering around pointlessly after a tiny white ball. Welcome to Hell, George.

25

IT'S NEVER VERY CONVINCING when successful people describe the hardships of their early years. I remember J. K. Rowling saying in an interview how, pre the global sensation that is Harry Potter, she used to sit in a café writing, because it was warmer than her bedsit. Nobody I have ever met gives a damn about this, but when you think about it, it's pretty unfair that we don't say, 'That must have been tough for J. K.' Because actually, it probably was. She wasn't to know at the time whether what she was writing was a masterpiece or a load of unpublishable, incoherent gibberish that nobody would want to buy. (It so happens that I am writing this very chapter whilst sitting in a café and I'll thank you to keep your snide comments to yourself.)

I don't expect anyone to be bothered for a minute that I had a rough time trying to sort out what I wanted to do with my life. So what? Who doesn't? Many have gone through similar experiences before settling down to, say, accountancy or a smashing career with Carphone Warehouse or Findus. All I'm saying is that there was a time in my adult life when I had almost no money. I seemed to exist on crisps and toast for weeks on end and one of my reasons for liking being a waiter was that I got proper food.

One incident stands out in my memory from this period of penury. I was in a convenience store and decided to go wild and buy some jam to go with my toast. By the time I got to the counter, I had thought better of this reckless expense and decided to leave the jam to one side, just pay for the bread and leave.

Unfortunately, somehow I dropped the jar and it broke on the floor.

There was no sympathy in the shop-keeper's voice, just a bored, flat 'You'll have to pay for that.'

I could have refused, had a big row and not paid, but I really needed to be able to continue using that store. So, the jam that I had so prudently decided to do without had to be paid for, but I would still have to do without.

There is an art to ditching goods at the supermarket checkout. I still occasionally have second thoughts about an item that's in my trolley and put it to one side, so that it misses its ride on the moving belt. But I'm unable to do so without first examining it and pretending to find some fault with it. It shouldn't matter, I know, but I don't want the checkout assistant thinking

I'm some kind of fool who can't decide what to buy and what not to buy until he's paying.

So, the unnecessary grain mustard in my hand gets a closer examination from me as my goods glide towards Kylie at the till. Now looking at the bottom of the jar, I shake my head slowly to register disappointment. There is, in my imagination, a hairline crack in the glass that will compromise the quality of the mustard and so, slightly crestfallen, I place the jar to one side, in front of the free magazines. It has nothing to do with suddenly remembering that I had that mustard before and didn't much like it. No. This is a quality issue.

I glance at Kylie, who rather than swiping the rest of my goods and dispatching them to the other end of her checkout counter is looking straight at me.

'Is there something the matter with it?' she asks, nodding at the grain mustard.

I had been happy to mime dissatisfaction, but now I have to explain. 'Yes, the jar is cracked slightly, so I think I'll leave it.'

'I'll get you another one,' she says, reaching for the red bell-button that will call over another assistant or, worse, a manager who'll want to inspect the mustard.

'No,' I say slightly too quickly, but at least it stops her. 'It's fine. I'll go without. I haven't got time.'

Kylie looks at me. We both know what's happened. I've changed my mind about one of the items that I put in my trolley and instead of saying exactly that, I made up a little story that wasn't true. Without a word she continues to swipe. The milk, the cheeses, the steak that will be served ungarnished. I guess it's her silence that cuts the deepest. If Kylie had taken me to task and insisted on looking at the jar herself it would have been easier than having to complete my shopping knowing that she was thinking that I'm just another twat who ditches stuff at the till.

Anyway, it so happens that I still live quite near to that shop where I dropped the jam. I use it fairly often. The owner is now greying and doesn't remember me from the jam incident. After all, it was twenty-five years ago. In fact, he is always pleased to see me, especially when I've been on the television recently. 'I saw you on *Haven't I Got News For You*', he says in his cheerful Bangladeshi accent.

'Oh right,' I reply, in a friendly way, not pointing out that it's *'HAVE' I Got News For You*, not 'Haven't'.

He says something about watching the television and then all of a sudden I came on. I suppose that's one way of describing the beginning of the programme. Anyway, he'd like to talk some more about the show and keeps calling it *Haven't I Got News For You*, which is annoying.

'What's it like to be on this show?' he asks, visibly desperate for me to furnish him with nuggets of gossip.

'Good,' I tell him, withholding all the insider

information that he would so like. I leave the shop, pleased that his jar of jam that he insisted I pay for a quarter of a century ago is now costing him in terms of fascinating conversation.

26

ON EITHER SIDE OF my desk I have a mains extension. Both of these have ten sockets, all of which are in constant use, meaning that the introduction of a new device requiring power necessitates the unplugging of another.

This is never an easy decision to make and often involves the following of cables back to the items that they bring life to. The computer and printer have priority status, as does the modem that connects me to the Net. But after that, everything is subject to my fickle mercy.

Depending on my mood, I might decide to kill off the radio, pulling the plug so that it falls silent, like cutting off the oxygen line to a deep-sea diver.

The electric guitar stares at me from its stand as if pleading for clemency. It was given to me as a present one Christmas by Jane. Arguably the best electric guitar ever made is the Fender Stratocaster, favoured by countless famous guitarists from Jimi Hendrix to Tony Blair and oh so many in between. It is *the* electric guitar to own. Prudently, Jane baulked at the cost of such an instrument, wondering whether my acoustic renditions of 'The Boxer', 'Blowin' In The Wind' and 'Yesterday' truly warranted further investment. Eventually she erred on the side of caution and purchased what is known in the guitar world as a Strat Copy.

As the name would suggest, this is a replica of the classic American icon, and the one that Jane gave me was made in Korea. It is identical in every respect except for one, which is that on the headstock it sports a name similar to Fender, yet not Fender, but in the same font that Fender is recognized by. It isn't fraud, because the attempt to blur the difference in names is quite transparent, as though the maker had known, in a calculated way, how much the human eye misses when it comes to reading joined-up writing.

Don't get me wrong, I was enormously touched and grateful when Jane gave it to me. Almost as touched and grateful as if she had given me a real Stratocaster. I mean, it's not like we're poor. But that's by the by. It's precious to me for different reasons and I would never in a million years think of getting rid of it. Even though there is a shop in Denmark Street that would do quite a good trade-in, enabling me, at last, to get a real one.

The problem with owning a cheap counterfeit version of the guitar you've always hankered after is that it

223

becomes an alibi. I attribute every botched note, rhythm-less song and wrong chord to the inferior fretboard which I have convinced myself that good old Leo Fender would not have allowed out of his workshop. My lack of talent is hidden away behind imagined technical flaws in the pick-ups or the controls.

How much better it would be if I didn't have these excuses for my inability to play properly. Presented with a real, genuine US-made Fender, I would have been forced to confront the truth and perhaps get on and do something constructive about it. Instead I waste more and more money on effects pedals that distort my ham-fisted strumming and achingly limited soloing, transforming it into something quite similar to what you hear on heavy-metal records. And the trouble with that is that heavy metal isn't my genre. 'Scarborough Fair' is depressing enough as it is, but played through a fuzz box with reverb, it's plain embarrassing.

So, quite often the Strat Copy gets unplugged and sits there with its back to me for days on end, unaware of the growing tension between us.

My camcorder has singularly failed to film anything since sports day two years ago. Sorry, but that's just not good enough, sitting on the side, gathering dust, idly winking its red blipping eye at me. My life has moved on since the impulse purchase of it, and it has not kept up. I don't wish to view its contents. A dozen eight-year-olds in the hundred-metre sprint. My kids don't look anything like that now and if the camcorder was any good it would have something a little more current to show me. I resent the implication of failure on my part when I think of the missed birthday party, that holiday in Cyprus, or when we had the snow. There is something very smug about the way that camcorder does nothing but remind me, by its unused presence, of special, wonderful events that I now have no record of, other than on the fragile loop of recollections in my mind.

I'm old enough to remember the cine-camera with affection; I can recall the excitement of looking back at the footage in a darkened room as memories flickered to life on the wall. The charm of cine-film is its way of endearing the past to us. It makes no attempt to compete against the present with high-definition quality and intrusive, boxy soundtrack. Instead, it teases the mind, beckoning you to travel back and recall the scene being shown.

So the camcorder was euthanized and buried in my box marked 'Gadgets', along with several dead mobile phones. Also in there was an early digital camera. Bulky and unattractive, it had a screen on the back no bigger than a postage stamp. Odd, looking at a comparatively sophisticated piece of technology that is already historical.

Out of interest, I decided to see if I could get it working, and after some searching found an adaptor that would fit it. As I switched on the power, it stirred and whirred from its sleep as the Minolta logo appeared on the tiny screen and it emitted a happy little jingle. I then connected it to my computer and was surprised that the photos it held came up on screen. It was quite an exciting moment. Like, perhaps, finding the key to a safe that you hadn't been able to open.

A picture of our two Dachshunds as puppies dated the camera's last use to seven years ago, their oversized paws and stubby muzzles recalling the infancy of the two now grown dogs asleep behind me on an armchair. It brings a twinge of sadness that I don't want to dwell upon. Not so much that they are no longer little, but that the past is what it is. Unchangeable and constantly moving away from me.

However, just as I was beginning to feel all maudlin and sad, up jumped a picture of someone from back then who really got on my tits big time.

Kenny and Kim were an Australian couple who came to stay with us. It's too long a story as to how that came about, but the basic fact is that it was Jane's fault, although she has yet to accept that fact.

Not that it matters. I know it's true, and that's enough for me.

I don't need to use these pages to settle a marital disagreement, because it really is no longer an issue.

But, if you must know, although Jane's parents are both New Zealanders, some distant members of her extended family seem to have ended up living in Australia. And apparently, if members of your family live in Australia and ask if you'll put up two of their friends who are visiting the UK, it's your responsibility to accommodate them.

There is something about Australia. Maybe it's because it's so unreasonably far away from everything that a subconscious sense of pity informs the way we treat its travelling citizens. Certainly if Kenny and Kim had come from, say, Cardiff or Sunderland, we wouldn't have felt the same duty to accommodate them, even though they would have been in just as much need of a place to stay.

And let me state from the outset that this anecdote is not a cheap device to excuse a session of Aussie-bashing. I've been to Australia several times and have always found it an interesting, almost worthwhile experience.

I don't mean to damn it with faint praise, but the fact is that nowhere can justify travelling distances like that. It makes more sense to be in an aeroplane for one hour and visit Paris than to be in the air for twenty-four hours, only to get out in Sydney. And I say that despite holding the opinion that Sydney is one of the greatest cities on Earth. But that doesn't change where it is. Fine if you're born there, lucky you, but if not, forget it. It's just so far away. What is the point?

Really, when you think about it, Neil Armstrong

must have secretly been a bit gutted when he got to the Moon and could see that it was basically a bit crap. After all that training and preparation, not to mention practically cacking himself at lift-off (I mean, who wouldn't?), to climb down the little silver ladder and realize that there wasn't that much to do there.

Admittedly, the odds are stacked against you actually enjoying yourself on the Moon. I know I'd be too preoccupied with how to get back to be able to savour the moment, let alone come up with a good quote. I'd hate to be remembered as the first man to set foot on the Moon with the words 'Is that it?'

'Yes, but what about the marvellous views from Space?' you say.

I don't remember *Apollo 11* having that many windows, and besides, it would have been incredibly cramped inside, and it's under those kind of circumstances that people really get on your nerves. I don't know if it happened or not, but I wouldn't blame Neil one bit if he got annoyed every time Buzz stuck his big head in the way and obscured what little there was to see.

Of course, when they got back they all said they had a great time, but you do that, don't you? First of all you forget the bad bits, and then you think you might as well say it was good because, at the end of the day, everyone paid so much money for you to go, and they're all so excited to see you that it would seem churlish to complain. I am right about this. Why else would they have stopped going? The fact is that several visits later, some astronaut was at last honest enough to say, 'You know what? I prefer Florida,' which opened the flood-gates of relieved agreement in the Space community and the annual Moon trip was quietly shelved.

So, anyway, Kenny and Kim arrived at our house with all their baggage, in both senses of the word. They were a bit older than us and, having no children or other commitments, had made the decision to travel around Europe and see the sights.

I am not good at having people to stay in my house, but at least the first day or so was lightened by the kids' excitement at having guests.

At breakfast, the day after they had arrived, Kenny and Kim discussed their plans for London. All the usual stuff: Buckingham Palace, the Houses of Parliament, the National Gallery and so on. As they did this I noticed with interest that they both cut their toast into two pieces and spread one half with jam and the other with Marmite, thus providing themselves with a savoury and a sweet course, all from the same piece of toast.

There was, needless to say, a discussion about the merits of Marmite versus Vegemite. Their prevailing assumption was that Vegemite was altogether superior but that Marmite was 'not too bad as a standby'.

The jam earned their approval, and they decided

between them that it was almost as good as a make that they regularly bought back home.

As for the coffee: that was excellent, nicer than the brand that they used to buy in Mudgee, their small New South Wales town, until, that is, they switched to a new variety which is the best coffee you'll ever taste. They promised to send us some when they returned.

'Thanks,' I said, adding 'I can't wait' as Jane's foot squeezed down firmly on top of mine beneath the table.

Their daily explorations of London pleased them generally, although they did consider many of the attractions to be 'a bit touristy', and they found it hard to recover from the idea of paying so much, 'pretty much fifteen dollars', for a hamburger at a restaurant just off Leicester Square.

It's funny how you can find yourself defending the pricing strategy of an establishment that you've never visited and almost definitely never would.

'Overheads, you see,' I reasoned.

'You'd never get away with it in "Mudge",' reckoned Kenny, and Kim completely agreed.

My suggestion that a restaurant in Mudgee wouldn't ever experience the need to offload exorbitant rental costs on to customers went unheard amid Kenny and Kim's description of a really good but inexpensive brasserie near their home.

Over the ensuing evenings I discovered much about Mudgee. It's an area made famous by its wine production. Nothing that they had tasted in England could compare, dollar for dollar, with a Mudgee Cabernet. Presumably that included the Pinot Grigio that I had opened and poured moments earlier.

They couldn't believe the price of Australian wines over here. They had seen a bottle of very ordinary 'Aussie Merlot' in an off-licence in Kensington that was four times what you'd pay for it back home.

I was about to point out the added expense of flying the very ordinary Aussie Merlot all the way here, when Kim continued, 'Then again, I guess part of that is because Britain doesn't produce any wines itself. At least, none to speak of.'

And Australian cheese is superb. They make their own fantastic Camembert. 'Probably better than your French equivalent that you'd get here,' was Kenny's verdict and I could see that Kim thought so too.

I announced that I was more of an English cheese fan, but, again, my views dissolved into the general chit-chat about Mudgee. I approached the fridge, thinking that I might reward my patience with a beer, but thought better of it, considering the conversation which that would doubtless trigger.

One morning, as she spread butter on her toast, Kim let me know that I was running out of Marmite.

'Oh right, thanks,' I found myself saying. 'I'd better get some more then.'

This might not sound like much of a triumph, but

being able to say 'I'd better get some more then' was a well-earned, if minor victory. From the moment that I saw the two of them tucking into it at their first breakfast with us, I had resolved not to eat any Marmite myself, at least, not so they could see. That way, responsibility for its depletion would land fairly and squarely upon their shoulders.

I needn't have troubled myself. The subtlety was lost on her.

'Well, don't worry yourself on my account, it's just I know how it is when you're out of something that you need,' said Kim.

'I don't really need it, but if you like it I'll buy some more,' I countered, wondering why I couldn't just let it drop.

'Only you might want to try Vegemite. It's pretty widely available here, I've noticed,' suggested Kim.

'I don't like Vegemite. It's not such good quality, I find.' God, that was bold of me. This was heading towards an argument.

Kim chuckled a slothful roll of soft, impotent laughter, as if my view was not worthy of anything more than a wordless dismissal.

Kenny came into the kitchen, smelling of the aftershave that he smacked his cheeks with each morning after performing his ablutions. In our bathroom. All fresh and smooth-faced, he was, ready for another day of trudging around museums and monuments, spreading his duty-free odour wherever he went.

'G'day, Jack. Is there any of that coffee going?'

As I poured him a cup, Kim got up and said she'd go and shower now, if there was any hot water left. Putting her plate in the dishwasher, she took herself upstairs. Kenny thanked me as he took the coffee, opened the fridge door and helped himself to a splash of milk.

Making toast, he told me that he and Kim were thinking of buying an inexpensive camper-van and travelling around a bit.

'Great,' I said, conscious that my next utterance should be delivered with less spontaneous joy.

They had found a copy of *Loot* on the Tube when they were coming back from Madame Tussaud's and in it was an advertisement for an old Commer van that had been customized. It had bunk beds, a calor-gas hob and a basin and was priced at £400 O.N.O.

'We figured it could be just the thing for getting around on a budget.'

I agreed, remembering not to sound too keen.

With some considerable encouragement over the following week, Kenny pursued the matter. It was a surprise to him, though not to me or probably anyone reading this, that the Commer had sold days ago. But I insisted that there would be other similar camper-vans to buy, if he worked hard enough at it.

Eventually, having spent several afternoons by the

phone, going through all the classifieds, ringing them up one by one, sometimes having needlessly long conversations with people who had already sold their campers, Kenny arranged to go and view an old Dormobile.

So, it wasn't long before the gently thumping rhythm of a VW engine became the dreaded drum-roll that announced their return from an excursion. Bath, Stonehenge, Cheddar Gorge and Oxford were all achieved in one trip, involving sleeping at night in the back of the 'V-Dub'. A few days of rest and map-study and they'd be off once more, looking at Hastings, Canterbury, Cambridge and the Norfolk Broads, before returning to tell us of their adventures.

August came and they drove to Edinburgh to immerse themselves in all the fun of the festival before driving, via the Lake District, to Liverpool, where they went to the Cavern and photographed each other standing next to a life-size cut-out of The Beatles. From there, a ferry to Belfast to stay with distant cousins, and then a leisurely drive down to the South, to Dublin, across to Galway and on to Cork.

Each return signalled a week at our house, during which mealtimes were spent hearing about the cities, cathedrals and National Trust houses that they had visited. Their knowledge of these attractions was garnered from the literature that was given out or, occasionally, a guided tour that they had been able to tag on to undetected. Kim kept a large rubber-banded stack of pamphlets from the places they had visited and was always quick to produce the appropriate one to support their description of a particular sight that they had seen.

As they told me all about Lincoln Cathedral one evening, I idly looked at the free brochure that they had picked up there and noticed that great chunks of their speech seemed to have been lifted verbatim from the hand-out. Gradually I became aware that their relentless tourism was purely an exercise in travelling the length and breadth of the country in order to tick off each place they stopped at from their list. It struck me as a somewhat cold and dispassionate approach that did away with the need for any sense of enjoyment or even appreciation. All that was required was tenacity and a near autistic absorbency of facts.

However, of more interest to me was my own participation in this arrangement. Why did I allow it? Two strangers staying in my house, using it as a hotel, coming and going as they pleased. Moreover, what was it that made me anticipate, with some degree of keen-ness, their return from each sortie and then find myself discouraging their next departure on the pretext that the traffic was bad or the weather unpredictable?

Jane healthily rejoiced each time they left and would put on a Kenny-and-Kim-have-gone celebration supper with candles and everything. Whereas I found myself slightly at a loose end, a bit restive and snappy towards the children.

The painful truth was that I benefited from their presence in the house. The more boring and objectionable they became, the more compelling I found them. It was good for me to have a focus for all my irritability. I felt as though some kind person had come into my life and installed an archive for my annoyances. There they all were, all my irritations, neatly arranged, cross-referenced, alphabeticized and indexed in two human filing cabinets. So long as Kenny and Kim were around, I felt that I would never be unhappy with anybody or anything else in my life again.

Alas, it was not to be. Eventually they became satisfied with their knowledge of these shores and decided to explore France, basing themselves at the home of the Thierrys, a couple from Lyon whom they had met on a boat trip up the Thames.

We later heard that this had not worked out so well. Although his wife was fairly friendly to begin with, Monsieur Thierry quickly grew intolerant of Kenny and Kim's constant to-ing and fro-ing and was unreceptive when they asked if they could simply camp in the street and run a power cable from the Thierrys' house to the Dormobile for heating and lighting, etc. So, having learnt at least some French, they drove on.

27

I'VE ALWAYS BEEN ANNOYED by those commercial vans you see around the place bearing the self-descriptive name of a business. You know the ones. 'The London Bed Company', 'The Real Ice Cream Company', 'The Ethical Cashmere Company'. Chirpy branding to invoke a sense of quality, nostalgia, tradition and earnest expertise. I doubt it. I doubt it very much, and every time I see one of these ridiculously optimistic vehicles my eyes just read 'The Plucky Out-Of-Work Public Schoolboy Showing Initiative Because He Thinks He Knows More Than You About Beds/Ice Cream/Cashmere Or Whatever But Doesn't Really So You'd Be Better Off Going To A Proper Shop Instead Company'.

As with nearly all of my resentments, my feelings about such businesses are completely unjustified and cannot be substantiated in court, or even a moderately challenging conversation. I just hate them and whenever I see one it ruins my day. Perhaps it's a type of twisted envy, the knowledge that, were I to start up a small business enterprise, I would choose a name like the ones I can't stand. I'd be the entrepreneur driving about in a Citroën Berlingo with livery proclaiming 'The Old-Fashioned Toffee Company' or some similar rubbish.

More likely, it's an unwelcome reminder of the time when I did drive a van. I was between restaurant jobs and fancied something that would get me out and about for a change. Through a friend, I got a position as a driver for the NHS, delivering incontinence pants all round Putney, Wimbledon and Roehampton. After all, that's what friends are for.

I should point out that other drivers delivered to other postcodes, and that incontinence is not and has never been, to my knowledge, confined to those three areas of south-west London. Having said that, it's surprising how many people wet themselves. Especially in Roehampton.

Don't worry, I won't use this episode as an excuse to write in a load of dodgy jokes, scatological puns and unkind stories. Nor am I heading towards a punchline that sees me delivering the goods in a van with 'The Nappies for Grown-Ups Company' graffitied on its side. In many ways, this was a sad job.

On my first day, I turned up at the depot, a single-storey sixties-style office building with a large annexe for storage on some tatty land off the Upper Richmond

Road. I forget where exactly, not that it matters. I don't imagine you were planning a visit.

So-and-so was 'Manager', but she was off sick, which meant we had to get our own schedules from her desk, and Thingy was late because of a bus strike but the store keys were in the second drawer down. Just load up what you need and go. It was all very slack, to be honest.

Stuart was another of the drivers. He quickly jumped into one of the vans, reversed it up to the store doors and started hurling packets and packets of incontinence pants into the back. As he did this he explained that it was a good idea to get there first so you got the best van. As far as I could discern, the best van was the one that didn't have torn seats.

It was pretty much up to me to figure out from the paperwork what I needed in the van and where it had to be delivered to. On my first day, the round took for ever, and when I got back Stuart was leaving, having completed his deliveries quickly and returned to the depot in time to complete his paperwork, have a cup of tea, use the telephone for various personal calls and generally hang around.

'I know why you took so long,' he said gleefully. 'You waited for them to come to the door. They take for ever and then they want to chat, you'd be there all day with some of them. Just ring the buzzer, leave it on the doorstep, take the used and go. If they haven't left it out for you it's their fault.'

He had a point. Much of my day had been spent waiting at front doors, listening for the tell-tale sounds of life. Opaque movement, a shuffling Zimmer, the mumble of somebody reassuring a cat as they made their way into the hall. Isolated people. Mostly old, some disabled or caring for somebody who was.

My experience, however, was that they didn't want to chat. Handing over a plastic sack of soiled goods and taking delivery of fresh supplies was not conducive to small-talk. It felt as though they were ashamed, but perhaps they weren't, and I was just embarrassed for them. Either way, the moment was always awkward.

As the day went on my van would take on the smell of stale urine from the collected bags of waste and I'd chain-smoke to mask it. It was always a relief to offload it all at the hospital incinerator and drive back to the depot, all the windows down, filling the van with fresh air. Occasionally, I'd remember what Steve had said at the leg factory and think that at least I'd rather deliver them than wear them.

With practice I found that my delivery round could be finished in about four hours, but Stuart and his mates warned me that I was working too fast now. They didn't want an agency boy like me making life difficult for them. In a couple of weeks, they reasoned, I'd be gone, but they were stuck driving nappies around London for the foreseeable. I would have to do as they did, take my time and then park up somewhere, read the paper, drink tea, whatever, just don't get back early.

Stuart suggested that I take on a little side-line. When I asked him what he meant, he confided that he finished his round in two hours, whereupon he'd drive to his brother's butcher's shop, fill the van with meat and do his round for him, delivering to various restaurants.

'What, so half the van is filled with sack-loads of, you know . . . And the rest of the van has fresh meat in, from your brother's shop?' I asked, very much hoping that I had got it all wrong. But I hadn't.

Sometimes, Stuart and I would share the round. He would drive horrendously fast, hurling the van round corners, running red lights and screeching to a stop for me to jump out, slide open the side-door, grab the required packages and drop them on somebody's front step.

In addition to dangerous driving, Stuart's hobbies included lorry-spotting. There wasn't a lorry for which Stuart didn't have the full technical spec, ready to reel off as soon as he saw it. Whenever we passed one he would list its make and model, country of manufacture, weight in tonnes, engine size, haulage capacity and so on. Then he would cross-reference it with the previous sighting of just such a lorry. "Nother Volvo F7, same as that one off the Upper Richmond Road. That's four of them we seen now,' Stuart would say, and I would agree that we had now seen four Volvo F7s.

'Jack. What's the most unusual truck you've seen this year?'

'Oh Christ,' I'd think.

'Gosh, I'm really not sure,' I'd say, knowing that he was expecting me to reciprocate with the same question. I really didn't want to know his answer, but it felt mean not to play along. So eventually I'd ask him, 'What was the most unusual truck—'

'Scania-Vabis LB 76,' Stuart would blurt out before I could even finish the question. 'They're not made any more. Saw it up in Gerrards Cross.'

'Wow,' I said.

'I know,' he said, adding after a few minutes of rare silence, 'Are you posh?'

'Why do you ask that?'

'You sound all posh. Did you go to university and all that?'

'No,' I said, wishing I had, imagining the type of conversations I might be enjoying at this very moment had I done so.

'Didn't you? You sound like you went to one. Why didn't you?'

Slightly awkwardly, I tried to answer his sudden, perceptive question. 'I didn't do very well with my A levels, so I didn't get in.'

'So you was going to go to one. So you *are* posh. I thought you was. Gonna be a doctor or something, were you?'

Even more awkwardly, I said that I had hoped to study theology and philosophy, which was true.

'Oh, right,' said Stuart.

I suppose, if I'm honest, I was surprised that he didn't ask me what theology was. But I was even more surprised by what he said next.

'Yeah, it's funny, really, when you look around you and you think about everything and how everything got here.'

'Yes,' I agreed.

"Cos when you really, really think about it,' said Stuart, 'it all came in lorries.'

'Oh Christ,' I thought again. Except this time, I might have said it.

28

PERHAPS THERE IS A term for the special kind of deafness that I suffer from when I ask directions from a stranger. Or if there isn't, we should invent one and fund some research into the condition. I would be happy to co-operate in the inevitable documentary that would be made for Channel 5.

Cut to: me walking down a street and asking someone the way to a particular address. As the passer-by explains the route I must take, I start to wonder how long it must have been before he regretted those tattoos. Words like 'crossroads' and 'lights' and 'second left' float unattached into my head and flutter down on to my consciousness like useless dead leaves. '. . . Then go straight on twenty yards, and it's in front of you.' He probably still likes the naked-lady one or he'd have covered it over with long sleeves.

'Thanks very much,' I say as I walk off in the wrong direction.

I should watch it. One of these days, I'll do that to someone, probably just like the tattooed man, and he'll think I'm taking the piss. He'll look around to see if it's all being filmed for a Channel 5 documentary, and – when he's satisfied that it's not – smack me in the mouth.

So it's a dangerous condition, this selective deafness. As I hope I've explained, it can actually lead to your teeth falling out. Early symptoms include being completely unable to remember somebody's name less than four seconds after you've been introduced to them, and going to a shop to buy two things and not being able to recall either of them without phoning home.

A lot of men believe in the cliché that women are poor map-readers and hopelessly dizzy when it comes to finding their way around. I dispute this. Not because that view is ignorant and sexist, but because I am a bad map-reader and if the gender theory is true it means that I have, basically, a female brain. And that doesn't seem right. Let's refer to the inability to read maps as 'maplexia'. No, actually, let's not. Anyway, my theory is simply that everybody is rubbish at map-reading, but only women get found out because men insist on driving.

Perhaps we'll never know, now that Satellite Navigation has spun into orbit and is guiding us all from above the clouds. Obviously SatNav goes wrong as well from time to time. Those Latvian artics don't get wedged into the narrowest lane in Devon by accident, but on the whole I'd say that SatNav has done more good than bad. That is, unless you belong in a relationship that is fundamentally flawed in a way that you never knew about because, until you got the SatNav, you were always so busy rowing in the car about directions. Now that that isn't an issue any more you have to confront the fact that bickering about B-roads and spending your holiday screaming at each other at roundabouts was all a big smoke-screen for the uncomfortable truth that you just hate each other's guts.

And in a way that's a good thing. Better out in the open and all that, so you can deal with the human disaster that is your marriage and end it as amicably as possible. Much better that than let it drag on and on until you're both so bitter and angry that your kids start bed-wetting because of the stress and you have to get solicitors to preside over a protracted and costly battle of possessions that is so depressing that you jump impulsively into a new relationship which, to begin with, appears to be the answer to your dreams but within months turns into a ghastly hologram of exactly what you had before.

Let's face it, that isn't what you or your spouse had in mind when you went into town that Saturday to buy the TomTom. But what's happened has happened. Time to get a divorce and move on.

My personal day of reckoning on the map-reading

front came in another break between restaurant jobs when I decided to be a dispatch rider.

I've ridden motorbikes from as soon as I could afford one. The house that I grew up in was at the top of a steep hill. Every time I cycled up it, straining with each rotation of the pedals, I would curse the topography of my home and the useless Sturmey Archer gears on my bike that only had three settings: 'hard', 'bloody hard' and 'Oh bollocks, I'm going to get off and push.' One day, I promised myself, I would get a bike that had an engine.

To this day I actively seek out hills; at the bottom I just have to twist the throttle to zoom up them, exercising little more than my wrist. It still feels like magic, especially if I have the added bonus of struggling cyclists to whizz past.

So when I first moved to London I was in thrall of the motorcycle couriers, weaving at hurtling speeds through the traffic. I was attracted to their grungy sense of purpose and maverick efficiency. Occasionally you'd see one parked up by a café, taking a break from the day's frenetic pace, feet up on the handlebars, using his parked bike like a chrome chaise longue. I could do that, I thought. One day I'd like to be a leather-clad Lone Ranger, racing round town, effectively my own boss at last.

Now was my chance. I had acquired a third-hand Honda CX 500 with full fairing. If bikes were horses then this was a retired, trusty old shire relieved no longer to be working the fields. Being a touring bike of sorts, it was built for comfort, but had an engine that would allow me adequate, if not show-off acceleration.

At the interview I was a little bit disappointed to see that the courier business was actually quite well run. I had expected a dingy club-room where bikers hung out and played billiards or something while they waited for a call-out. I imagined that I'd walk in and be pointed to the back room, where I'd have a brief chat with the controller, who would turn out to have links with the mob and we'd hit it off straight away and that would be that. But no.

It was all coordinated by a middle-aged man called Dean from an unlikely-looking office just off Old Street. Being late because I couldn't find the place might have counted against me so I said that I'd witnessed an accident and had to wait for the police to give a statement, which could quite easily have happened.

'Bike?' asked Dean.

'Yeah, I've got a CX.' He'd know what that was.

'No, I mean was it a bike? In the accident?'

'Oh right. No, it was a Jag; went into the back of a builder's van. No one hurt, but it messed the Jag up.'

It was the scenario that I'd thought up as I revved around Shoreditch looking for the office. When I rang for the job they might have warned me how long Old Street is and mentioned the fact that they were situated in the crack down the middle of the *A–Z*. Dean was glad that there were no bikes involved in the crash because, in his words, 'We always come off worst, even if it's not our fault, which it almost never is.' As he said this he hoisted up his left leg and rapped on it with his knuckle as if knocking on a door. The noise was the same.

'Blimey,' I said.

That was all the encouragement Dean needed to recite the terrible story of when he was a courier, on his way back from a drop in Birmingham, and got stuck under the wheel of a tanker that veered into the fast lane as he was overtaking it on the M40, and how the medics had to operate at the scene of the accident before he was airlifted to hospital, where he stayed for three months.

'Took them two days to find my leg. They reckon a fox got it, or a badger. Dragged it away, ate what it could and left the rest of it in a ditch.'

'Oh, God' isn't much of a commiseration in those circumstances, but it was all I could come up with, without coming up with my breakfast as well.

'Hence the desk job,' said Dean. 'No. You did the right thing, stopping. No one stopped when I had this happen.' As he spoke, Dean gestured again towards his hollow leg.

I probably said something like 'Right,' but basically it fell a bit quiet after Dean had told me his story. I briefly considered telling Dean that I used to make artificial legs, but thought better of it. From his point of view it might not have seemed such an amusing coincidence.

Then he cheerily said, 'So you want to come and do a spot of courier work, then?' as if he hadn't spent the last ten minutes telling me a very graphic story all about why nobody in their right mind would want to be a courier.

'Yeah, sounds great,' I said.

I was issued with a walkie-talkie and a fluorescent over-vest with the name of the courier company printed on its back. At least I looked like the real thing. After a couple of days of daredevil delivery work and macho bike-banter I'd be a hardened, grimy-faced biker-bandit, born to be wild. Hell's Angels would nod approvingly, feeble pedestrians would dive out of my way and female receptionists would reach for their Diet Cokes when I appeared in their foyers, package in hand.

For my first job I had to go to a depot at the back of Euston, pick up a large cardboard tube which I imagine had a poster in it and take it to a shop in Covent Garden.

Tying that thing to the bike was what held me up most. When I called in from Long Acre to request my next job, Dean said they'd all thought I'd done a runner. I tried to explain that it was a bit of an awkward parcel, but he ignored me and said I had to 'get my arse up to Manchester Square' to pick up a letter from a solicitor's office and get it over to an address in White City. I fumbled through my *A–Z* and tried to memorize the route, which I did efficiently enough to have to stop only twice on the way. In fairness, one of those stops was to listen to Dean's stupid voice squawking like a parrot inside my jacket.

One thing that was playing on my nerves a bit by now was Dean's insistence on radio protocol when speaking on-air. You had to say 'Roger that' instead of 'OK' and every speech had to be concluded with 'Over'. Personally I thought it all sounded a bit childish, like we were pretending to be policemen or something.

'Not being funny, Jack, but can you go a bit faster on that heap of Jap crap you're riding around on? Over.'

The difficulty for me here was that I couldn't witness another accident and have to wait to give a statement again, because the chances of that happening twice in one day were so remote. Obviously the chances of it happening once were remote enough for it not to have happened in the first place, but at least Dean had bought it. He wouldn't a second time, I was sure.

Nor could I blame any kind of technical problem with the bike. Much as I loved motorbikes, I'd never really taken the trouble to learn what's what on them and I knew that Dean's cross-examining would quickly demolish any alibi that I came up with.

I was left having to admit that I was slow, which left me exposed to one of the things that I most hate in life: taking advice. I really didn't care what one-legged Dean felt that he could teach me about riding my motorbike faster.

'You've got to push yourself. Set yourself time limits, deadlines for every job, and don't let up. Don't just plan the route you're on, plan the next one. To be completely frank, you've just got to go faster, Jack. Over.'

'Roger, will do. Over.' It's humiliating being given a talking-to over the air like that, because you know that all the other riders can hear it as well. I was wondering if I was the only one thinking, 'Yes, thanks for the tip, Dean. Can I refer you to our previous conversation in which you described riding very fast and ending up in an ambulance? Or at least most of you ending up in an ambulance. Over.'

At lunchtime I found myself near Old Street, so Dean called me in. It wasn't a happy occasion. Dean said that he was disappointed that I had only completed four local jobs that morning.

'Yup, still got both legs though,' I didn't say.

'I know. Sorry, Dean. I'll be much faster this afternoon,' I did say.

Dean softened and said something quite kind about wanting to give me a fair chance, and gave me a job which involved riding out to Ickenham and back to the office in an hour and a half. To be even kinder, he started to give me directions up to the A40. I had never heard of Ickenham, so I really should have listened.

As soon as he said 'Western Avenue', my mind closed

down and began to wonder if it had been a fox or a badger that had eaten his leg, and whether the policeman who found it spent any time looking for the rest of the body. Suppose the accident occurred on the border between two counties and the police forces from those two counties didn't talk to each other. It wouldn't have been impossible for the leg to have ended up in a different county and for the police there to have concluded that there was a bloody great man-eating badger in the area.

And I pondered how much confusion it would cause on the airwaves if Dean was called Roger instead of Dean. I might have to say 'Roger Roger' to him if I was agreeing to a request in a friendly way. How many times could the word Roger be used in a sentence comprising only of that word? I reckoned if I was being instructed to jump on someone from behind who was called Roger but whose surname was also Roger, and the instruction was coming from someone who coincidentally had the exact same name, and I was happy to comply, then I could justifiably construct the sentence 'Roger Roger Roger? Roger Roger Roger.'

'. . . But don't miss the slip road because there isn't another exit for two miles. Do you reckon you've got all that?' he asked, scratching his real leg.

'Roger – I mean Dean – I mean yes,' I answered.

Dean was starting to look confused. Nothing he said made any sense to me and now the circle was complete. Nothing I said made sense to him either.

'Alright, it's quarter past two now. You get back by three forty-five and we'll take it from there,' said Dean, pressing a parcel the size of a shoebox into my hands. I didn't know what he meant by 'We'll take it from there,' but it sounded as though I was on some sort of last-chance mission.

I started the bike and left, got round the corner and stopped to look in the A–Z, wishing I'd actually listened to his directions instead of thinking up the 'Roger Roger' stuff.

One tricky thing about motorcycling is that it's really hard to get your clothing right for the whole day. A freezing autumn morning might dupe you into wearing extra layers for a day that turns out to be as warm as summer. Black leather absorbs and retains the sun's heat. It wasn't long before I was tugging at my jacket zip for ventilation on what was turning out be one of the warmest days of the year, despite it being mid October.

After half an hour I was uncomfortably hot and lost, somewhere near Wembley, from what I could tell. I knew that Ickenham was north-west so I was basically in the right area and for the third or fourth time I pulled over to check the map. The streets and roads started to swim around underneath my finger, their names gliding into one another as I urgently tried to make sense of what I was looking at. For whatever reason, I was – temporarily, I hoped – completely unable to read.

Then I had a really good idea.

Looking around for a reference point that would help me plan my route onwards, there, to my left, was a Tube station. I thought that what I would do, seeing as I could no longer read effectively, was use London's fine underground train network to deliver the parcel. What difference would it make to Dean?

Happy with my decision, I locked up the bike, took the parcel and headed for the platform. Luckily my Tube pass was still valid from a spell of door-to-door selling that I had done the previous week. I didn't even need to buy a ticket. Things were looking up.

A glance at the map in the entrance of the station showed me that Ickenham was on the Metropolitan line, and within a minute or so I was on a train. I soon discovered that the Metropolitan line forks into two as it heads north-west. In an ideal world I would have realized this before jumping on to the train headed for Watford.

However, the world is not ideal, as I was soon to appreciate. Even I could see, from the simplified map above the carriage windows, that a train that stops somewhere called Northwood cannot possibly also include Ickenham on its travels. I was on the wrong train, looking at my watch, tugging at my thick clothing in the cloying warmth of the carriage, wondering how I was going to deliver the wrapped-up shoebox and return to Old Street within twenty-five minutes.

I got off the train and on to another one that was

headed the other way. I got off that train at Harrow-on-the-Hill and waited in the stale heat of the platform for the Uxbridge train that I knew would stop at Ickenham.

Yes, I did feel conspicuous in full leathers and helmet with a radio-set on my shoulder. Yes, I did get some looks, and yes, some school kids thought it hilarious to ask where my motorbike was. I gave them a withering look that probably made them realize that I had a very good reason indeed for being on the Tube dressed like that. Thank God I wasn't getting on their train, I thought as it slid away, carrying the rude little bastards home, flicking V-signs at me as they glided by.

Then came the announcement. The Uxbridge train was delayed until further notice. Now I was stuffed. I decided the best thing would be to get back to my bike, maybe find a quiet road, lay it on its side and fake an accident.

Briefly, I toyed with the possibility of somehow obtaining an amputated leg and leaving it alongside my 'crashed' motorbike, causing a Lucanesque mystery as to my whereabouts. That would get Dean onside for sure, but then I'd have to go and live abroad and if he ever spotted me whilst on holiday, say, in Rio de Janeiro, I'd have to pretend that my perfectly good leg was bionic, or something.

Not that it mattered because I couldn't find the bike anyway. The problem being that, because of the rude school kids and the heat, I had overlooked the fact that

I had not observed the name of the station where I had parked up and got on the first train.

The game was up. Even if I knew where the bike was, I would never get back to Dean's office in time, let alone deliver the package as well. I considered ditching the package, chucking it somewhere or just stuffing it in a bin, but I was worried in case it was something quite important like a fresh transplant kidney. I hated the idea of a fully scrubbed-up surgical team hanging around the renal unit at Ickenham General, if that exists, waiting for me to burst through the swing-doors so that the operation could begin. I couldn't live with it on my conscience that someone died because I threw their kidney into a skip. There was only one thing for it: contact Dean and explain that I'd been in an accident. I could say that my bike was a write-off and had been taken straight to a scrapyard, or that it had burst into flames and reduced to a pile of ash.

Unfortunately, I was either out of range or I'd taken so long that the batteries had run flat. Either way, the radio-set wasn't working. I found a phone box and thought that I'd ring Dean. I could always stamp on the radio and say that it got damaged in the accident and that's why it wasn't working.

I wonder how many packets of Polos have been bought by people who really only wanted change for the phone, or, for that matter, how much money newsagents have made that way. Perhaps it's a huge amount, more than you could imagine, and that's why they won't change notes for you. Maybe it's their main source of income, selling things to people that they don't really want, exploiting their need to park or make phone calls.

If this is feeling like an overly long story, believe me it is, I lived it. The next thing was that I didn't have the phone number for the office. Nor did I have a pen with which to note it down.

Back to the newsagent to buy a biro, which I could have bought instead of the Polos that I didn't want, but never mind. By then, someone else was using the phone, so I had to wait for what seemed an eternity while he finished his call.

I rang Directory Enquiries and scribbled, with my new biro, the very number that was, as it happens, printed on the back of my fluorescent vest.

When my coins tumbled through the slot and I was connected, I asked to be put through to Dean. But when he answered, for some reason I found myself unable to pretend that I'd had an accident. It seemed in bad taste, considering what he'd been through with the fox and the badger and everything. Besides, most people who have been in an accident at least know where it happened, so I just said that I'd got really badly lost.

'What are you, sick or something?' he said.

'No, I just – I don't know, just couldn't find it.' I sort of mumbled the rest of the story, but when I got to the newsagent bit he butted in, rather impatiently, I thought, 'Alright, stay by the phone box. I'll send someone.'

Dean went up in my estimation when he said that. Here was somebody with a contingency plan, a strategy for coming to the aid of stranded couriers. For nearly a whole day, I had been a loyal employee and now Dean was showing me that he appreciated that by sending help.

I stood around with the packet in my hand until, about twenty minutes later, a courier arrived and relieved me of it. As he put it in his top box he said, 'Dean wants the radio back.'

I could see that this was a sacking of sorts. Their loss, not mine, I thought. The biker took my radio and said, 'And the . . .' gesturing to the fluorescent vest. He took that as well and without a word sped off into the early evening.

So that was that. All I had to do now was find out the name of the Tube station where I parked my bike.

29

FOR THE MOST PART, I find it funny when people can't be bothered. It doesn't matter to me what they can't be bothered with, I just find that attitude humorous.

As I write this I can see two Council workers in the street outside whose job it is to clear the compacted snow from our pavements. One has a shovel, the other a broom. Neither man is holding his implement with both hands, preferring to push lethargically at the ice with one hand only. This leaves a hand free to make a phone call, in one case, and to eat a Twix, in the other. Possibly I should find this more annoying than I do, but it is quite funny. Two grown men who can't be arsed. I know that my impulse, if that was my job, would be to throw myself at the task with all the gusto I could muster, but when you think about it, that's not especially commendable. Maybe it makes me a bit sad.

No, I enjoy witnessing the arrangement that these two characters have struck with the Council. In a nutshell: they said that they would clear the snow and the Council said that they would pay them to do so. The end result will be that the Council will pay the men, but the men will not have cleared the snow, knowing full well that sunlight and time will destroy the evidence of their indolence. Something about that makes me laugh, which is just as well, because I see so many examples of this on an everyday basis that if it didn't make me laugh, my blood would probably burst from its vessels.

Some years ago I was banging on to my children about something or other. Oh yes, that's what it was: initiative and how with vim and endeavour anybody can make a go of things in life and that it is unnecessary for a fit person to descend into poverty. Much of this was lost on them, especially the boys, who were only one at the time and hadn't yet learnt to worry about life.

As I was saying this the doorbell rang. Two teenagers were asking if I wanted my car washed for ten pounds. Obliged by the timing of their visit, but also charmed by their ingenuity, I felt it only right to engage their services.

Back in the kitchen I made full use of this happy co-incidence by pointing out how well those young men would do in this world with their sense of enterprise and readiness to roll up their sleeves.

A short while later, the doorbell rang for a second time. The two entrepreneurs were standing there, eager to show me that my car was cleaned and ready for inspection. I looked at it, gleaming like new on the other side of the street, and cheerfully paid the tenner, plus a small tip, wishing them good luck in a patriarchal way as I did so.

After about an hour, I had to go out, which is when I discovered that the teenagers had only cleaned the parts of the car which were visible from my front door. The side of the vehicle that was hidden from view was as filthy as ever; a clear border existed from bonnet to boot, calculated to deceive anybody looking at the car from the precise angle of my house.

'Why did the men only clean a bit of your car, Daddy?'

'Oh, because that's all they had time to do, I expect, darling. Come on, seat-belt on.'

'Will they come back and do the rest of it tomorrow, Daddy?'

'I doubt it, my sweetness, that's what the world is like. Full of people who want to cheat you. As I was saying earlier, the important thing in life is not to trust anyone.'

'Daddy, I think the car looks silly now. Silly car, silly car, silly car . . .'

I'd like to be able to report that I wised up after that incident and never again succumbed to the sly ways of the con-artist. But admit it, that's not what you want to read. You're hoping that I was naive and stupid enough to get shafted again. Well, lucky you.

For a long time now, my Novembers have been marred by having to spend very nearly five pounds on a diary refill for my Filofax. It always annoys me that I should have to spend so much on a few bits of paper, so imagine my delight when, walking down Oxford Street one late-autumnal day in 2006, I was approached by an apparently destitute Eastern European lady with a small child who was selling Filofax 2007 diary refills for only two pounds.

So I bought one. Obviously, I was aware that they were, in all likelihood, stolen. I'm not stupid. Just unethical.

They had to be stolen for so many reasons it hardly bears thinking about.

Well, alright, for one, why would an esteemed and sophisticated brand such as Filofax suddenly decide to abandon the comparative comfort of W. H. Smith's and, instead, employ an asylum-seeker to wander around with a sports holdall full of diary refills in the hope that people would see this as an improvement in their service?

Secondly, if you had to sell stolen goods to feed your children, these are exactly the sort of goods you would end up selling. Stolen goods are, by their very definition, completely random. Nobody in their right mind would deliberately choose an obscure line of stationery that would only interest a tiny minority.

No, they were nicked. No doubt about it. And to be honest, I didn't mind in the least. After all those years of being (in my opinion) overcharged for my annual refill, it was payback time. As I tucked the packet discreetly into my inside pocket, I resolved that in future I might make a point of buying stolen things more often because they are so much cheaper.

Admittedly you run the risk of disappointment. Like the time when I bought a bumper-pack of AA batteries for just five pounds from someone at a market stall. They were as flat as the out-of-date pancakes being sold next-door to him. Obviously he'd just re-packaged a load of old discarded double As. And no, he wasn't there when I took them back the following week. At times like that you just have to be philosophical and think, 'If that's what he has to do to make a crust, rummage around in rubbish all day, looking for old batteries so he can rip off decent people like me, then I feel sorry for him.' Thieving bastard.

So, I got home with my diary refill, put it into my Filofax, and some three months later – a week into the new year – I turned the page to discover that only the top page – i.e. week one – was for 2007. The next eight months slipped back into 2006 and by the end of the year the weeks and days had dissolved into one long blank, as though the pages themselves could no longer be bothered to maintain the pretence.

Really, I should have been cross with the Eastern

European lady, but, in all honesty, I felt that I had got my money's worth when you consider the labour involved, the fiddling about with cellophane packaging and the sheer originality of it. And I rather liked the delayed disclosure of conceit that the plan involved. As if she was thinking, 'By the time my crime is discovered, civil war in my country will be finished and I will have made enough money to go home and buy own business. Perhaps stationery shop.'

I felt more than a hint of admiration for the woman. It was pretty harmless as scams go. It's not like she was selling fake pharmaceuticals that turn out to be made of rat poison, or counterfeit spare parts for Boeing 747s, like fuel pumps that transpire to be made out of bits from a lawnmower. I mean, that really is naughty. How can some people live with themselves? One hardly dare consider the possible consequences of such deceit. It's awful enough when you hear about a plane crash some-where in the world without having to lie awake at night thinking, 'Hope it was nothing to do with that fuel pump I sold them.'

You would never guess, however, just by looking at me, that I was once the victim of an even worse ruse than any of those.

Not long after we moved from that little house in Tooting that we bought from the vicar – that's right, the one who tricked me into buying his fetid, stinky bog-hole of a dwelling (God, it's a wonder I trust anyone) –

I was singled out and targeted by a completely ruthless con-man. What is particularly hurtful is that I was in such a good mood when it happened.

When he knocked on the door, I was so replete with the joys of life that I was actually in a vulnerable state, like being drunk or something. I can see that now. We now lived in genteel Balham and our second daughter, Phoebe, had just been born.

'Any knives sharpened for you, Sir?' That was his opening line. I could have said 'No' and shut the door in his face, but as I say, I was intoxicated with *joie de vivre* and wanted to share my good fortune with the rest of humanity. I was also thrilled at the quaintness of having a genuine itinerant knife-sharpener come to the house. What a lovely area I had relocated to. No doubt the muffin man would be round shortly. Then evening would fall and it would be time for the street-lights to be lit by that gentleman with the top hat and long pole. Charming.

'Any knives, kitchenware, scissors, garden tools you'd like sharpened, Sir?' This time I noticed his soft, trustworthy Irish brogue and thought what a pity it would be if his craft were to die out due to the yuppie gentrification of an area that had traditionally provided my visitor with an honest living for generations, to be sure.

And, on a practical level, I had noticed that one or two of our kitchen knives had lost their magic of late.

Only the other day, making a sandwich, I had tried to slice a tomato and struggled to make the blade puncture the fruit's skin. Yes, it was high time that all of our kitchen knives were honed back to the professional condition they had been in when I bought them.

So I handed them over, a great bundle, scissors, secateurs and all, carefully lowering them into his held-open canvas bag for him to 'take to the van parked around the corner there'. To be sure.

At this point you will be thinking that I never saw him again. After all, I've already told you this was a scam. However, you're dead wrong. I saw him about half an hour later when he knocked at the door, empty-handed, and said that all the knives were done and that his son was just finishing off the garden tools for me and could he take payment now so that when his son delivered them back in a minute he wouldn't have to worry about the money.

Evidently, I didn't question the logic of this idea – after all, there isn't any – so I got my wallet.

'That's forty five, call it forty for cash. Thank you, Sir.'

Clever. I'm being robbed, but it's a bargain. The sleight of hand: I haven't got my knives back and I am being charged more than I expected, but suddenly I don't question any of that because I'm getting a deal. I'll be able to tell my wife that I haggled, wore him down and struck a good price, not like the idiot next door who probably just told him flat 'No thanks.'

So I handed over my forty quid and off he went, folding the notes into his breast pocket, to tell his son to get a move on.

'He's learning the trade, Sir. He's good, mind, but he needs to step it up.'

I nodded with approval and waved him cheerio, pleased at the thought that the skills of an honest trade were still being handed down from one generation of the working class to the next for the benefit of their intellectual superiors.

A moment ago I told you that you were wrong to think that I never saw him again after that. And, as I went on to explain, you were wrong. But if you were to think that again now, you'd be right.

The police were very casual about it all. Not as concerned as I would have hoped. I did get a follow-up call from the case officer, but it wasn't terribly helpful. Apart from anything else, he picked a bad time. You know what it's like when the phone rings and the baby's crying and you're just coming in with the shopping. New knives, mostly, scissors, secateurs, that kind of thing.

Anyway, it turns out that the Irish knife-sharpener plays this trick all over London. Apparently, what he and his imaginary son do is drive around until they/he sees a removal van unloading, makes a note of the address, and soon afterwards pays the newcomer a visit. There is something psychologically disarming about settling into an unfamiliar area, and he knows this. To be sure.

30

WITHOUT ANY DOUBT, BURGLARY constitutes a major violation of your rights as a citizen to lead a peaceful and safe existence. Especially aggravated burglary. You know, the kind where they break stuff that they don't need to break, tip your recently tidied stationery drawer into the toilet and scrawl words on the walls that the children ask you to explain. I know, because that's what happened to me.

Admittedly, in my case, not all of those things happened. There was no actual graffiti or toilet business and, to be fair, they didn't technically break anything, but that doesn't make what did happen any less traumatic.

One warm summer's day, I innocently left the sash window at the front of our house slightly open to let in some cool air. Just a couple of inches, and there was a lock to prevent the window being lifted any higher. What it didn't prevent was the pilfering hand of a passer-by reaching in and taking my cordless telephone from its base-unit. It's hard to imagine a more senseless crime. What could he possibly gain? Unless he returned the next night, crouched down in my front garden and used the handset to call a premium-rate number. Even then, what would he do when the battery ran low? Hope that one day I would leave the window open again so that he could slip it back on to the base-unit for a sly recharge? Yeah, right. Dream on, mate. From now on that window is staying shut.

That's the effect of crime for you. I felt utterly violated and our house will never truly feel like home again. But if you're reading this in bed, please, don't have nightmares. Crime of this sort is incredibly rare. And funny, according to the desk sergeant at my local police station when I went in to report it.

Anyway, two months or so later, when the chaos and upset of the break-in had given way to a fragile calm, small unimportant tasks became a distracting comfort like never before. I found that traumatic memories of having to throw away a perfectly good base-unit, only to discover you can buy replacement handsets, flickered away for moments at a time as I focused on the minutiae of life.

I have a small set of wooden tongs that magnetize to the toaster, designed specifically to stay in that place just so they are right there when you need to pick the hot toast out. After several years of being pulled away from their metal home at about the same time every morning, the wooden tongs fell to the worktop, leaving a small round magnet stuck to the side of the toaster.

So, a trip to the corner shop. Superglue. A walk back, rehearsing in my mind the process of gently squeezing a small bead of the glue into the circular hole on the back of the tongs and then placing the magnet into it. Not too little, because then it'll happen again at just about the same time as the new superglue can no longer be found and I'll have to buy some more, having used hardly any of the last lot. And not too much, or it'll ooze out and look all amateur and crap. Like some idiot did it. Probably nobody will know how rubbish the mend is, but I will. I won't enjoy using the tongs, knowing that I botched the job. And it has to be toast in the mornings, because I don't like cereal.

Or I could unscrew the cap now, in the street (nobody's around), and shoot the lot into the lock of someone's car door. It would be random, pointless and a very bad thing to do. No. I am really so far from being the type of person who would do something like that, so why would the thought even occur? I clutch the tiny bottle tighter in my hand and hold my wrist with my other hand as if it needs to be restrained.

Now I'm preparing to glue the magnet back into its rightful place. I do it well. The trial run in my head paid off. I thought it through, considered all the possible complications that might arise, executed the task and hit pay-dirt. And I'm pleased that I didn't squirt the glue into someone's car door. Although I did at one point feel the need to pull the tongs apart to see where they would snap. But I resisted, because I didn't want them broken and I used to do that a lot with pencils and rulers and so on. It's quite inconclusive.

I didn't squirt the glue into someone's car door because basically I'm one of the decent people who don't do that kind of thing. Even if I do think of it. And I'm one of the decent people because I was brought up that way. Knowing that you only use glue to do good things and that other people's property is to be respected. Not ruined with glue.

Which brings me back to the burglary that I was talking about before the tongs incident. I guess whoever robbed me just isn't one of the decent people. But a small part of me worries that he might be, that like me with the glue and the car, he considered just walking past my window, but instead of walking past, he stuck his thieving arm in and helped himself to my phone. The trouble with that theory is it makes me understand him more and hate him less. So I'm not going with it. He's just a bastard.

The reason for telling you all this is that while I was so successfully repairing the tongs and considering a career change to art restoration, I was quite involuntarily drawn into a debate about knife crime. This was being conducted by a member of that strange friendless breed, the radio talk-show host. In this instance an excitable Irishman to-ing and fro-ing between Margaret in Derby and Carl in Southwark.

I was aware that Carl was probably quite stupid because he had to be told to turn off his radio while he was on the line, because the delay would make it impossible for him to take part properly. It took a tiny bit too long for him to understand.

Margaret in Derby remained a mystery throughout. Basically, she thought that young people were stabbing each other a lot because there wasn't enough to do and that if we built more sports centres and suchlike then they could all go swimming or play five-a-side instead. I don't know what she meant by 'suchlike'. Maybe youth clubs or Army cadet training. Probably not amusement arcades though, because that brings you back to people stabbing each other.

Anyway, Carl in Southwark felt that that wasn't the way forward at all. It went like this:

Excitable Irishman: Carl in Southwark, what do you think about that? Margaret in Derby's saying 'provide more facilities and knife crime will disappear'.

Carl in Southwark: Yeah, well, it's the same old story, isn't it?

Excitable Irishman: What is?

Carl in Southwark: Oh, you know. Throw money at them, all that sort of thing.

Excitable Irishman: You don't think that'll work? Why's that, Carl?

Carl in Southwark: Just won't, will it?

Excitable Irishman: Margaret, Carl says your sports centre won't work. That you're just throwing money at them. What do you think of that?

Margaret in Derby: Well, I think it will.

Excitable Irishman: Carl in Southwark, Margaret there's calling you a liar. What have you to say to that?

Carl in Southwark explained that he wasn't lying and then Margaret in Derby denied calling him a liar, which prompted the excitable Irishman to suggest that Carl was calling Margaret a liar.

Some conversations are circular like that. Like Sky News. Leave the room and come back ten minutes later, and you won't have missed anything because it's on a loop going on endlessly until some dreadful event somewhere in the world changes the rhythm of the news. And the sick thing is that part of you actually welcomes it. Carl, Margaret and the excitable Irishman are still talking like that somewhere on the airwaves. They might have changed their names but everything else will be the same.

These days, makers of news programmes are obsessed with filling their reports with vox pops. Little sound-bite clips of the man or woman in the street, caught unprepared but undaunted by the prospect of addressing the nation. When asked, issues of global concern are deftly shrunk to 'terrible' and 'awful' by those who are seduced by the presence of a camera into thinking that their comments will in some way add to our understanding of events.

It didn't occur to me that the events of 9/11 were in any way undesirable until, a couple of days later, a commuter in Bromley High Street explained on the news that hijacking passenger planes and flying them into buildings was shocking. A woman in the same report went further. She was out shopping, but said it was a diabolical thing to have happened.

Up until then, I don't suppose that I'd given the attack on the World Trade Center all that much thought. So thank heaven for those ordinary shoppers for keeping me in the loop. Naturally I could see the disadvantages of being in the skyscrapers or indeed the aeroplanes, but I hadn't gone as far as forming an opinion about it one way or the other. Without their insight I might have watched the news that day and just thought, 'Oh well, hey ho!'

Maybe it's time for us to insist that our news-makers level the playing field when it comes to vox pops. It just isn't fair that snazzy correspondents are allowed to highlight their slickness by inserting clips of uninitiated punters blurting out knee-jerk adjectives. Those journos know too well that nobody likes a smart-arse, at least not until they've been forced to listen to a dullard first.

Reporters should at least be made to tone down their appearance so that members of the public look less ridiculous by comparison. If Jeremy Paxman was made to present *Newsnight* wearing tracksuit bottoms and a cap-sleeve T-shirt then the poor old vox-pop speaker might stand a chance of looking less hopeless. Likewise, give the commuter some make-up like the presenter has, so that his forehead is not aglow with sweat and his oily chin doesn't catch the light.

Of course, in reality, my response to the events of that day was much like everyone else's. Although at one point, seeking an escape from the horror of it all, I flicked through the channels and eventually found a station that wasn't covering it. Instead, they were showing an old episode of Alan Titchmarsh doing up a tatty garden and the awful thing is, I got sort of interested in that as well, so I found myself switching back to him once or twice when the news footage became too repetitive.

In case you're wondering, Alan Titchmarsh was doing a really nice makeover of this couple's garden while they were away for the weekend. Their daughter had organized it all and they burst into tears when they saw how nice it was with the new decking and water-feature and everything. In a matter of hours their shabby old garden had been completely transformed. A bit like what happened to the world that day. Only what happened to the world was bad, not good. As I said to the radio interviewer when they rang me for a quote.

31

I ENVY THE ABILITY to talk to people. Getting strangers to open up and say more than they mean to requires a kind of seduction that I'm not capable of. This isn't false modesty, in case you were thinking, 'Of course you're capable of it, Jack. You can do anything you turn your hand to, you can.'

OK, so you weren't thinking that. My point is I couldn't do what the Excitable Irishman does. I know because I've tried. Not on the radio. Or on television. No, much worse than that.

Up until my mid-twenties, although the restaurant business had provided me with a living that was enjoyable enough, it never completely anaesthetized that deeper sense of aching for something else. In my quest to find what it was, I tried pretty much everything.

Tuesday's *Evening Standard* had a double-page spread of miscellaneous situations vacant that varied from driving jobs to leafleting, from selling magic herbal pills in a magic pyramid-selling scheme that could make you millions, to the more obscure little notices that hinted at easy fortunes if you'd just call this number. It's easy for me now to look at advertisements like that and wonder who they attract, forgetting that once they attracted me.

One Tuesday I ran my finger down those columns of promises, vaguely recognizing each one. There was the shop job, the delivery job, the standing-in-the-street-wearing-a-sandwich-board-saying-'Golf-Sale'-job. There was hospital portering, car-valeting, cold-calling, labouring, night security, office-cleaning, shelf-stacking, courier work. I had done them all.

Market research shone from those dreary pages like a gold tooth in a tramp's mouth. It sounded respectable and sophisticated, interesting too. Here was a job with prospects. In all probability, this would be the moment that I'd look back upon as being fateful, not only for me but for the market-research industry itself, which was about to be turned on its head and revolutionized by that kid who answered the ad. Most likely a biopic would eventually be made, depicting me as a Howard Hughes type, only more enigmatic. At the end of the film, it would fade to black. No music. No need for it. Just a few words explaining where I now live (south of France) and how market research continues to thrive thanks to the great work that I had done. So, knowing this to be a turning point in my fortunes, I lifted the phone and wound the dial. Ring ring.

I got an interview. Just like that. 'Can you come in and see us tomorrow?' Clearly an omen that this was the thing I'd been waiting for all my life. For so long I'd been doing odd-jobs and waiting tables, when all along, the world of market research was waiting for their new Messiah to arrive.

Now all I needed was my suit and to find out exactly what market research was. Which, ideally, I would have done before the interview.

This took place in a dispiriting open-plan office, with long empty desks of telephones, their numerals almost erased by usage. The odd photocopied form lying neglected on the floor. Beige swivel-seats with cigarette burns. Phone directories lying open with line after line of names and numbers biroed out. Bored doodles spirographed into the margin and sometimes on the desk. It all felt as if some sad primate had been caged there.

In response to my interviewer's question 'What makes you interested in market research?' I offer one of several non-answers that have proved invaluable over my years of job-hunting.

'I like working with people.'

He looks at me, expecting more than that. So I choose a crayon out of my imaginary box of bullshit and start colouring.

'And I'm looking for a new challenge,' I continue. 'You know? A job where I can learn and contribute at the same time.'

He's listening, but not totally buying it.

'And so my uncle suggested market research,' I add. 'Really recommended it, so here I am . . .'

'Great, glad to hear it,' says the man with the nicotine fingers and worn-out telephone. 'What has he told you about the business?'

Good question. A fair question. He has a right to know. What has my fictional, non-existent, just-made-up uncle told me about market research?

'Well, he's a lawyer actually, in New York, and he got to know about it through friends and acquaintances, and so what I've heard from him is probably not one hundred per cent accurate, but it was enough to get me interested'

He grins as if to say I've passed the test. 'No, fair enough,' he says. 'Let me tell you a little bit about it and see if it tallies with what you already know.'

It was that easy. Now he was saying all the stuff that he'd asked me to say, and all I had to do was agree and nod.

At the training session one week later, held in the large, modern foyer of the Lyric Theatre in Hammersmith, my suspicions were confirmed. Market research is about stopping people in the street and asking them if they prefer Daz or Persil. Obviously it varies. The makers of Daz and Persil are not uniquely insecure and competitive. Sometimes it's Mars bars or Snickers and sometimes it's coffee or tea, but you get the picture.

If the person you approach does stop, you have to ask them a list of other questions like 'A lot, quite a lot, not very much or none at all?' and 'Extremely satisfied, satisfied, not very satisfied or not satisfied at all?' Then when you've done your quota of, say, fifty questionnaires, to include at least fifteen males aged 18–24 and at least twenty females aged 35–45, your work is done.

After lunch, which wasn't provided, we split into groups and practised asking each other if we preferred Daz or Persil. I was with a nervous man from Egypt and two women who knew each other already, so when they asked each other questions it was like they were cheating. The man from Egypt told me he was returning to market research after three years studying business management.

'Time well spent,' I said.

And he said 'Yes' as if I'd meant it.

Then, at three thirty, that was that. I had qualified. No actual degree, but I did get an ID card in one of those plastic envelopes that you hang round your neck. All I had to do now was return home and await further instructions.

I heard nothing the first day, but still told people

that I was in market research. Despite knowing by now that it was a lousy job, it still had a certain ring to it as far as I was concerned. I buried my feeling of disillusionment and, as usual, defaulted to the comfort of a fantasy existence.

I'd been recruited into MI5. I was what is known as 'a sleeper', infiltrating the neighbourhood, watching, waiting, lying low. Any time now, my handler would make contact, two chalk marks on a lamp-post, a note concealed in a book at the library. Classic dead-drop scenario.

The businessman who parks outside my flat each night at around nine won't know anything. He'll get out of his car, the way he always does, pull his briefcase from the passenger seat, two soft thuds in quick succession, the fail-safe double-tap, and he'll quietly crumple to the pavement as I melt back into the evening's shadows, adjusting my jacket so that the bulge under my arm is unnoticeable. It's a grubby business, arms-dealing, and he should never have got involved.

I don't hear his wife scream until I'm round the corner. She heard his car, but not the familiar clunk of the door that usually followed. Something wasn't right. Like waiting for the other shoe to drop. She went to look from the window and then, rushing outside, approaching in a panicky blur, reached her husband lying by the car, rolled him over and saw the blood on the shirt that she had ironed only last night. Nothing will get that out. Not Daz, not Persil. Nothing.

So, I eventually get a call from the market-research company. They don't want me to shoot anyone but they do want me to find out people's attitude towards cereal bars. I have to go to their office again, where I had the interview, and pick up all the questionnaires. The man who interviewed me doesn't work there any more but Brenda introduces herself and says that she'll be my coordinator. My mission, should I wish to accept it, is to ask eighty people the same set of questions about what they eat for breakfast and what their thoughts are about a new type of confectionery bar made of corn flakes.

For this, I can knock on doors or ask people in the street. Good luck, Jack. When you've read these instructions, eat them.

After a morning of having front doors shut in my face, I was eventually invited in by a man wearing a dressing gown. He was about forty, a bachelor I'd say. He asked me if I'd like some chocolate. I declined and asked him what he usually had for breakfast. 'Why don't you stay and find out?' was his response. I made my excuses and left.

The Arndale Centre in Wandsworth was a shopping mall that has now been pulled down and rebuilt to create the altogether smarter Southside. But in the early eighties the Arndale Centre was an interesting model of what I think Britain might have been like after a catastrophic nuclear accident. People would waddle or shuffle but never just walk. They were rude or horribly familiar, never just civil.

Anyone under the impression that childhood obesity is a new phenomenon never went to the Wandsworth Arndale Centre. Bloated dadless families wandered from shop to shop, bleating after each other, pushing buggies around. A shaven-headed boy squeezed into a stained England strip lags behind and is shouted at. He wobbles into a lardy trot to catch up whilst, head angled upwards towards the Perspex sky, he lowers a metre of red liquorice into the puckered hole in his face.

'What you fucking looking at?' Mummy asks me.

Sensing that as an unpromising start, I decide not to trouble her with the questionnaire.

There is a fountain at the intersection of the mall with McDonald's cartons bobbing in the yellowing water. The place has a sickly smell that wafts from an olde worlde mobile sweet stall where a woman in stripy dungarees and a white nylon pork-pie hat spins candy-floss. The aroma blends with the general Big Mac bouquet to create instant nausea in anyone unversed in the Golden Arches menu.

Apart from the olde worlde sweet stand and McDonald's, I only remember there being card shops at the Arndale. Countless card shops with their aisles and aisles of cards for all occasions. More categories than there are days in the year, from birthdays to exam results, engagements, marriages, births, christenings, anniversaries, deepest condolences. The whole of life's rich experience expressed in corny couplets and swirling sentiments.

Of course, card shops don't just make their money from the cards, profitable though they must be. Some bright spark deduced that when a card is given, it is often with a present, so why not sell those as well? The management must have agreed because they soon diversified and now stock all manner of gifts. Mugs, key-fobs, cuddly toys, that kind of thing. All of which are graced with a compliment ('World's best nan') or a joke ('When God made men he was practising'), something soppy ('Begin every day with a hug') or something sincere ('A listening ear, a hand to lend, throughout the years you've been a friend. Thank you.')

Perhaps the very same bright spark also surmised that when a card is given and a present is given, it's often at a party, so why not sell stuff for that as well? Banners that say '21 today', fancy-dress outfits and champagne bottles that are really bombs which burst forth with streams of paper tape, glitter and sweets. It's only a matter of time before he realizes that a car will be needed for getting to the party, as well as a house to go home to afterwards. And a sick bucket for when you finally get round to opening the card. My God, the possibilities are endless.

Generally, normal sane people do not want to stop when someone with a clipboard and an ID card tries to start up any sort of dialogue. In truth, I remember none of the excuses given for not obliging. As a rule, refusal was transmitted with a blank, bovine stare.

I suppose we all have our own methods of avoiding people with clipboards. In my case, these range from a confident 'No thank you' to pretending I'm foreign and don't understand or that I'm extremely ill and need directions to the nearest hospital. The point is, I never stop for them.

In my defence, I'd like to explain that they are invariably chuggers, those abnormally extrovert students who would like you to sign a direct-debit mandate for some charity, a percentage of which they keep, although they don't tell you that. At least I was doing it for honest reasons. I was keeping all the money I made.

After twenty minutes or so of standing in the Arndale, peacefully going about my lawful business of harassing people, I was escorted from the mall by a security guard, who had as much charm as you'd expect from someone who has ended up as a security guard in a downmarket shopping mall. My guess is that it wasn't his first choice, but he was asked to leave Hendon Police College after only two days. Either way, it turned out my business wasn't so lawful after all. Not without a permit.

So I loitered close to the entrance and tried again. When conducting a market-research survey, you are at the mercy of the public. They dictate whether or not you complete your work and get paid, and certainly how long it will take. And I will always be grateful to those kind, ordinary working people who took time in their busy day to cooperate. Both of them.

Because the fact is that almost without exception, the people who agreed to stop and answer my dull questions were strange. By that I mean anything from oddly gentle, sweet-hearted souls whom your best instincts tell you to protect and look after, to the plain frightening.

'Excuse me, Sir, I'm conducting a survey on behalf of a well-known cereal brand. I wonder if you'd mind answering a few questions?'

Sir is about five foot ten and very thin. In my heart I know that I've made a mistake in stopping him. His suit trousers are too short, flapping around his ankles like loose sails. His walk has too much spring in it. Too much bounce. Nobody sensible walks like that. On hearing me ask if he'd mind answering a few questions, his eyes light up and a grin spreads across his face. Here we go.

'I'd love to,' he shouts. People look at us. I hold my clipboard so that it's obvious and they don't just think that we're mates. He tells me, before being asked, that his name is Neil and asks me mine. I can't lie because of the ID card in its plastic sleeve.

Trying to dampen his enthusiasm, I calmly explain

that the company I represent is developing a new type of cereal bar and that his answers will help them to best determine the needs of their customers.

Having tactfully established whether Neil has a job (astonishingly he does), I run through the first set of multiple choice. 'Suppose you didn't have time for breakfast at home one morning, would you (a) take food such as a piece of toast or fruit from your home and eat it on the way to work, (b) buy something to eat on the way to work, or (c) get something to eat at work?'

Neil puts his hand to his chin and considers his options, then shouts, 'Sometimes I go home on the bus,' adding something about sitting at the front because it feels as though he's driving. I think that's what he said. To be honest I wasn't really listening. I was trying to work out how to get away from him.

But it wasn't going to be that easy. 'Well, thank you for your time, Neil, you've been most helpful,' I say, knowing that it won't work because, in case you haven't guessed, Neil is as mad as a bag of ferrets. Worse still, he likes me and he thinks that I like him. Why else would I have started up a conversation with him?

'You've got loads more questions,' he yells. 'You haven't asked me that one. Or that one. Ask me that one.'

I realize that talking to Neil is like opening one of those joke mustard jars when a big plastic snake springs out and you discover you've been tricked. There is no mustard and the snake won't go back in.

I say that he doesn't need to shout and he asks why. Because we're standing next to each other, is the gist of my argument and he sees my point. Except instead of simply lowering his voice, he raises his finger to his lips and goes 'Shhh' in a way that makes me feel more embarrassed than when he was just shouting at me.

Nobody has ever told Neil that he stands too close. That he should back off, give people some space, or they won't like you. I am not a microphone. You don't need to talk into me. Our arms do not need to be pressed together like conjoined twins. Perhaps it is this mistake that has caused his madness. He is a space-invader and humans can't handle that, any more than Neil can handle the constant rejection that his tendency has yielded. Standing too close has made everybody in his life reject him. Closeness, the thing that he craves, is the very thing that makes him repulsive to others. Perhaps that innocent, correctable quirk of gauche familiarity is, ultimately, what has brought about his insanity. If only someone had told him.

On Neil's insistence, we continue with the question-naire. I grind out the questions, and Neil thrills at each one. It's a quiz, it's fun. My lack of patience doesn't disturb him. Only me. I find myself wishing Neil no harm, whilst simultaneously wishing that he simply didn't exist.

Then, just as we reach the end of the form, Neil walks away from me, literally in the middle of an almost enjoyably crazy answer. I assume that he has decided to chase one of the grimy pigeons that are pecking at some chips that have been dropped nearby. They'd certainly been bothering me. But no, he keeps walking – long, bouncy, loping steps, past the pigeons, across the road, and jumps on to a Routemaster that is pulling away. He must be going home, I think, as he waltzes his way slowly to the front.

For my part, you can't deny that I started off in my career of market research with the best of intentions. Nonetheless, I returned home from the Arndale Centre with a thick wad of untouched forms and only fifteen that I'd managed to get completed. It could have been sixteen if I'd relented and approached the guy in the torn parka who loitered nearby all afternoon, clearly desperate to be interviewed. I ignored him deliberately. Firstly, just out of pique. Secondly, because he looked even madder than Neil. And thirdly, it emboldened me that, technically, a queue was forming.

That evening I transgressed the first rule of market research and filled in the remaining questionnaires myself. Not callously or with mal intent. I still cared about the integrity of the survey. I went to the trouble of not only inventing interviewees with postcode-correct addresses, but I gave them all little personalities that I hope came through in their answers.

Kenneth, for instance, hadn't bothered with break-fast of any description since his wife died, so he was 'not very interested'.

Carol declared herself to be wheat-intolerant and said that she would be 'very interested' in buying a gluten-free cereal bar. It felt strange being a woman and I worried that something weird might happen. My mind might get stuck like a scratched record and I would become Carol. It wasn't sexual or anything. Just depressing, being a woman who was allergic to so many things. I can be a fussy cow at times.

Susan was on a diet so wanted to know if there would be a low-calorie one. (Yes, I know, another woman, I was short on my quota, OK? Anyway it's just a form, it's not like I put a dress on to do it.)

And so my evening was spent. When my flatmates returned from work, they were recruited into my multi-persona world with the promise of a beer or glass of wine, depending which character they drank in.

Now all that data would enter the cereal manufacturer's system. Those answers would influence, in some way, future products and how they got marketed. In a boardroom somewhere, a year or so after my research, a young executive would give a presentation about a proposed new range of snacks. More astute board-members might ask to be reassured that the questionnaire had been correctly worded so as not to lead the interviewee; that enough people were questioned in a sufficient variety of locations. Almost certainly, however, nobody around the table would think to ask whether the people questioned were mad or not, or whether they actually existed or were merely the creation of a rogue surveyor.

And so the cereal bar got the go-ahead by a show of wise hands. The board had commissioned their market research, studied the results and liked what they saw. None of them will ever know that faddy Carol, anorexic Susan, bereaved Kenneth and all the others were formative in the process. Their opinions counted as much as anyone else's, irrespective of the fact that Carol was just a twenty-three-year-old bloke in a basement flat in Earl's Court, or that Susan wasn't really on a diet because she had already reached her target weight of nought point zero, and that Kenneth was no more alive than his wife.

Much less will they know that poor, potty Neil thought, with a considerable degree of excitement, despite my best efforts to explain, that this new cereal bar was going to be a place where you go to eat corn flakes and make friends. Now there's an idea. I wonder how many people would frequent a place like that. How can we find out?

32

I SOMETIMES WONDER WHETHER our lives are affected more than we think by fraudulent market research.

It could well be, for instance, that somebody faced with a pile of questionnaires about what the public would like to put on a piece of crispbread came up with a set of bogus answers that led to the invention of cottage cheese.

'What I'd like,' said imaginary Rebecca, a twenty-three-year-old secretary from Cheam who enjoys walking and is currently single, 'is some sort of lumpy, off-milk product that looks like albino sick.'

'Why not put some chopped chives in it, or bits of pineapple?' suggested made-up thirty-two-year-old solicitor's clerk Gordon. 'I'd buy that.'

And so the go-ahead was given, and against all odds, cottage cheese (why that name? Don't even go there) took off and we bought the unlikely product in tub-loads.

Similarly, how else could patio-heaters have been thought of? Quite possibly a simple survey about our jumper-wearing habits was hijacked by a sarcastic student with a rucksack full of forms to forge. Filling in the seventy-fourth questionnaire about what you would do to stay warm outside on a cool evening, he understandably allowed his imagination to take over. The answer 'put on a jumper' was beginning to sound repetitive. So instead, he came up with 'I hate wearing jumpers. I wish they'd invent some sort of burning beacon that you could sit under until your hair singes and your friends start to pass out because of the fumes. I'd definitely buy one of those.'

And I can only imagine it was a medieval market-researcher who first convinced his gullible masters that there would be a demand for the game known as real tennis. This, of course, is the eccentric ancestor of modern lawn tennis and is played in a four-walled court resembling a film-set for Henry VIII. It's the kind of game that only appeals to proper toffs or those sad enough to want to pass themselves off as one. Which may explain why I recently invested a great deal of time and money in it.

In case you have never played it yourself, the basics of real tennis are as follows: along one side of the court is a sloped roof that extends at right angles around both ends. Service consists of knocking the ball on to this pitched roof and seeing it roll round, bounce off the end wall and drop from the slope into your opponent's end. I used to really like that bit.

Receiving service at the 'hazard end' is as much a matter of anticipation as anything else – watching the serve, following the ball around the roof and gauging how it will bounce and where it will drop behind you. The balls are made of cork and covered in Melton cloth and are similar in size to their modern cousins, but because they are not pneumatic, lack their keen bounce. Therefore the challenge is to get your trusty wooden racket underneath the ball after it has dropped to the floor and hook it away, back to your opponent. That racket, by the way, is asymmetric, having a slight curve at the neck so that the head, similar in size to that of a squash racket, appears to be tilting.

The net is higher than a conventional tennis net, with a more pronounced dip in the middle. Most pleasing of all is the thick crimson velvet band running along its top. The rules are ingeniously complicated, and apart from some aspects of the scoring, bear very little similarity to lawn tennis. I won't go into detail, partly because I never did quite understand them and partly because . . . well, no, *entirely* because I never did quite understand them.

Any novice must, however, become familiar with the game's enchanting terminology. Tambour, dedans, grille, last gallery, penthouse and 'half a yard worse than six' are just some of the aspects of the game that need to be fully appreciated. Although, as I've already stated, I didn't.

But I enjoyed my new lexicon; it sounded erudite and sophisticated. I'll make no bones about it, I was attracted by the game's exclusivity. For me it had an air of decadence that surpassed the usual meanness and vulgarity of competitive sport. Here at last was a sporting pastime that would fulfil all my requirements – i.e. it was good fun but nobody was going to take it too seriously. Or so I thought. Furthermore, it was quite in order to wear long white trousers, which I felt gave me the appearance of a pre-war Wimbledon ace like Fred Perry.

I had found my sport.

The coach was a nice enough chap whose nickname was Binky. Initially, I let that pass, as I was so keen on the game, but after a few lessons it did start to annoy me that he was called Binky. There seemed no need for it. Perhaps it wouldn't have got to me if his surname was Bink. I would have thought, 'Fair enough, doesn't matter, let it go.' But his surname wasn't Bink or Binks or anything remotely like Binky, so, naturally, that became a massive distraction.

After feeding me a basket of balls for me to return, Binky would approach the net and start explaining various rules of the game.

Binky was English, but had spent much of his childhood in Paris because his father was a diplomat. That fact is not as irrelevant as it may at first seem, because it meant that when talking about real tennis he was able to grace the French terms of the game with a perfect French accent. 'Tambour' or 'dedans', for instance, in the context of an otherwise classic English pronunciation, sounded slightly silly.

Moreover, I didn't know whether to follow suit or to stick with my English renditions. As I had found out during my time in France, I have a fairly good ear for accents, so I started doing the same as Binky. I would find myself asking him, 'How many points for getting *la grille*?'

Then it worried me that Binky would think that I was taking the piss. Or worse, that I thought it was cool the way he pronounced the French words so accurately and that my copying him was an obvious sign of admiration.

I knew that I was starting to sound a bit affected, but I couldn't go back now. Not now that I had shown that I could speak French quite well.

Every time Binky approached the net to deliver another of his talks, my mind would wander. Is he aware that he pronounces the French words that way? How would 'Binky' sound in French? My guess was that it would be pronounced 'Bonkee'. Perhaps I should say 'Thank you for le lesson, Bonkee.' It was becoming increasingly difficult to concentrate.

Somehow I managed to survive my introduction to

the game and graduate to actually playing against other people who had also discovered the mysterious, cloaked world of real tennis. Having used a club racket until now, I felt it was time to commit and buy my own, which at some considerable expense I did.

My first game was against Susan. She was a retired engineer and flew light aircraft for a hobby when she wasn't thrashing me at real tennis. I was going to tell you about our match, but now I've spoilt it by telling you the result. Susan had a friend called Gabriella who came and watched, clapping whenever she scored.

A week later I was set up to play against Robert. It turned out that Robert's right arm was missing. (Obviously Robert knew already. It's just that that was the first thing I noticed about him.) I was so anxious not to patronize Robert by deliberately losing that I resolved to play as well as I could. If this was a proper story, he would have beaten me. I was going to say 'hands-down', but you know what I mean.

As it happens, after not very long at all, I beat him easily. The fact is that he really wasn't very good at it, which surprised me because, ironically, my expectations had been raised by his disability. As soon as I met him and saw his one arm I thought that he would obviously be exceptionally good even though he had this problem. But, not to put too fine a point on it, poor old Robert was useless.

Anyway, it made me feel uncomfortable, and the

worst thing is that Robert seemed really crushed. He looked at me as if to imply that I should have let him win, considering he only had one arm, etc. I was gracious about it. I said well tried and let's play again some time, but Robert was so despondent in defeat that all he could do was grunt. It left a bad taste in the mouth.

With only twenty-five courts in the UK and forty-five worldwide, finding people to play against isn't that easy. Robert disappeared from the scene after that game. I asked about him but nobody knew anything. At least that's what they said. I was starting to get the feeling that word had got around about how I had broken brave Robert's spirit and that he needed protecting from me, the bully-boy of real tennis.

'What? Jack beat him?' people were saying. 'What's the matter with Jack anyway? What's he trying to prove? Everyone lets Robert win. He's only got one arm, for Chrissakes.'

When I bumped into Susan and Gabriella having a beer in the club bar, they acted in a slightly hostile manner, which just confirmed matters. Even Binky seemed a little insouciant. Definitely un peu non-chalant towards moi.

I played one or two more matches after the Robert incident, but my fondness for the game had peaked. I was never going to fit in with the likes of half-French Binky, one-armed Robert or stunt-flyer Susan. My days in the cloistered world of real tennis were over, and I knew it. The stupid-shaped racket tilts at me quizzically from the umbrella stand in our hall, reminding me, each time I leave the house, of yet another failed adventure.

Taking up an obscure, near-obsolete sport is not a great idea. Regardless of how much you like it, it is a waste of time. Perhaps I should have realized that and have only myself to blame. As it is, I spent a fair amount of my children's inheritance trying to learn a skill that is enjoyed by so few people that a game of doubles pretty much amounts to an international convention.

You might as well go to night-school and study A-level Welsh, or buy a village post-office as a long-term investment.

33

It was 1986 and, having abandoned the idea of becoming a market-research mogul, I had reluctantly returned to being a waiter, this time at a restaurant called Jakes in Fulham. I was sharing a flat with Alice, my latest girlfriend, an out-of-work actress who also worked there. The flat was a rental that Alice had acquired before she met me, so it always felt more like hers, not that anyone would have wanted to own it. We had a mattress on the floor and kept our clothes in bin-liners to protect them from the damp lino.

Situated between the six-lane section of the Talgarth Road at the front and the railway lines at the back, it was the noisiest place I had ever stayed. To compound matters, the guy upstairs was a keen amateur rock drummer who was clearly convinced by the theory that practice would one day make perfect. Until then, he was going to bash away as though his mother's life depended on it. Sometimes at night I'd close my eyes, trying to sleep, and all I could think of was that someone had wound up a giant version of one of those tin monkeys and left it up there.

In the centre of the flat was a windowless bathroom, which was the only quiet room in the place. Next to that, to the rear and overlooking the Tube trains as they trundled into Baron's Court, were a small galley kitchen and Daniel's room.

Daniel, at the time, managed Jakes. He had trained as a ballet dancer in San Francisco, was half French, half American, and had decided to eschew any further training in favour of the restaurant bohemia that he had been drawn to as a student. His great gift was the joy that he got from looking after people. Customers loved his wild, camp good looks and witty banter, but also his attention to detail and natural ability to combine efficiency with fun. Everybody who was lucky enough to work with him had much to learn, not just about waiting, but how to enjoy life. I wish I'd paid more attention.

His flaw was a generosity that compelled him to pour free drinks for regulars, making him popular with them, but less so with the owners, Michael and Anthony.

Most of the waiters in that restaurant were flamboyantly gay. In the mornings, one of them, Seb, would pass the time telling me and anyone within earshot stories of his eye-watering nightlife. He was pathologically promiscuous, taking different lovers every night of the week, usually having met them in one of the notorious pubs in Earl's Court, just up the road. The details of these encounters were completely porno-graphic and don't bear repeating, mainly because in print they could never be as amusing or disgusting as when Seb was recounting them.

Sometimes, while the rest of us busily set the tables and polished glasses, Seb would provide entertainment, going through the alphabet listing the men he could remember having sex with.

'Three Andrews, one Angus, an Adam, no, two Adams, Aaron, he was nice, Alfie, married, oh another Andrew, Alan. I've had loads of Alans, for some reason. I don't think anyone called Alan is straight, do you, Jackie?'

That's what he called me. I didn't mind at all and found it preferable to 'sister', another nickname he was fond of.

At other times he'd pull his T-shirt off and wrap one of the tablecloths around him like a strapless ballgown and stand in the window impersonating Shirley Bassey, singing 'Big Spender' for passers-by.

But one day, Seb just upped and left, having worked there for five years. He claimed to be in love with a KLM air steward, Adelhelm (a first in the As, which struck Seb as portentous), whom he'd met on a recent flight to Amsterdam. He was going there to live with him and possibly retrain as a flight attendant.

Knowing his track-record for relationships, I don't think any of us thought that this was a plan destined for success, but Seb was hugely missed when he went. Often we would tell each other stories of his antics.

They were not innocent times, the eighties, but they were ignorant. I don't know what happened to Seb and can only hope that he slipped through the net that was beginning to close in on a good many of his friends.

Often, the restaurant would have stag parties in the basement. These were usually mad and messy affairs but the service charge would boost our tips considerably, which meant that we relished the business. That is, unless the revellers became uncontrollably drunk. It's one thing clearing up a merrily flung meringue, but splattered puke was beyond a joke. Acting quite autonomously, I created a Vomit Clause on the booking slip that allowed me to charge huge amounts for dealing with any incident involving sick.

A typical stag involved strippers who would arrive at around ten p.m. and perform for the men, who were, of course, well drunk by then. The routines were usually pretty corny but always provoked salacious roars of approval as each garment came off. Diners in the more sedate upstairs room would wonder what the noise was. So long as they didn't wander down there looking for the loos, it didn't matter.

The girls would often arrive and work in pairs. They were coldly businesslike and dismissive of any of the staff, other than Daniel or whoever was managing. Maybe they found it easier to block out as much human interaction as possible to make everything feel less real. They would go to our locker-room to change, and emerge in the gaudy circus-wear of their act, smelling of the freshly applied baby-lotion that made their glabrous skin glow in the candlelight. Now they were flirty and gregarious, they were sexual, signalling their illusive availability. They were in character.

On the back stairs they would drink red wine, leaving rich lipstick kisses on the rim of the glass, and smoke a cigarette, treading it into the floor with a sequinned shoe when they heard their cue music starting up. I liked that atmosphere. It felt like being backstage, part of a show.

A really clever stripper could control the room from the moment she went on. She had an instinct for timing and attitude that would create an atmosphere of mesmerized respect. She was to be idolized, and the men behaved protectively towards her, becoming childishly doting as she toyed with their tipsiness and excitement until the moment when the music finished and she could slip away.

More often it would be a less restrained affair. The inebriated party-goers would lose all their inhibitions and the women would find themselves fending off their drunken gropes.

But there were occasions when a deal was struck.

Usually two girls would perform a more blatantly pro-
vocative set to effect maximum desire amongst the men,
who would then negotiate sex. Between them they
would have a collection which might raise several
hundred pounds so that the priapic groom-to-be could
then be led by the girls into the toilets for, well, sex
presumably.

Not that full-blown debauchery always required the
presence of a professional. One Saturday night the
restaurant was fully booked, with a hen night in one
part of the basement and a stag in the other. It goes
almost without saying that they were from different
weddings, but inevitably, as the evening grew more and
more rowdy, the two began to merge until it was one big
fraternizing party.

A game of forfeits spread among the guests, each
participant seeming to raise the stakes so that the
challenges quickly advanced in luridness from kisses to
snogs, gropes and further.

Each time I went through the room to get to the
kitchen, the atmosphere had become more charged;
until one of the waitresses said to me, as I waited at the
pass for an order, that I should take a look at what was
going on.

Basically, matters had progressed to such an extent
that the bride-to-be was now, as the tabloids so
delicately put it, 'performing a sex act' on the groom-to-
be while everybody cheered them along.

This would be merely a sordid detail added to my memoir to titillate and entertain any unsavoury types whose hands this book might fall into, were it not for an interesting footnote.

Some time later, I was at a New Year's party at a friend's house. Queuing for the buffet, I got chatting to a talkative fellow called Owen who worked in the City. He was telling me what a great Christmas he'd had in Val d'Isère, but that he couldn't go again at Easter as he was going to St Lucia to do some sort of scuba-diving course. Suffice it to say that in no time at all, he'd made my life seem very boring indeed. But it was about to brighten up considerably. Because at that moment he was joined by his wife, who looked me up and down and said, in a kind of sneering way, 'Do I know you? Haven't I seen you somewhere or other?'

'Quite possibly,' I was able to say, adding helpfully, 'I was a waiter at your hen party.'

34

ALICE SUGGESTED A HOLIDAY. Her brother had rented a small house in Lindos and was happy for us to chip in and share. It had probably been three years since I'd taken a proper break. My life had been a constant stream of menial jobs, almost always with no time off in between.

Everything about the Mediterranean is seductive. We hired a motorbike and travelled around a little, but in fact its best use was for accessing the quieter beaches a mile or so down the coast. I shouldn't romanticize the place. I know that, even then, Lindos was touristy and in many ways quite tacky. During the day it was less obvious: the place looked like a busy fishing town with its tiers of whitewashed villas rising from the beach up the steep hillside. Apart from the sunbathers and children playing in the water, it showed few outward signs of being a place that had evolved over a short time into a thriving holiday location.

In the evenings, as darkness fell, it was a different story. Those quaint whitewashed villas became luminous with the lurid floodlights of a hundred night-clubs as their DJs obliterated the contented cicada chorus with the muffled boomy rhythms of their Bose speakers and microphoned implorings to have a good time. The sloping cobbled lanes seemed to be brimming with pissed Brummie girls and Essex boys, high on cheap cold beer and sweet cocktails, staggering off to the next bar.

It was probably our third day before I realized that the early mornings were so quiet because most of the town's visitors were sleeping off hangovers. At around two o'clock they would start to surface. Shutters would open hesitantly and gradually they would emerge, shorted and flip-flopped, for an afternoon down on the baking sand, burning, stretched out on a towel with an airport novel and Piz Buin, before hitting the nightlife again.

Soon after we arrived, I became aware from various conversations with bartenders and waiters that a film was due to be made in and around Lindos. They were advertising for stand-ins. This, I later found out, is somebody who literally stands in for an actor whilst the camera crew do all their measuring and rehearse their shot. Out of curiosity I went along to the production office and, before I knew it, found myself being interviewed.

If nothing else, I was a good interviewee. The man who spoke to me said they needed a stand-in for the lead male, an actor called Kenneth Branagh.

'You don't need any experience, but you do need to be the same height as Ken. He's five foot ten. How tall are you?'

'I'm five foot ten as well,' I said. And that is true if you allow a two-inch margin of error, which is hardly anything and only reasonable. Besides, I thought, there's a fair chance that this Branagh bloke is lying about his height too.

So the job was mine. Work would begin a day after I was due to fly home and would continue for ten weeks, during which I would be needed on set all the time. Having booked the cheapest possible deal, I was unable to transfer my flight, but didn't worry too much about that. What I needed was to find some accommodation, which involved going round the various holiday reps' offices and asking if they could help. In the end, someone had an empty room that I could have for the first week at least, so I went with that. Alice returned to England at the end of our holiday and I began my assignment the next day.

The work was un-taxing. Just a matter of watching the scene being rehearsed, remembering what Branagh did and then copying it while he went off to change, get made-up or just sit around. I would stand, kneel or sit, as the focus-puller drew out his tape-measure and made careful notes, calculating how the required shot could be achieved, then marking the small white wheel on the side of the camera with various gaugings so that, during action, he could studiously pull different focus settings, leaving the camera-operator free to concentrate on his frame.

I was fortunate that the director of photography, and therefore the person in overall charge of the lighting and camera-work, was Chris Menges. Over the ensuing weeks I learnt from people of his extraordinary career and great reputation in cinema, which at that point included *Kes* and *The Killing Fields*, which he had just completed. Fortunate because his gentle authority had a calming influence on all around him and seemed to create a good working atmosphere.

I soon expanded my brief and helped with whatever I could. There was always gear to be carried, for instance, but mostly I usurped the incompetent runner by fetching drinks and snacks for the artists, and generally became absorbed into the daily rituals of the set.

Often I would be needed to help hold up traffic so that a shot could be completed without cars passing through the background. It wasn't long before I noticed that locals, with their tractors, towing vegetables to market, delivering goods in their trucks or going about their business in their cars, were always happy to oblige by waiting and switching off the engine for a minute or two. After a couple of rows with bolshie Englanders protesting their right to enjoy themselves without being stopped in the road, I suggested to the production manager that it would be better to adopt a policy of-letting holiday-makers pass. Though wildly discriminatory, it was successful and so my range of duties expanded.

The movie, as yet untitled but later called *High Season*, was a comedy adventure of sorts. It has to be said that it was a turkey, but for me this was a magical time. It felt as though I was waking up.

It had a good cast. Alongside Kenneth Branagh were Jacqueline Bisset and Lesley Manville, James Fox and Sebastian Shaw. Also starring was the magnificent Robert Stephens, who, as far as anyone could tell, wasn't sober for a single minute of his time there.

Most tricky were the night shoots, which couldn't begin until two in the morning when even the night-clubs were obliged to be quiet. Stephens would be called from his villa at eleven or twelve in the evening and would arrive on set high as a kite. The best strategy seemed to be to sit him down with a coffee and hope that he would be patient until he was required.

As one particularly quiet and fragile scene was being shot on the roof terrace of an old villa, Stephens, who wasn't in the scene, looked on quietly from his deckchair in the shadows behind the camera, dormant like a subdued beast. From the corner of my eye I noticed one of the Greek technicians silently offer him a cigarette, which he accepted, pulling it from its packet without a sound.

The scene, a difficult and sensitive one, was finally going well after several aborted takes and a great deal of anxious discussion between each one. Everyone held their breath as the dialogue rolled out faultlessly, the actors hit their marks and the camera glided noiselessly on its tracks.

Stephens held the unlit cigarette under his nose to smell the tobacco. Clearly alerted by its unfamiliar scent he looked at it quizzically. Realizing it was an obscure Greek brand of dubious quality, he threw it on the ground.

'FUCK OFF!' he screamed at the man who had given it to him.

Branagh and Manville almost jumped, as if transported violently from the moment that they had so painstakingly created.

'Cut,' called the director wearily.

'Sorry,' slurred a contrite Stephens. 'Sorry, everybody. Sorry, Ken. Lesley, so sorry, darling.'

It was decided that it would be better to abandon any hope of using Stephens that night and I was chosen to escort him back to his villa. I had volunteered to do so, my years of restaurant experience having taught me about handling the worse-for-wear. Even drunk, he was great company, swaying about, reciting long pieces of Shakespeare and telling stories of life on the stage. (I've since worked with a number of actors who worked with him, and from what they told me about his drinking I'm amazed that he could remember anything at all.)

'What are you going to do with yourself?' he asked without warning.

'I think I want to act,' I replied. A pretty brave admission, looking back, and one that surprised me as much as him.

'Act?'

'Yes. I want to perform. To be on stage.'

'Sit down,' urged the drinker.

And so we sat in the middle of one of Lindos's myriad cobbled lanes which stretch down through the little town to the sea-front like the veins of a withered hand, and talked for an hour or so. Drunk as he was, he was still lucid. Besides, it was hard to tell where the drunkenness ended and the theatricality began. Asking me whether I'd 'studied', before I could answer he pronounced, 'Chekhov. You must do Chekhov. Dear boy, it is the blood of theatre.'

'Should I go to drama school?' I asked.

He shrugged. 'Doesn't matter. Come and work for me. I'm doing *Vanya* when I get back to London. I'll give you a job. Call me. You'll be good, I can tell these things. You've got the face for it. I'm right, you know. You'll work hard, like everybody does, but you'll be good. I can see.'

Knowing that he was talking in his cups, I took this

with a pinch of salt and thanked him. He was insistent, however, telling me where he'd be rehearsing, making me note his phone number and saying that I was to telephone him 'as soon as I get away from this fucking awful film. Christ, what a fuck-up.'

Laughing all the way, he demolished the script, hamming up each quote and ending each line with a raspberry of derision or imploring the heavens in his gravelly, soulful voice, as if playing to an invisible audience, 'For the love of God, what utter shit.' He was hilarious, and I knew that the next day he wouldn't remember any of it.

I was right. When I finally returned from Lindos, knowing full well that his offer would come to nothing, I nevertheless rang the number he had given me and was told by the woman who answered that Robert was not able to help. I don't blame him one bit and remain grateful for the generous encouragement he gave me that night. His words stayed with me, as does the memory of the time I spent in his company.

Having returned to England, finding myself back at Jakes, back on the treadmill, I realized that I had changed and that I would no longer be content to drift without direction. But things have a habit of getting worse before they get better.

35

Suffering from an uncharacteristic moment of enthusiasm, I signed up for juggling lessons at the City Lit in Covent Garden. I went to a few, but quickly decided that I didn't like it. The only remotely entertaining thing about juggling is when it goes wrong, and I could already do that.

A lot of the other students were amateur dropouts hoping to find a point to their lives and an excuse to go to festivals for ever, or they were disappointed forty-somethings trying to reinvent themselves in some way. I don't mean that disparagingly, but learning to throw beanbags around isn't ultimately going to brighten up your life, or anybody else's.

Marion was an example. Her partner had left her after a twelve-year relationship which had produced one child, Josh. Now that Josh was five, she was having some me-time. I only went for a month or so, but over that period alone Marion changed from frumpy dumpee into a dyed-haired, patchouli-smelling trainee busker with an annoying tendency to start crying in the middle of a conversation. In the fourth week, despite unceasing practice, she still struggled to keep her third ball airborne for more than two throws. All I said was that she should think about the diabolo instead.

Boo hoo. 'I'm a failure, everyone thinks so.'

It was the final straw. I'd wasted enough time hanging around with these types, learning their useless and impractical skills. Decisive action was needed. I switched to Unicycle Class.

It was attended by two others. One of them, Stuart, was a self-styled eccentric who had decided that the world would be a better place if he were to commute to work perched on top of one wheel. I don't know if he ever mastered the art, but suspect that he probably did. He was that kind of person – lonely. However, I very much doubt that it would have brought about the expected instantaneous joy in passers-by. Grafting flowers of enjoyment on to the dull creeping ivy of reality almost never produces the hoped-for result. Like the merry murals of a children's ward, the forced hilarity of *It's A Knockout* or Christmas decorations in an office, seeing a grown man unicycle to work somehow only worsens everything.

My sincere hope is that Stuart eventually bumped into Marion at a trapeze-for-beginners taster session, that they fell in love and realized that life is not enhanced by desperately trying to ape the seemingly carefree existence of travelling performers. Nor can you sweep away your underlying depression with a broom called 'fun'. Who knows, they might have discovered this, run away from the circus and gone to live happier lives in suburbia.

The other pupil in Unicycle Class was Graham, an embittered actor who felt that this might be some kind of breakthrough skill. That, with 'unicyclist' on his CV, directors might actually sit up and take him a little more seriously.

Nobody in Unicycle Class wanted to ask the obvious question: why? And in a way it would have been inappropriate. I don't mean this unkindly, but the fact is that Graham was a loser. He really was. He smelt of failure. Two minutes was more than enough time in his company to know that you didn't want to be in his company. He had an anger that presented as a complete absence of generosity. When Stuart spoke of his dreams and ambitions, pathetic as they were, Graham was scornful and doubted their value, as if his own chances were directly threatened by another's unconnected plans.

Yet, for all their ridiculousness, I could not bring myself to disdain my acquaintances at City Lit. As much as I felt I was different from them, I knew that I had something in common – that, like them, I was seeking something in my life that I felt was missing.

For me, the urge to perform was a persistent nuisance-caller rather than an unhinged stalker. At times I would have done anything to rid myself of its attention, to hide in normality from its quietly increasing desire.

My urge was anonymous and without form, hard to define, hard to complain about. The stalker is perhaps simpler to deal with. It demands immediate action that will propel you into changing your life for ever. My nuisance-caller allowed me to drift with no direction or firm sense of purpose, but at the same time refused to be ignored.

'Graduating' from this three months of training, I decided to try for real drama school. I applied for RADA, stood in front of the auditioners and dried. I had chosen a speech from Shaffer's *Amadeus* in which the composer Antonio Salieri rejects God and vows to destroy the boorish Mozart. From the first word, I was floundering. There is a terrible sensation that you can get on stage when it feels as though you are standing next to yourself, watching and hearing all the excruciating hesitations, fluffs, flaws, mumbles and fidgeting. The words of the piece that I thought I had memorized began to evaporate in my mind before they could be spoken, like bubbles bursting in the air as you reach out to them. I paused and switched from Salieri to Henry V with as corny and unwise a choice of monologue as it could be possible to make. My throat became parched as the man behind the desk and his assistant watched, completely expressionless. I crawled to a wounded, pathetic end and stood there awaiting judgement.

In the event, what the man behind the desk said was worse than the stinging dismissal that I was dreading. He looked up from my application, smiled sympathetically and said, 'Thank you.'

My attempts to impress at the London Academy of Music and Dramatic Arts, at the Central School of Speech and Drama and at Webber Douglas Academy of Dramatic Art were similar, if not quite as good.

The trouble is, I was crap.

Wanting an unbiased opinion, I got in touch with Lizzie, an actress and an old friend from my days in the restaurant at Covent Garden. She heard me read and confirmed my diagnosis that I was crap, but helped me to sort out the speeches and turn them into something presentable. I was persuaded to try again, this time for Mountview, a drama school in north London. Once more unto the breach.

Now I knew what to expect and, although terrified with nerves and the smarting memories of my recent flops, I was on top of the material, both the Shakespeare and the modern.

I was offered a place at Mountview, bless them, but by then, a bit like Groucho Marx and the club that he refused to join, I had decided I didn't want to attend the type of drama school that would have me as a student, so I declined.

Much of what alarmed me about the prospect of going to drama school was what I had observed at the auditions. Naturally (although it was surprising to me) there tended to be a strong emphasis on singing and dancing. This didn't sit well with me for two reasons – singing and dancing.

Instead, I attended a series of acting classes at a drama studio in north London for a few months. They were quite good, although I think it wasn't the lessons themselves so much as the sense that I was moving my life in the right direction that I found encouraging. The course was designed to give students a taster of as many different facets of professional acting as possible. Naturally, some of the coverage was perfunctory and infuriatingly vague. But I particularly loved the character work, which was over far too soon, giving way to all the song-and-dance nonsense that everyone else got excited by.

I'm sorry to report that after about a week I fell out with one tutor. Zoë refused to have me in her comedy lecture because she thought I was scowling at her. It wasn't true, not to begin with anyway, but once she'd accused me, it was hard not to look pissed off. I wondered just how unnerving I could look if I tried. Shortly afterwards, she asked me to leave the class, which I did willingly. More fool me. Who knows how things might have turned out if only I had swallowed my pride, toed the line and learnt to smile at an audience.

Actually, I fell out with two tutors. The music classes exposed my inability to sing in tune with pianos. And I do blame pianos. I'm no virtuoso guitarist, but I can play enough to provide myself with accompaniment and can achieve what I'd describe as provincial town-busker standard. Bad but passable. However, put me with a piano and I sound like a dying ox, baying and yelping his last. When I asked if we could have another instrument to sing to, Gary, the pianist, got shirty and pointed out that the West End was unlikely to abandon the piano in the near future, so I'd better get used to it.

Alright, I suppose I fell out with three tutors, if you include Richard. Significant time was devoted to acting workshops, which always ended with a sobering talk about how hard it is to get work in the industry. Richard, who turned to teaching because he'd achieved his lifelong wish to appear in a big London musical, *Guys 'n' Dolls*, said that it was a good idea to go to auditions dressed for the part.

Very reasonably, I thought, and indeed seriously, I asked if that applied for costume dramas and, say, sci-fi parts. Should I, for instance, dress up in a Space-type outfit if I found myself going up for an Isaac Asimov adaptation? Was it worth investing in a Tudor costume for Shakespeare roles? Or some wacky braces and big glasses in case children's television had a recruitment drive? I mean, I didn't relish getting on the bus like that, I explained, but if it was going to put me at an advantage over the other auditionees, then I'd be prepared to do so, certainly.

I didn't intend to make everybody smirk and titter. That was their doing. Richard looked at the ceiling, pursing his lips in a self-controlled way, and then said something along the lines that Zoë and Gary had warned him about me and qualified his suggestion by explaining that he meant that if it was the part of a businessman, put a suit on. That kind of thing.

He looked as though he could happily slap my face, so I left it at that. But I wondered if I would ever be in a classroom situation where the teacher didn't eventually end up hating me. Probably not, I thought. And it's not all my fault.

36

ALICE GOT A PART in a play about Hiroshima and was busy
with rehearsals in preparation for the Edinburgh Fringe.
I would have helped her with her lines, but the entire
thing was in Japanese so I was of no use. I know if it was
me, I'd have been making it up as I went along, but
none of the cast liked the idea, or me once I'd suggested
it.

After the relative fun of my acting course, I hit something of a slump. Back at the restaurant it was the same
old same old. Having sampled a different, more fulfilling life, it became very hard to turn my back on it and
return to the monotony of catering. Waiting on long-
drawn-out business lunches that would blur into
evening service. Frantic Saturday nights that could keep
us until three in the morning re-setting tables for
Sunday lunch so that we could get a lie-in and not have
to be back in until eleven. Week in, week out, the work
could become an endless cycle. Seb had left and now

Daniel too had gone travelling. Everybody was on the move except me, because I needed as many shifts as I could get to live on, having raided my savings to pay for the acting classes.

During the week there would be only two of us on at lunch. Usually, my new colleague was Mitchell, a traumatized, gay cathedral organist who had abandoned his hometown of Johannesburg because South Africans were so homophobic, which I might add was a surprise to nobody except Mitchell. An intellectual, essentially, he spent his free time going to recitals and art galleries, the theatre and cinema. Consequently, his conversation was reasonably uplifting. He was too intelligent to be dull, but sometimes I'd wonder what I was doing with my life, working six- and seven-day weeks, shut away in this bistro with damaged refugees of one sort or another: strippers, drifters and struggling actors. I wondered if this was to be it. I would become a career waiter like Adolfo, never quite managing to vault the confines of my circumstances. It seemed like a very real possibility, if not probability, at that time. I had nothing to fall back on: no degree, no training, no A levels even.

What I know now, and didn't know at the time, was that when you have nothing to fall back on, the only way is forwards. Of course, the other thing that I didn't know was that I was close to making a decision that would change my life for ever in ways that I could not have dreamed of.

August was looming and Alice and I discussed the idea of me travelling with her to Edinburgh and maybe helping out behind the scenes. Perhaps the atmosphere at the Fringe would be inspiring, I thought.

The Hiroshima play involved the actors talking, as I said, in Japanese, about their lives, whilst at the same time making and eventually covering the entire stage with paper houses and buildings to create the impression of a city. No prizes for guessing that the city gets destroyed at the end of Act Three. This was achieved by a bright light being shone into the audience's faces as all the cast rolled around the stage in slow motion, squashing everything. The whole city. Construction would start all over again at the beginning of the next performance.

After a couple of preview shows at arts centres in London, the cast were worried about being able to make enough buildings in the time allowed by the script, so it became necessary to have quite a number of pre-folded houses to help with the process. I offered my services, but after my comment about making up the Japanese, as well as one or two ill-judged quips about 'explosive situations' and the play being good 'but a bit flat at the end', my offer was unanimously declined. Anyway, the truth was that I really couldn't afford a three-week holiday, no matter how much I dressed it up as vocational. So, as Alice left for the Fringe with all her friends, I got on with working at the restaurant.

She didn't sound the same on the phone. The distance felt more than geographical. Calling her at the apartment she was sharing with the cast and other actors seemed intrusive. I sensed that being there was fun and taking my call wasn't. And when she phoned me it was as if a meter was running, a clock ticking, time being marked until she could reasonably say goodbye and go. I could hear, in her cracked, short answers, the sound of broken love.

Inevitably, the final conversation came. Two people talking through wire, one in an empty London flat, the other sitting on the busy stairs of temporary digs. Four hundred miles apart and talking about needing more space. The words were awkwardly handed over, like a child surrendering stolen sweets. And it was finished. What a bombshell.

Sorry.

The next forty-eight hours were spent in a haze of misery. My immediate resolution was to get out of Alice's flat before she returned. I was too proud to stick around where I wasn't wanted. I rang a friend, Emma, whose house I'd lived in for a while a few months previously. Thank God the room was still available, and, more to the point, she was good enough to let me back. I'd left under a bit of a cloud last time.

Surrounded by boxes and bags of my belongings, waiting for a mate to turn up with his van and help me move, I looked around the noisy flat on the Talgarth

Road. I'd been dumped, I had a rubbish job, almost no money and absolutely no prospects to speak of. I'd hit rock bottom, and not even a very impressive one at that.

I don't know why it occurred to me in all that gloom, but I promised myself that I would now do at least one thing that I would not have done had I still been in a relationship. I took the packet of Daniel's French cigarettes that I'd helped myself to, lit one, and thought about what that might be. By the time I'd finished my smoke, I had decided.

For ages I had been meaning to visit the Comedy Store in Leicester Square.

37

I JOINED THE END of the queue that slowly shuffled forwards every few minutes down the stairs into the small foyer area where you pay. I got my ticket and went through the swing doors into the club itself. The Comedy Store was a long, low-ceilinged room with black walls and a bar to the right. Beyond that was a slightly raised seating area forming the back of the stalls. Otherwise, the room was set out with rows of red plastic chairs that curved round the small stage in the centre. The place smelt of spilt beer and last night's cigarette smoke. As it filled up with a new audience, and the atmosphere of an impending live show built, the odour of booze and fags revived itself and began to smother me.

The house-lights dimmed and the Friday-night crowd whistled and shouted in the dark as the compere, Neil Mullarkey, was introduced over the PA. He bounced on stage to lively applause and after a few well-aimed jokes about various people in the audience, introduced the first act of the night, the Brown Paper Bag Brothers, a double act comprising John Hegley and Otis Cannelloni. It was daft, surreal and very funny. For the first time I heard the intense roar of laughter that the Comedy Store audience could produce. More importantly, this was comedy that seemed to be about life as I saw it and not just a sequence of recited, second-hand jokes. So many things came together in those first few minutes. The anticipation, the surprise, the sense of jeopardy that a live show generates.

Next to be introduced was Jeremy Hardy, who stood at the microphone in a shabby cardigan. Holding a pint, he delivered a blisteringly funny twenty minutes. With stories from his childhood and withering observations on everyday life mingled with scathing satire, he had the audience eating from his hand.

Later, interviewers have been incredulous that I had been oblivious to the likes of Ben Elton and Alexei Sayle in the very early days of the Store, but when you spend most nights working in a restaurant or an underground kitchen and don't have a video recorder, you can easily miss out on everything. All work and no play made this Jack a dull boy, but suddenly something had stirred in him.

Before announcing the interval, Neil Mullarkey reminded the audience that there was a chance for open spots to try out at the end of the show and that if you fancied having a go performing in front of everyone, then to come up and see him during the break. As soon as he said this, my mind began spinning with the idea. Could I get up and have a go? How would it feel? What would I say?

I didn't have a clue, but I was filled with the overwhelming sense that these new comedians had somehow started without me and that I would put that right. As everybody else made for the bar I noticed a small group of people waiting around the dressing-room door at the far end of the room. When Mullarkey emerged he started taking their names. Obviously these were the people who wanted to get on stage and have a go.

I suddenly realized that this was the starting point if you wanted to be a comedian. I couldn't help myself, I had to get closer, hear what they were saying, find out how it all worked. Before I knew it, I was telling the guy in front of me that I was going to have a go, whilst an inner voice was screaming at me 'You what?'

As my turn to put my name forward got closer, I became more and more nervous. In that brief moment that exists between action and abortion, I turned and walked away. Infuriated by my cowardice, I looked round to see if I could change my mind but it was too late. He'd gone.

All through the interval I listened to the conversations around me and noticed how much people were talking about the acts that they'd just seen, repeating lines and discussing how funny they had been. I had come to the Comedy Store expecting a show and had been introduced to an entire scene that I was almost completely unaware of.

But now I had chickened out and hated myself for it, sitting through the second half wishing that I'd had the guts to go for it. As the final act of the night finished, Mullarkey came back on and introduced the first of the novices. As far as I could tell, they were a mix of painfully naive show-offs, university revue players and actors in search of work that would count towards their Equity Card. Their offerings were usually prop-based and involved wearing stupid clothes. Potentially, there's nothing wrong with that, but even then I could see that in the context of what is basically an audition, props and costume could easily expose a vulnerability. The only thing worse than a joke that doesn't work is being left standing on stage wearing that joke for the rest of your act.

I remember one of them wearing a raincoat and a hat made from a kitchen colander with plastic flowers sprouting from it. Dismally wacky. One after another, they were introduced, and left the stage a minute or two later to a sympathetic ripple of clapping, having achieved at best the occasional laugh, and only then for the wrong reasons. If that was the worst that could happen, what did I have to lose by coming back another day and having a go? I was annoyed with myself for not having put my name on that list.

As the show finally ended and the audience got up to leave, I had an increasing sense of regret that I had let that chance slip by. I decided to try and put it right. As the room thinned out, I plucked up the courage to ask the guy at the front desk when the next open spot would be.

'You can come back and do the late show if you're mad enough,' he said.

I hadn't appreciated that there would be a second show that night, starting just after eleven o'clock. To the man's great surprise – and mine, I might add – I bought my ticket there and then, saying that I wanted to go on, if I could.

'Fine,' he said, scribbling my name down. 'See you at eleven. You have to be here before the show starts.'

As we spoke, one of the try-outs I'd just seen was leaving, climbing the stairs and being comforted by her friend. I did feel sorry for her, but my God she had been terrible.

I made a mental note of how embarrassing it would be if I did really badly, to have to exit the building by walking the entire length of the room through the milling crowd with people pointing and saying, 'Look, that's him, that one who thought he was funny but wasn't.' My plan was to have my motorcycle helmet close at hand, so that if things got really sticky I could put it on and escape unrecognized by making out that I'd just delivered a pizza to the dressing room.

For an hour or so I wandered around the West End, taking in the night-life. I was desperately trying to think of something funny to say when my turn came to step on stage. Damn, why had I got myself into this? And yet something was telling me not to run away. My stomach was in knots. It felt like I was in a bad dream. I had, for some bizarre reason, put my name down to perform at the Comedy Store when I didn't have a single thing to say, let alone an act. It's the kind of thing that you wake up from, sweating, heart thumping, hugely relieved to realize that it was just a nightmare.

I couldn't think straight. Nothing remotely comedic came to mind, and worse, the mingling smells of the burger stalls in Leicester Square and the strong whiff of rich garlicky food from Chinatown was making me feel sick. I sipped water and paced around like a vagrant, racking my blank mind for something funny to say.

I thought of opening with 'It's like Piccadilly Circus out there.' A bit corny maybe, so I dismissed it. In hindsight it would have been a reasonable line to use. I was subsequently to discover that most comedians who do the Store think of it at some stage. Other lines occurred to me, but I couldn't settle on any decision. I remembered a great joke but somehow it seemed totally wrong. I felt that the whole point of the Comedy Store was to show new comedy and new writing, not just re-worked gags. Not that that was helping me now.

The clock ticked away, each minute seeming to drag me nearer and nearer to my fate. Eventually, I could put it off no longer. The audience had gone in and the show would be starting any time now. Of course, it wouldn't have mattered a jot had I not returned. It's not like I would have been missed. But as far as I was concerned, act or no act (and as I was all too aware, it was the latter), I was due on stage.

The late show at the Comedy Store is a different creature. The audience had already had a full night out and should have been heading home by now. Instead, intent on prolonging the drunken fun of it all, they had made their way here. The atmosphere was different. The excitement of the audience was volatile and uneasy. They were delirious at the outset, but were swift to heckle if not pleased with what they were getting.

The line-up had changed a little. The Brown Paper Bags closed the first half triumphantly, but the opening act had been a comic who wasn't on the earlier show. He struggled to get the crowd's fickle attention and, when he did, struggled to make them laugh. All too often, a punchline was greeted with a sarcastic 'Ha ha ha,' but he just about won their approval by the time he left the stage.

Before the interval, the same announcement was made for those wishing to do an open spot. The very

mention of it brought a great gladiatorial roar of anticipation from the crowd. By any sane standards I should
have slipped out at that point and never gone back, but
I was possessed by the urge to get on that stage.
Knowing how it had felt earlier to renege, I could allow
myself no alternative.

As the second half of the show began, the tone of
the crowd became even more unpredictable. I could
hardly bear to watch. I made my way to the toilets.
Sitting in the cubicle, doubled up with gastric spasms, I
could hear the succession of drunken revellers talking as
they peed and burped away, cursing the previous act
and swearing to give the next one a hard time. It didn't
help my nerves.

Eventually I was able to go back into the room just
as Mark Steel stepped on to the stage. Within moments
he had conquered the audience with an assured pro-
fessionalism and devastating treatment of the first few
hecklers who were stupid enough to challenge his
authority. He was topping the bill and he was storming
it, the place rocking with great explosions of laughter.
Back to the toilet.

As the official show drew to a close, I approached
Neil Mullarkey. I'd already spoken to him earlier to
make sure that he had me on his list. He was very
friendly, but by that point I was practically paralysed
with nerves and when he asked me to confirm my name
I could hardly utter the words 'Jack Dee'.

There was a brief hiatus as much of the audience filed out. It was one in the morning and, I'll admit, it was a relief that so many were leaving. Unfortunately, those left were the ones who were no longer able to stand or who just hadn't quite had their fill of booing and shouting, deprived by Mark Steel's winning performance.

So we few try-outs assembled near the side of the stage to await our turn.

The bloke who went on first instantly annoyed the audience with such a feeble joke that I'm embarrassed that I still recall it. He stepped up to the mic and said, 'Right. Let's get one thing straight.' Then he stuck his leg out rigidly and said, 'There, that's quite straight, isn't it?'

'Fuck off!' screamed at least nine people from the remaining audience. But he didn't. Instead he got some clothes pegs out and started clipping bits of screwed-up paper to the microphone cable and asked, 'Have you ever noticed how everything on cable is rubbish?'

'You're fucking rubbish. Fuck off!' came the response, followed by a wave of derisive laughter from all.

Undeterred, he came back with 'So, anyone here from north London?'

Silence. A long, uncomfortable, deliberate, concerted silence. Without conferring or forewarning, the room had made a decision of its own not to oblige, but to leave the 'entertainer' dangling in the spotlight. Lenny Bruce once said, 'The audience is a genius,' which until that moment I hadn't fully understood.

The conspiracy of silence continued.

'No? Surely someone. Come on now. Who's from north London?'

As he floundered over this, a chant that began as a lowly murmur developed into an outraged and truly hateful insistence: 'Off, off, off, OFF, OFF, OFF, OFF, OFF, OFF, OFF, OFF, OFF, OFF, OFF, OFF, OFF, OFF, OFF,' it went, as feet were stamping and the thunder of venomous rage rolled around the room.

The unknown comic actually had the balls to say, quite chirpily and in a manner that suggested a complete inability to learn from this experience, 'Alright, have it your way. Thank you for your time. Enjoy the rest of the show. Cheerio.'

Next up were two girls. I can understand the temptation to form a double act. You have company on stage, somebody to share the burden or maybe bail you out of a tricky situation. More importantly, there is the promise of a stage alchemy which transcends the boundaries of a solo performer. The potential for a duo who can create and act out comedic scenes whilst engaging the audience is, of course, enormous. Sadly, none of this was accessed by the two girls. Their comedy gambit was to produce a packet of Tampax and throw the contents into the audience. This was done in the absence of any explanation or accompanying joke, but instead in the desperate hope that it would somehow produce laughter.

The booing started from the back of the half-empty room and several of the tampons were thrown back at them. One of the girls yelled into the microphone something about the audience being a bunch of yuppies, which got derisory shouts of approval from the very people it was supposed to sting.

Chaotically, they rambled on, attempting a sketch involving two posh mothers talking about their children. Each line missed its target and vaporized into the hateful atmosphere that now existed.

'You're not funny! Fuck off!' screamed someone from the darkness.

'Bring the last bloke back,' shouted another, causing a tidal wave of mocking laughter.

On they struggled with their dismal skit, now ignored and trying to be heard above the swelling jeers.

I wasn't enjoying their failure. They didn't deserve success, or even still to be on the stage, but more to the point, these two were messing it up for me. By the time I got on, the audience would be like a pack of salivating hounds, closing in on their quarry. Not that I was in a position to be confident of my own credentials. I was about to be summoned into the very same arena, having never done it before in my life and still not knowing what the hell I would do or say when I got up there.

Eventually they conceded defeat and left, abandoning all dignity as they gathered up the failed props that were strewn around the stage. I wish I were a big enough man to say that I felt sorry for them, but I was too busy working out how I could escape the building in the next twenty seconds.

Knowing I was next on, I positioned myself so that I would be able to get on (and off) the stage as fast as possible. I'd noticed that there was always a short ripple of applause upon the introduction, no matter how inexperienced the act, but that the performers created an unnecessary problem for themselves by not getting to the centre of the stage quickly enough, thereby losing that initial energy of expectation that exists when anybody walks on stage with a sense of purpose. It was just a hunch, but I had decided that to get to the microphone before that sprinkling of support died away would be an advantage.

All I had to do now was figure out what to say. In my mind I had rehearsed a dozen ideas, but none of them gave me any confidence. I thought of jokes that I liked but somehow felt sure that just telling a joke, the kind you would tell to your mates, would be a mistake.

Maybe the best thing would be to say that I was here on work experience and wanted to see what it would feel like to be a tosser. At least head into it and hope-fully get a laugh by owning up to being no good. But perhaps that would make the audience uncomfortable.

I had some stamps in my wallet and thought of sticking one on my forehead so I could go on saying I was a post impressionist. No. That was a terrible idea. Worse than those two girls.

The more I tried to think, the more lost and clueless I felt. I had less of a plan now than two hours ago when I was walking round Leicester Square.

Sorry for the flashback at this point, but here it is. When I was about twelve my older brother Dave brought home a Fairport Convention album called *Babbacombe Lee*. It's a concept album about the true-life story of the eponymous John Lee, who, wrongly accused of a murder, is sentenced to death. The night before his execution he had a strange dream that he would come to no harm and the next morning he was led to the gallows. With the leather strap biting into his wrist, the noose was tightened around his neck as the priest whispered the last rites. However, the trapdoor beneath his feet failed to open when the hangman pulled the lever. A second time, he tried and failed. Then, after Lee was removed, the doors swung open with their deathly clang. Positioned again and with the rope refastened, the executioner struck the lever, only for the apparatus to fail a third time. It's a cheerful song.

According to the story, one of the peculiar laws of

capital punishment in this country was that the death sentence was nullified should the execution fail three times. I doubt whether poor John Lee was in any fit state to speak at the time, but had he been able to, I like to think that he did so in as cocky a voice as possible, preferably with a really annoying remark as he was being led away from the gallows, like ''Ere, I think I can see what's jammin' it. Oh well, too late now. See ya.'

In an act of consummate Victorian compassion, the then Home Secretary commuted his sentence to life imprisonment. Nice one.

The story haunted me from the moment I read the sleeve notes and I became quite traumatized by the very thought of execution. I don't know if it qualifies as a phobia, as it still seems to me to be an eminently sensible dread.

Waiting for my name to be called felt like sitting in the condemned cell. It's a dramatic analogy, I know, and if you're reading this on Death Row I apologize for being insensitive, but that's honestly how it felt at the time.

Finally, the appalling moment arrived when Mullarkey came to the end of his link, looked at a note in his hand to remind himself of my name and said, 'Please welcome Jack Dee.'

Trusting the autopilot that you have to rely on at such moments, I let my legs walk me on to the stage. As planned, I reached the microphone before silence fell and I had to speak.

About three feet in front of my face, suspended from the ceiling, were two spotlights that obliterated the rest of the room so that all I could see were the powerful lamps, burning into my squinting eyes.

'Hello,' I said, immediately startled by my own amplified voice. I gathered my senses as much as I could and was pleased to find that I was able to think quite clearly. The trouble was that I still didn't have a plan.

With nothing better to say, I filled the silence with a very throwaway 'It's great to be here,' delivered with complete innocence.

There was a brief pause and two or three people laughed, I guess at the perceived insincerity. Again, the audience is a genius and they were way ahead of me.

My mind went blank. I had nothing to say, but somehow I wasn't so fazed by that. As my eyes adjusted to the intense lights, the waiting faces of the audience seemed to take shape and emerge from the blinding whiteness. I looked around, slowly. As I did so, a few people tittered but nobody spoke. They were unsure if this was a deliberate part of the act. They didn't know what I would say next. Like me.

A heckler broke the moment with 'Tell us a joke.' Laughter. This is where I lose them. The game is up.

They will know that I have no jokes and no business standing there, wasting their time.

'Come on, tell us a joke.'

Without any premeditation, I just said, quite belligerently, 'No.'

And the audience laughed.

Bolstered by this, I started on the one thing that had come to me moments before stepping on stage. I had been surprised that the first of the try-outs had thought it a good idea to interact with the audience by asking a direct question like 'Anyone here from north London?' My instinct had been that that could only work if the audience felt confident in the comedian and were not worried about being drawn into his failure. But it triggered an idea.

'Anyone here from Finland?' I asked.

They sat there with expectant grins but, of course, nobody was.

I waited until it looked awkward for me and said, 'Well, that's my act buggered then.'

To my utter astonishment, this got a really good laugh. (Admittedly, you had to be there.) The audience were laughing at my joke and it felt to me like an epiphany. On stage, however, such moments are short-lived and I soon saw that I was indeed buggered. The one thing that I hadn't considered happening had just happened: it was going well and now I didn't know how to handle it.

I forget how I got myself off stage. I know I didn't top the gag about Finland and was kicking myself for not having more up my sleeve. I stepped back down into the comfortable darkness as Neil Mullarkey took the stage for a final time to say goodnight to the audience and announce who would be on next week. I felt someone pat me on the back. I thought my legs would buckle from the relief of it being over. I sat down. A man came over and asked, 'That wasn't bad. How long have you been going?'

'That was my first time,' I said.

He looked at me for a moment.

'Come back, I'll put you on again.'

'Thanks,' I said, wondering who he was, and he was gone.

As I was climbing the stairs to leave, I passed Neil Mullarkey.

'Well done,' he said genuinely. 'That was Don Ward who just spoke to you. He owns the Store.'

I love London in the early hours of the morning. Perhaps because it still always reminds me of that turning point in my life. Homeward-bound revellers and street-sweepers, the first of the delivery lorries making their drops, party-goers staggering down the road arm in arm. Night coming to an end. A new day beginning. I got to where my motorbike was parked and unlocked it. Putting my helmet on reminded me of my contingency plan to use it as a disguise so that I could leave the club without being spotted. It hadn't been needed after all. I started the engine, kicked up the stand and twisted the throttle.

Accelerating down Whitehall, I let out a long scream of exhilaration. This was it. I felt that I had found the missing piece of the jigsaw. I knew that I was going to be a stand-up.

38

I'VE NEVER BEEN TO a psychic, although I know one or two people who have. Without fail, they come away amazed that the clairvoyant has been able, with her mystic powers, to tell them so many accurate details of their lives, simply by looking at them.

But then, when I question them further, it turns out that these insights aren't so mystical after all.

'She just looked at my hand,' explains my friend, 'and said that I had a scar on my knee, and that I got it when I was a child, which is incredible because I have got a scar on my knee from when I fell over when I was eight.'

'Wow. Amazing,' I say, not wishing to spoil the moment by adding that just about everybody has scarred knees from falling over as a child. 'Did she also say that you were going on a journey this summer? A long journey to somewhere hot?' I ask.

'Yes, funnily enough she did,' says my impressed

friend, by now wondering if I too possess psychic powers.

Had I gone to a psychic back in the autumn of '86, the same clairvoyant would no doubt have told me that there was a love interest on the horizon, another stunning forecast to make about any young person. I wouldn't have believed her, dismissing it as another catch-all prediction. But, in my case, she would have been right.

Back at Jakes and much buoyed by my recent inauguration into the comedy scene, I threw myself into work again. The harder I toiled, the faster time would fly before I'd get my chance to go on stage again. The restaurant was usually busy, which also helped the evenings pass more quickly. I always enjoyed it when the last of the customers paid and left and the place was set up, made ready again for tomorrow's lunch. My final duties of the night involved restocking the wine, beers and mixers, cleaning the mighty Gaggia and polishing endless glasses as they emerged wet and glistening from the washer.

A girl, about twenty-one, very slim, brunette and attractive, came in and sat at the bar. I was sorry that we were closed and said so, but she interrupted me, saying that she hadn't come in to eat, but to meet her sister Tracy, who worked there.

Naturally, I knew Tracy well, so I poured her a drink

and we started chatting. She told me her name was Jane. I told her my name was Jack.

Jane worked as a receptionist at a hotel in Queen's Gate, a boutique hotel where one of the porters was definitely stealing from customers' luggage and the other receptionist was on the game. Jane had briefly been night manager at a large Bed & Breakfast on the Seven Sisters Road. On her first shift a man had thrown himself from a top window and was only found the next morning, dazed and crawling around in the car park. The job before that had been in a hostel for the homeless, which she left because it was so depressing. Most of the proprietor's income was from the Council, who paid him to house people, but he was incredibly mean and insisted that at breakfast they could only have half a fried egg each, so she left.

Worst of all though, she told me, was the job before that, which was in one of London's hundreds of small, grotty hotels. A man had checked in with his male lover and the next morning, when the maid couldn't open the bedroom door, Jane pushed her way in. The man was lying on the floor, dead, with his trousers round his ankles and an armchair on top of him. The armchair was arranged so that the leg of it was firmly rammed in the dead man's anus. The male lover was gone, nowhere to be seen. Jane called the police and they said she did the right thing.

Before that, she had worked in a holiday camp in

Selsey. A Pontin's type of place. She hated it and immediately got another job locally, renting a small caravan to live in, which she had loved.

I really liked Jane. She had history and attitude and an unreasonable opinion on most things and she seemed to have had almost as many crap jobs as me. But to be honest, I wasn't looking for a new relationship. I was worried that it would distract me from my ambitions in the world of comedy. When Jane rang me one lunchtime and asked if I'd like to meet for dinner that night, I found myself saying that I was too busy, maybe some other time.

'Screw you then,' she said and hung up.

I liked that. And when she stopped coming into the restaurant to meet her sister and sit and chat with me, I realized I was missing her. So a week later I called her back. Charm is a wonderful thing, I always think. I wish I had it, but at least I'm an accomplished groveller. I managed to convince her that I regretted having been so nonchalant and asked her if she still wanted to meet up.

We were, as Jane had foreseen and I hadn't, a good match. Before long we were sharing a basement flat in Redcliffe Gardens.

I quickly discovered that it was a good place to sit and write. The stone floor in the kitchen would keep me just chilled enough to concentrate and the fumes from the Calor gas heater caused sufficient nausea to stop me from falling asleep in its fuggy, warm glow.

In the weeks that followed, I returned as often as possible to the Store so that I could get on stage and try the material that I was thinking up during the day. You learn everything the hard way when you're a comedian. If a thing doesn't work, then you get booed off and are left floored and demoralized for a whole seven days before you can get back up there and have another go. Sometimes the 'spot' went well enough to maintain my hopes, but often it would end less happily. I would exit the stage with the crowd's jeers ringing in my ears, knowing that I wouldn't be able to sleep, eat or breathe properly again until I'd returned and fared better. For once, this wasn't a fad or an imaginary persona I was adopting. I had discovered something central to my being, which I knew that I could not live without.

On those occasions when my performance was good and achieved that wonderful crashing roar of an audience's laughter, it felt like being able to fly. When it went badly and my nerves got the better of me, or I was shouted into impotent submission by a determined heckler who recognized a rookie when he saw one, it was like being shot down. Sometimes one of the paid comics would give you a tip or just a supportive nod, which could be enough encouragement to build your confidence up again for the next time.

I learnt to live in that strange vortex of arrogance and diffidence that governs the comedian's psyche. You get on stage because you believe you have something that the audience doesn't, and you stay there for as long as you can convince yourself and them of it. At an early point in this process I can remember giving myself one rule: never get booed off for the same thing twice.

One Saturday night, I was introduced on stage and I opened with a line that I'd been nursing all week. The line was 'I don't usually work here . . . I'm a stunt double on the Sooty Show but I'm giving it a rest 'cos I've got a sore arse.' I felt sure it would get a laugh and was looking forward to trying it.

I got to the mic and surveyed the room, then said, 'I don't usually work here . . .'

And someone just shouted, 'Well, why don't you fuck off then?'

Which, twenty-five years later, I'm man enough to admit was a reasonably good heckle. The audience, however, were quicker to recognize its quality and it brought the roof down. I was done for. Nothing I could say was even audible. I mumbled and stumbled, trying to win them back, but I was done for. Why should the audience give this unknown a second chance? I could sense the compere edging closer to the side of the stage, a sure sign that this week's long-awaited go was about to end ignominiously.

The lesson? Don't leave a pause in your first joke like that again. At least not with such a bloodthirsty crowd. It was like setting up my own heckle. Get your first line in quickly, with confidence, so that they know that you have the authority to stand there.

Nick Revell, a headliner at the time, approached me after a particularly savage mauling. I was in the back room, licking my wounds, reeling from the shock.

'You know what you did wrong?' he said.

'No,' I replied, indignant that he felt it had been my fault. I'd been heckled, I'd answered back, and the room had turned on me like a pack of hyenas. That makes it their fault for being arseholes as far as my analysis went.

'You were aggressive. The guy was a wanker, but with your face, if you get genuinely aggressive, you look threatening and the audience won't have that.'

Nick was right, and although I had many more terrible experiences doing those midnight open-spots, I made sure that my responses to any jibes from the audience remained humorous rather than defensive or offensive. It was an important change in my approach and helped to reduce my natural dread of heckling, so freeing me to concentrate on my delivery and material.

For several months, this was my life, hanging around, watching and learning from the good comedians and going on whenever I could. Often my fellow try-outs would suffer horrible defeats on stage and come off vowing never to return. Others might do better and make me realize how much work I had to do if I was to succeed. It was like being at school and we were that year's intake. Mark Lamarr was in the same year, as were Lee Evans, Jo Brand, Hattie Hayridge,

Brenda Gilhooly, Frank Skinner, David Baddiel, Eddie Izzard and Sean Hughes. If we were the fresh intake and I'm allowed to stretch the analogy, the established comedians were like the upper sixth, somehow so sophisticated and accomplished. And yet their presence served as a reminder that I was now on that ladder myself and might, just might, get to be up there one day, as one of the comedians chalked up on the sandwich board outside the front entrance in Leicester Square. Genuinely, without a moment's thought of fame or fortune, what I wanted more than anything during that time was to have my name written on that blackboard. I wanted to be listed with the comics that I watched and admired so much. I wanted to be one of them. That was my new burning ambition.

Soul-destroying knock-outs could soon be assuaged by a promising minute at the late show. That minute would become three minutes the next weekend. Then such a triumph could be built upon and extended so that it formed the core of what was emerging as my first 'set'. With gags that could be relied upon to work (almost) consistently, surely I was on my way to achieving my goal and having my name written up beneath the likes of Arnold Brown, Arthur Smith, Lee Cornes, Norman Lovett, Jerry Sadowitz, Jeremy Hardy, Mark Steel, Paul Merton and so many others.

One night Brenda Gilhooly asked me which other clubs I was doing. I know that it sounds implausible, but I really had no idea that there were any other clubs. She thought this was hilarious and told me to buy *Time Out*, London's listings magazine (there was also *City Limits*, which no longer exists), and take a look. She was right. London had at least ten other comedy clubs. I could maybe approach them as well and try my stuff there.

This was quite a breakthrough. I got myself a copy, went to a phone box with a pocketful of coins and worked my way through the various clubs, most of which were rooms above pubs, just as the Comedy Store had once been.

Open-spots became possible and I often found the atmosphere in these places much gentler, realizing that, if anything, I had had a baptism of fire when I first stepped on stage that night at the Store.

Jane accompanied me to some of these gigs, giving feedback from her perspective. I didn't always welcome it. I was too busy beating myself up over a gag that I'd forgotten to do or a heckle that threw me off balance. Nevertheless, I think that we both now appreciate how useful it is in our marriage (sorry, I forgot to mention we got married and had four kids) that we met and got to know each other during this hiatus between waiting and fame. No pun intended.

On a more mundane note, I still needed an income, but wanted a change of scenery from Jakes. More importantly, I needed a job that would allow me some flexibility so that I could remain focused on my writing and open-spots. So I took a daytime job in a basement bar called Corks, just off Oxford Street, leaving evenings free to go off and explore these little clubs and get my face known.

But getting gigs was a slow process and after a few months I was starting to become dispirited. A pattern was emerging of going along to a club, doing a successful five or ten minutes, but then not getting the longed-for paid gig. I began to suspect that one or two of the less scrupulous 'owners' of clubs were taking advantage of newcomers by asking them to do endless unpaid performances because it obviously suited them. Also, there was a problem that certain clubs were niche-driven and therefore hard to infiltrate.

Nonetheless, for now the task was to get as much experience under my belt as possible. Thanks to comedy, my attitude to life had a new value. It was almost as if I had been writing jokes without realizing it. A good observation had the potential to be turned into something that would make an audience laugh. In that respect, I was developing an instinct for what would and wouldn't work on stage.

At school I always had an intuitive feel for what joke would make which friend laugh the most. Though not aware of it at the time, I was in the habit of indexing people according to their sense of humour. Now I was becoming conscious of an emerging sensibility for comedy on a larger scale.

But there was a big problem. While the material was alright, I sensed that my performances were falling short of the mark. I've always believed that real comedy is about what happens between the jokes; that special ingredient that has the audience chuckling before you open your mouth and laughing beyond the content of your act. Perhaps, subliminally, I was remembering my experience as a ventriloquist's dummy on my brother's knee, when the actual jokes were the last thing that mattered. I got more and more frustrated that the success of each gig that I did corresponded precisely to how good the material was and nothing else. It was as if it wouldn't have mattered who was on stage delivering it. I began to think that I might as well phone the jokes in, or at least pursue the idea of writing comedy, perhaps for other comedians to do. It was a depressing conclusion considering my initial passion, but I just couldn't stand the thought of being so mediocre.

I told Jane that I was thinking of giving it all up and trying to write for a living instead. She was against it and said that, considering how hard I had worked to get the four bookings that I had left in my diary, I should go along and do them anyway. Reluctantly I agreed, although had it been down to me alone, remembering how low I had suddenly become, I think I would have rung and cancelled.

In fact, by the time I did the last of these short spots, I'd had it with the whole stand-up thing. All it had come down to was: get on stage, tell a joke, get a laugh, joke, laugh, joke, laugh, you've been a great audience, good-night.

It may sound unreasonable for a comedian to complain about the audience laughing at his jokes, but for me it was always supposed to be about so much more than that. I'd once heard an American say, 'A comic says funny things, a comedian says things funny,' and that had sort of stuck. I, personally, was not being funny for the audience, even if the gags were OK. It was sad, because I had really got a sense of that talent when I first started, but somehow I'd lost it. Perhaps it had never been there in the first place and I had imagined it all. My mind was made up. It was definitely time to quit. Just get through tomorrow's gig and that will be that.

So with a heavy heart I turned up at the pub. There, in the window, was a pathetically cheerful sign yelling '!!!Friday night is Comedy Night. Upstairs. £2.50!!!' I've always hated exclamation marks.

I climbed the stairs and said hi to the compere, some useless tit I'd seen before and didn't like. I looked around me as the lights dimmed and the show started. This was the litmus test. Would the spotlight on the mic stand in the centre of the stage stir me from my lethargy and disillusionment?

No. I didn't want to be there and I didn't want to do the gig.

The first act died. A bloke my age embarrassing the

audience with a series of bland observations about yuppies and growing up in the seventies and Action Man figures and being on the dole. They clapped politely, but I felt like going up and kicking him. This particular club used to put the try-outs on in between the paid acts, so I was on next. The compere introduced me and on to the stage I shuffled, relieved that it was nearly all over. Just do your ten minutes one more time and then you're free to go and maybe try your hand at writing, or just go back to waiting tables. I was so pissed off to be there that I switched to auto-pilot for the first line. It was meaningless anyway.

'Good to be here. What a great comedy club,' I mumbled disingenuously.

A brief silence. And then the audience laughed.

Taken aback, I instantly realized that what I had done was exactly right. No attempt to be funny or sincere. Suddenly it was like another voice that was speaking from inside. Just keep talking. See what happens.

'I'd like to thank the compere for that introduction and the guy who was on before me. He was brilliant, wasn't he?'

The room was filling with laughter, and so it went on. I maintained the miserable attitude and the material worked better than ever before. I could do no wrong. I left the stage to huge applause and the next act really struggled, which, if you're in this business, I'm not proud to say, is always a joy to behold.

Trying to work out the reason for this unexpected triumph, I soon realized that it wasn't so much what I had done right that evening, as what I had been doing wrong for the last few months. My original instinct when I first stepped on stage at the Comedy Store was to be deadpan. It's my natural expression anyway, and I intuitively knew that it would be my best bet, comedically. But in the following weeks and months, seeing so much very good comedy and becoming more and more anxious about having to follow the professionals, I'd slipped into the (for me) bad habit of trying to appear cheerful. I cringe to think of it, but I would say a line like 'I'd like to thank the compere for that introduction and the guy who was on before me. He was brilliant, wasn't he?' as sincerely as possible, without a hint of irony or sarcasm, and think that I could ingratiate my way into the audience's affection. It had been a gradual abandoning of my natural comic asset in favour of a manufactured showbiz smarm that, for some extraordinary reason, I hadn't even noticed. With this correction to my delivery, I felt like a proper comedian: it wasn't just the jokes that were getting laughs.

Now that I had re-found my style, I was back on course. So long as I remembered to rely on my natural downbeat delivery and didn't bolt on any artifice to it, then being on stage felt completely right to me. It was where I could enter into the heightened reality of performance that brings something special out of you and at the same time draws the audience into your world.

But despite this return to form, I still wasn't getting the bookings that I needed. Typically, I would do well at an open-spot, the promoter would promise to phone to talk about a paid gig, but then I'd hear nothing more about it.

'So what made the difference?' you ask.

The stupid answer, and one that demonstrates just how thick I can be, is that I came up with the radical idea of buying an answerphone. The first day that I set it up and came home to it, there were several messages from various bookers trying to contact me. Perhaps I could have saved myself six months of grafting had I thought of getting a machine earlier, but that's life.

Not that the money was great. My first paid engagement was at a place called the Square in Harlow, for which I got ten pounds. You may laugh, but in those days ten pounds was actually still bugger all. My ambition remained to get my name on the Comedy Store blackboard, but I now realized that that would be a sign of turning professional, i.e., making a living as a comedian. I was all too aware that it was going to be a long, slow haul.

At times the struggle to get paid gigs seemed hopeless. The combination of endless late nights travelling to an increasing network of clubs, plus a demanding day job, was exhausting me.

Every comedian will relate to the experience of going along to a packed gig on the promise of a door-split (a share of the takings, but not including the bar, which was always the proprietor's), doing a great show, encoring, and then being handed thirty quid by the owner, usually with the words 'Is that OK?' I wish now that I'd turned around and said 'No, it isn't OK, you fucking parasite. Give me my money.' But at the time I didn't want to jeopardize my chance of a return booking.

In the following years, I found it ironic that the Comedy Store and Jongleurs in Battersea, which by then were gaining a reputation for being 'commercial', were the only two venues I knew of which were entirely straightforward and transparent about their booking policy and the money that they paid. They also happened to be the toughest places to succeed in and so it became convenient, if you weren't suited to such places, to label them pejoratively.

For me, ultimately, stage-time was far more important than financial gain. Besides, I was starting to do really well wherever I went and was enjoying myself too much to care about the money.

Not that everybody opened their arms to welcome me. I rang the Hackney Empire and asked if there was any chance that I could try out at their comedy night. It was a gig that I really wanted because the place boasted of its reputation for promoting new talent and several comics on the circuit had told me to give it a go. Excitedly, I rang and asked if there was any chance of a try-out.

'Not really,' said the woman on the other end, in a drab, right-on voice.

'Oh. Any reason for that?' I asked. I'd never encountered flat refusal before.

'I just think there are too many of your sort around.'

'What sort?' I asked.

'You know, white, middle-class males,' she droned.

'Generally, or on the circuit?' I wondered.

'I think you know what I mean.'

I asked if I could send her a tape of a recent show.

'You can, but I'll probably just put it in the bin,' she said helpfully.

I was saddened that I wouldn't get a chance to play such a famous old theatre and didn't understand her attitude towards me. However, I needn't have worried. About three years later, having made several television appearances, I received a call from the very same woman. She had either forgotten our original conversation, or had attended a racial equality enlightenment workshop, of which there are many in Hackney, and decided that my career in comedy should no longer be blighted by her hatred of fellow white folk. Anyway, she wanted to know if I could do a benefit to help with the upkeep of the theatre.

'It's a chance to give something back,' suggested the familiar nasal voice. I thought that was nice of her.

39

I GOT A CALL FROM Captain Fracas. He and his partner, Bubbles La Touche, were organizing a gig in Bradford with the Crisis Twins and the Sea Monster, and would I like to come along? It's a door-split minus exes. Sounds great, I said.

I knew Fracas and La Touche from doing spots at the club that they ran, the Ealing Comedy. Uncharacteristically, they had got themselves organized and arranged to hire a minibus to keep costs down. So it was agreed that I'd meet up with the Sea Monster outside Baker Street Tube station and the charabanc would pick us up there. God, I'm glad Jo Brand ditched that name, the Sea Monster. And I dare say she is too. So we stood in the street and chatted until eventually the rest of the troupe pulled up and away we went up the M1.

That gig was the first traditional working-men's club that I ever played. In its heyday it was, no doubt, the vibrant and packed centre of the community's social life. But now it was a dismal, long room with twenty or so punters who could have walked straight out of a Mike Leigh film. The floor was covered with threadbare carpet-tiles now tacky with the grime of old bitter and trodden-in crisps. Next to the bar, two men played darts, concentrating on the thump, thump, thump of the cork as each shot landed. Then the lazy quickness of subtraction, a drag on the cigarette, a sip of the pint, as the other took aim.

A large woman sat on a bar stool in front of the fruit machine, hypnotized by the spinning wheels and the flashing 'Go' pad, which she would press with her left hand while her right hand was poised to drop the next coin into the slot. Nothing would come of it, of course, but there was just that slight chance of three identical cherries coming to rest in a line, triggering the winning chorus of bells, sirens and flashing lights as the tray at her knees flooded with jangling silver. Click, click, click. Nothing. Should have maybe held the strawberry. Maybe not. She knows what she's doing.

Others looked on in silence, sitting at the Formica tables with their half-empty glasses on stained beer mats, occasionally tapping their cigarettes into burn-marked ashtrays. In fairness, a double-act like Captain Fracas and Bubbles La Touche was never going to thrill on a night like this.

The dotty, undisciplined whimsy of two sweet-natured eccentrics was just about tolerated by their regular audience, who always knew that better was yet to come in the form of a proper stand-up. But to a gathering of hardened, disillusioned men and women on a Thursday night in Bradford it was only going to gain a disbelieving stare. One old boy at the front, no doubt remembering brighter evenings of comedy, hurled some abuse, more out of disappointment than anger. His was the expectation of what he and his club had always known: a man in a dinner jacket telling jokes one after another about his fat wife, a couple of Irish fellows looking for a job or a Pakistani who goes into a pub. Crude, yes, racist, sexist and every other ist, very probably. But it was reliably funny to the audiences of its day.

It's wrong to paint all the old comedians with the same brush, however. Most of them were competent joke-tellers, some were very funny and original and the occasional one was exceptional and memorable. I'd suggest that this is a ratio that applies to our generation's current circuit, so it's not a particular indictment. My point is that the really fine comedians of thirty or more years ago have all been classed as one type, which is unhelpful when looking back at the change that took place in comedy at the very end of the seventies. There is hardly a single modern comic I know who does not refer to Eric Morecambe or Tommy Cooper as a favourite. So there never existed an automatic dislike of the old school that I was aware of. The antagonism was towards the vast lower echelon of cheesy journeymen in grubby tuxedos, reciting reams of tawdry gags, many of which would be the same as those told by a dozen other stand-ups on their circuit.

Coincidentally, while I was writing this chapter, I took a day off because I had to go to a meeting at the BBC. I bumped into Jo Brand and told her that I was writing about the Bradford gig, which she also remembered because it was the first time that we met. She reminded me that the man who ran the club had said before the show that, come what may, he always turned the lights off at ten thirty. This turned out to have unfortunate consequences.

The Captain and Bubbles hastily brought the intro to an underwhelming end, gathered their hapless, deployed props and brought on the Crisis Twins. To be completely honest, I don't recall anything about their act, as I was nervously preparing to go on next, mentally running through my material and adding ideas that I thought would work.

I was well received and started to improvise with the old guy at the front, which got laughs and gave me the confidence to throw in the new pieces that I'd thought of before going on.

It was only when I came off that I realized that it was twenty-seven minutes past ten. I had overshot my fifteen and left Jo with only three minutes on stage before the plug was due to be pulled – which is exactly what happened.

As a penance, I drove the bus most of the way home, getting back to Earl's Court at about three in the morning. Jo has since become a friend, but on that occasion she was pretty unhappy with me. So unhappy, in fact, that she was still banging on about it some two decades later. Suffice it to say that on the way back from Bradford there was a bit of an atmosphere, what with that and John and Simon (the Crisis Twins) arguing in the back about anything that came to mind, the way only double-acts can.

Not long after that gig, Captain Fracas (I can't remember his real name and forgot to ask Jo. If you see her, you ask) called to suggest that I take over running the Ealing Comedy for a couple of weeks. It sounded like an exciting proposition since it would give me the opportunity to compere, something that I'd always liked the idea of, as it seemed an ideal way of trying out snippets of new material between each act. Jane came along to help. She set up till at the door with a small float and took the fee from the few people who came in. There were about nine or so, which is obviously less than ideal. Even less ideal was that none of the acts that I had booked had bothered to turn up. I was beginning to see the Captain's reason for wanting to take a break.

The showbiz rule has always been that if the audience outnumbers the acts, then the show must go on. Well, sorry to disappoint by not finishing this anecdote with 'so I went on and did a two-hour improvised show, and in the audience was the head of Channel 4 and he came up to me afterwards and said . . .' That is not what happened. I chickened out of attempting to do the show alone, mainly because I felt that it would just be more honourable to own up, admit that none of the comics had turned up, explain that the show was cancelled and say that everyone would get their money back on the way out.

Shortly afterwards, in the now empty room, I unplugged the PA system, wound the cables and put the chairs up as Jane counted the float back into the tin.

'That's weird,' she said. 'I'm down by £4.50 from what I started with.'

We sat on the bus, glumly wondering who had robbed us, when it dawned on us that on the way in, everyone had got the concessionary ticket price for being unemployed, but on the way out they'd all mysteriously got jobs and asked for a full refund. As I've already said, Lenny Bruce reckoned that the audience was a genius. Well, sometimes it can be a bastard as well.

But then, trundling along the Uxbridge Road in the whining double-decker, rain streaking the windows and blurring the vibrant shop lights outside, I looked at Jane and realized that I loved her in a way that I'd never known before.

40

I'M ALWAYS BEING ASKED if there was a moment in my early comedy career when I knew that it was going to work out. It wasn't a particular show that I did, although many stick in my memory as important to my development, some of which I have already described to you. In the end the moment was quite undramatic, but to me, no less amazing for that.

I had kept on with the day job in the bar, occasionally having to go to my boss, Paul, and ask for a couple of days off so that I could take a gig in, say, Manchester or Liverpool. He'd always make out that this was incredibly inconvenient but then let me go with a genuine 'Good luck.' It felt as though everything had turned 180 degrees since my days of working in Covent Garden. Now I was the one with a second career beyond the restaurant.

If nothing else, I was always a very hard worker (once I'd left school), and I'm grateful for that quality.

Had my nature been more bohemian, I would have missed so many extraordinary experiences. More crucially, I would have missed several formative years of ordinary experiences. I had no idea at that point just how much my life would change, nor how close that change was standing by, waiting to hurl me into a new world.

From midday, the large basement at Corks would fill with local business people ordering snacks and cold beers to have at the bar, or sometimes a more leisurely sit-down meal in the restaurant area. Regulars were friendly and liked to chat, staying later than they should, having that last bottle of Becks before they hit the office again. I didn't let on about my secret comedy career, partly because, if I flunked and ended up working there for the next ten years, I didn't want to be reminded of it by the Oxford Street lunchtime boozers. A lot of the time a big part of me believed such failure was more than likely.

I was in the middle of a really busy Friday lunch service, opening and serving beers and bottles of wine as fast as I could. The place was heaving with a bunch of suits who had just spilt out of some conference at a nearby hotel, their heads giddy with sales targets and turnover talk. Several of them were pretty blunt in their manner, but I was used to that from the thousands of people like them that I'd served over the years, not to mention my more recent nocturnal sorties to the Comedy Store.

As I struggled to keep up with demand, the phone behind the bar began to ring. I ignored it, thinking whoever it was would hang up. When they didn't, and the noise of it became unbearable, competing with the babble of delegates baying for beers and chardonnay, gin and tonics and Martinis, I picked up the receiver and put it straight back down again. The relief of the endless ringing having stopped was short-lived. By the time I'd served the next customer it had started ringing again.

'Three Becks and a glass of white wine,' said a forty-something in a damp, striped shirt, sweat beading on his red brow, as he waved a tenner at me.

Against my professional instinct, I said that I'd have to answer the call.

'Look, can't you serve me first,' protested Sweaty Boy as his fist scooped into the bowl of nuts like a mechanical digger. 'I mean, bloody hell, what's wrong with you?'

But it was too late. As he carried on with his rant, I picked up the phone.

'Corks wine bar, how can I help?'

'Is that Jack Dee?' The voice sounded like a chirpy barrow-boy.

'Speaking,' I said, gesturing to the impatient customer that I'd be serving him in a moment.

'My name's Addison Cresswell. I met you on Sunday when you did your open-spot down at the Tramshed.'

The Woolwich Tramshed was a great venue to play and was run by Addison, who had quickly established himself as the number-one impresario of the new comedy scene. It was an accomplishment even to get a try-out at his club, so this could be an important call. He might be about to offer me a paid gig. My appearance there at the weekend had gone well. It was a great little space with banked seating that came close to the stage. Ideal for stand-up.

The man at the bar clicked his fingers. '*Garçon*,' he said and his mates laughed, reminding me of Wilton Reid and his cronies.

But now, all my attention had switched to the voice on the phone. This could be great. A paid gig at one of the toughest venues to crack. My mind raced with the possibilities. Once it got round that I had done a proper gig at the Tramshed, other bookers would sit up and think seriously about taking me on.

'What are you doing for representation?' he asked.

'Sorry?'

I wasn't sure what he meant.

'Who's your agent?'

'I haven't really got an agent, I'm sort of looking after myself,' I explained, trying to come across as confident, but knowing it sounded a bit amateurish and hoping it wouldn't put him off booking me.

'Well, do you want to meet up and have a chat about it?'

It took me a moment to figure out what he was saying.

'I look after Julian Clary, Jeremy Hardy . . .'

I knew very well who he had on his books.

The penny dropped. He was saying that he would be my agent. More customers were waiting restively to be served and I knew I'd have to deal with this smartly. I'd started the conversation hopeful of getting a gig and now I was talking about a move that could change the course of my life completely. I knew from countless green-room conversations that Cresswell got all his acts on to the university circuit. They were tough gigs to do, but it was constant work and the best training you could subject yourself to as a comedian at that time.

I took his number and agreed to call him after lunch. As I put down the phone, I knew that that call was a real turning point in my life. It could very well mean that I'd never have to do another open-spot or pull another pint again.

Not that I was able to savour destiny's angelic chorus for long.

The man who had called me *garçon* was now fuming. 'How can a phone call be more important than your customers?' he demanded.

I'd put up with all kinds of crap from people like him for so many years that I couldn't remember the beginning. I knew now that it was all over. That phone call that I'd just received meant that I could finally give up the day-job and make a living as a comedian. I could say anything I wanted to this sweaty oaf who was standing in front of me and it wouldn't matter a jot.

I looked at him for a moment, then said, 'Sorry about that. What was it? Three Becks and a white wine?'

Index

Dee, Jack, 1–377

FREE AUDIO DOWNLOAD READ BY JACK DEE

For your **FREE** 50 minute audio extract of Jack Dee reading from his book *Thanks for Nothing*, visit:

www.dontgetdeestarted.co.uk/freeaudio

You can also enter our competition for your chance to **WIN** one of five Jack Dee Live Stand-Up Collection DVDs.

See website for full terms and conditions